Flying Low

1956-1980

A memoir by

Brian K. Bryans
Captain, U.S. Navy (Retired)

Flying Low
1956—1980

A memoir by

Brian K. Bryans
Captain, U.S. Navy (Retired)

ISBN 978-1-105-38439-4

Fourth Edition

Other books by B.K. Bryans:

Those '67 Blues
The Dog Robbers
Flight to Redemption
Brannigan Rides Again
Trouble in Tucson
Arizona Grit

Most of them are available on Amazon.com at:
https://www.amazon.com/author/b.k.bryans

You are also invited to visit the author's personal website at:
www.brianbryans.com

Dedication

For Pat . . . who followed me through twenty-four Navy moves and tumultuous times . . . except when she was leading the way.

Forword

The lieutenant glared at me. "Did ya ever fly Corsairs, sonny?"

No, I had never flown a Corsair, the famous gull-winged, four-bladed prop plane that had fought so well in the skies over the Pacific and Korea. I was a junior jet jockey, and one of my comments to that senior pilot had shown that I didn't fully appreciate the piloting skills required of that earlier era. I had erred.

Our house contains many high-quality models of the jet aircraft I've flown, and a model of one airplane I never flew: the Corsair. My wife bought it for me because "Did ya ever fly Corsairs, sonny?" became a family saying useful during minor disagreements.

So now—to the F/A-18 jet jocks that cruise at Mach 1.5 with satellite navigation, smart weapons, and automatic carrier landing systems—I pose these questions:

"Did ya ever fly Skyhawks, sonny?"

"Off a 1950's Essex Class aircraft carrier?"

"At night?"

1

"There I was, flat on my back at twenty thousand feet."

That lead-in to an old fighter-pilot joke suddenly took on new meaning to me. I was inverted, falling backwards through twenty thousand feet, and the airplane's controls were useless. How in hell could anyone get in that fix?

It was one of those crisp, clean, autumn days in southern California, the kind you could still find there in 1959. I was on a routine post-maintenance test hop. My job was to run one of the squadron's A4D-2 Skyhawks through a series of controlled tests designed to make sure the mechanics had put all the pieces back together in the right places. Although this was not like what real test pilots did for a living, I relished the designation as one of the squadron's maintenance test pilots. This was big stuff. I had over six hundred hours of flight time and figured I was a damn good pilot. I was about to be humbled.

I finished the last maneuver listed in the test booklet strapped to my kneepad, jotted down all the parameters, and checked the clock. I had fuel and time for about fifteen minutes of fun and games before I had to start my descent back into NAS (Naval Air Station) Miramar.

The Douglas Aircraft Company's A4D Skyhawk was a terrific little delta-winged jet designed to carry and loft a nuclear weapon down range at someone you didn't like very much. The loft maneuver is nothing more than a half-Cuban-eight (two thirds of a loop with a roll upright on the back slope) where the weapon is released on the way up. The nuke then flies an arc in the original direction while you and the plane reverse course and run like hell. The maneuver is started with the aircraft right down in the weeds after a low level penetration to avoid enemy radars, so we always practiced this at low altitude.

U.S. Navy Photo

A4D-2 Skyhawk

Now I'd done this maneuver dozens of times, but always starting from an altitude of less than a hundred feet above the ground. Now I was idling along at three hundred knots at twenty-five thousand feet. I decided to see if I could do a loft maneuver at this altitude.

Pushing the throttle up to a hundred percent power, I put the plane in a gentle dive to pick up speed while I scanned the area for other aircraft. (In those days there weren't many up that high, but you never knew.)

I leveled off at twenty thousand feet, set my course due north, and moved the control stick smartly back into my lap to get the standard four-g pull-up. Everything was normal for about three seconds, and then it turned to deep *kimchi*.

It's a well-established principle that when airflow across a wing becomes too slow to sustain flight, the aircraft stalls. What happens next varies a great deal from one airframe to another and from one situation to the next.

In my vast prior experience (six hundred plus hours, remember), airplanes that stalled pitched over nose down and lost altitude. If you were in a relatively stable airplane and made all the right moves over the next few seconds, you could recover with nothing worse than the loss of some altitude. If not, you went into a spin, a much more exciting maneuver with the aircraft nose down in a rapid rotation, much like when water swirls down a drain.

If you were truly unlucky, you did this upside down in what is called an inverted spin. Inverted spins throw you away from your seat, unless you are strapped in very tight, and they can drive blood into your head until you "red out." Naval aviators are trained to handle stalls and spins, even inverted ones. They are not trained to handle what I had.

The A4D and I went from normal flight to absolute nothing so fast I didn't even feel the stall. By absolute nothing I mean that we were suspended at a point in space. The airspeed read zero. The flight controls flopped around with no effect.

At that moment it dawned on me; despite my many qualities, I could still screw up big time. Wisdom arrived: *Of course you can't do a loft maneuver at this altitude, you jerk; the air isn't dense enough. Any idiot knows that.*

And then the aircraft began to move. It didn't pitch over. It didn't roll. It just slid backward, like a ship sinking stern first.

Now I'd been here several times before in the Grumman F9F-8 Cougar. That plane tended to run out of airspeed whenever you went straight up for any length of time. So I wasn't too concerned; I had altitude to spare. I'd wait for the nose to fall through, the airspeed to build up, and the aluminum to fly again.

The EGT (Exhaust Gas Temperature) soared beyond limits as the engine, still at full power, fought the sudden reverse flow of air, so I throttled back to the idle position. The airplane rewarded me: it rolled over onto its back.

Great. Now I slid backward while I was upside down. Why in hell didn't the nose fall through? It always had in the Cougar.

But the damn airplane didn't do any of the things I expected. If it acted like a stall, I could handle it. If it pitched and went into a spin, I knew what to do. If it only behaved and went nose down, that would be great . . . but it didn't.

Then the tail began to make slow swings from side to side, like a pendulum. Little points of light danced around the cockpit, the sun's reflections from the mirrors. It was very quiet. I was at zero-g; the force of gravity didn't pull at me. The controls were still useless, like the arms of a rag doll.

The altimeter unwound . . . down to eighteen thousand feet, then seventeen thousand feet. The rule driven into every student naval aviator's head in those days was (and probably still is), *if it isn't flyable at ten thousand feet, get out.* This piece of wisdom passed through my consciousness several times while I teased the flight controls and watched the altimeter unwind.

Finally, passing twelve thousand feet, my tugs on the control stick began to pay off: I got a nibble. It felt like a sunfish that chews on the worm while it debates whether to take a real bite. I played with the fish . . . and got a strike.

The horizontal stabilizer bit the air as the altimeter slid through eleven thousand feet, and then I was able to work the nose down below the horizon. When the airspeed indicator came up off the stop, I pushed the throttle forward and waited.

As the altimeter passed through ten thousand feet, I should have ejected, but we were about to fly again. Any thought of leaving that nice warm aluminum cocoon was dropped.

With a welcome roar, air rushed over the canopy, and the little A4D flew again. I rolled the plane upright and, for the first time, became aware of the mountain peaks only a few hundred feet below me.

For the second time in less than two minutes, I realized what a bonehead I was; the emergency ejection altitude is supposed to be ten thousand feet *above ground level*, not ten thousand feet on the altimeter.

When I got back to Miramar, I described the scenario in detail to the Douglas tech rep who worked with the squadron. He'd never heard of such a maneuver, but he promised to research it.

About a month later the tech rep took me aside. "Congratulations," he said. "The Douglas Aircraft Company says you're the only pilot they know of who has managed to recover from an *inverted falling leaf* in the A4D."

So, my grand adventure didn't end that autumn day in 1959. Of course it didn't start there either; it began four years earlier.

"All of you who are independently wealthy please sit down."

A whole bunch of the kids around me did. Not me. About two hundred of us still stood in the school's auditorium. Some craned their necks to see which ones had taken a seat.

"Okay," the dean of the College of Agriculture went on, "those of you who are certain to inherit a ranch or farm from your folks, take your seat."

There was a massive shuffling sound. I was stunned. Only about thirty of us were left on our feet. This—whatever it was—did not look good.

The kindly old dean shook his head. "I've been studying the economics of ranching and farming in this country, and it's not good. Sadly, those of you still on your feet have no business being here. You'll never be ranchers or farmers. It just won't happen. I urge you to pick up your books, walk out of here, and find another career path. I'm sorry, but that's the way it is."

Now the seated ones turned their heads to stare at those of us who still stood: we, the excommunicated.

I took the dean's advice, picked up my books, and walked out into the bright spring sunshine. I crossed the University of Arizona campus, head down, future shattered. I had spent much of the last few years on horseback, and I'd planned to spend the rest of my life that way, but the dean had just killed that dream.

Fine, I thought. I'll drop out of school, join the Navy, and run away to sea. I'd be eighteen in two months, and that was a good age to leave home.

The Navy recruiter's office downtown was crowded, and I wound up number seven in line at that sailor's desk. While the recruiter lied to the first kid up, my eyes drifted across the rack of pamphlets arrayed against the wall next to me.

A pale blue booklet featured a dark blue jet airplane on the cover. The title read, *Wear Navy Wings of Gold.* I picked it up. Inside was an artist's rendition of a beach scene: blue waves and white sand. Pretty girls in scanty bathing suits surrounded a guy in a dark blue uniform with gold stripes on his sleeves and gold wings on his chest.

Two minutes later I was hooked. I clutched my new dream and bolted from the recruiter's office. After all, if an American boy can't be a cowboy, he darn well ought to be a jet pilot. I would fly.

That night I did the math. The Navy required sixty semester hours of college to get into the NAVCAD (Naval Aviation Cadet)

Program. If I went to summer school and took a max load in the fall, I'd have sixty by January.

To give myself some back up, and to gain experience on the tests I'd have to pass, I also applied for the (brand new) Air Force Academy, the Naval Academy, and advanced Air Force ROTC. Each of these applications required a battery of tests that were only given on certain dates.

I scheduled the NAVCAD tests for last. It worked. By the time those tests rolled around that next winter, I had taken so many spatial orientation, math, vocabulary, and psychological tests that they seemed like old friends.

The Navy flew me from Tucson to NAS Los Alamitos (near Los Angeles) for the written tests. Twenty-four of us spent three hours in a cramped classroom bent over the multiple exams, and then we waited another hour for the results.

Finally, the sailor in charge came back and announced the results: only two of us had passed all the tests. But I was one of the two.

It was obvious from the slide rule on his desk that the fellow to my right, who had *not* passed, was an engineering student. He picked up the slide rule, fumbled for its case, then turned and said, "Congratulations. What engineering program are you in?"

"None," I said. "I'm an Aggie."

The poor guy snapped his slide rule in half.

Since I had passed, the Navy flew me back to Tucson in a TV-2 jet trainer. The pilot strapped me into the rear ejection seat, then grimaced as he plopped the large suitcase onto my lap. He knew—and I soon figured out—that if we had to eject, the suitcase would kill me.

Whisper quiet, we cruised east above a floor of fluffy white clouds that the sunset behind us slowly turned crimson. I was a happy boy.

Tucson is home to Davis-Monthan Air Force Base, a Strategic Air Command (SAC) base at the time; so to save the expense of another trip to Los Angeles, the Navy asked the Air Force to give me the flight physical in Tucson.

I passed everything except the blood pressure test; mine was way too high. The young Air Force flight surgeon was sympathetic and explained that it was the result of my obvious case of nerves. Nerves? Just my entire life was on the line here. Why have nerves?

He put me on an examining table in a dark room and told me he'd be back in a little while to test me again. It was a long time before he came back. So long, in fact, that I fell asleep.

Pressure on my arm brought me awake. "Congratulations," the doctor said when my eyes focused on his grin. "Your pressure is fine now. You passed." God bless him for that. I wonder if he would have been so accommodating if he thought I was going to fly for *his* outfit.

"Hey, Brian!"

I turned my head to see who had called my name, and drove my dad's 1954 Buick Super into the light pole in the middle of the parking lot at Johnny's Drive In. There went the travel money that was set aside to take me to NAS Pensacola, Florida, the hub of naval aviation flight training. I had to sell my saddle for plane fare. Fitting.

I got off the bus from the airport in Pensacola on a beautiful spring evening. The South was in full bloom. It was March 5, 1956.

For some reason, I'd brought my guitar. The bus driver pulled the guitar case out of the lower storage space and handed it to me.

Up the street about a hundred feet were three teen-age girls. One of them glanced at me, noted the guitar and my long, wavy hair, and screamed, "It's Elvis." The girls charged me, making primal noises at the top of their little lungs.

I stepped back and tried to put the driver between them and me.

He just stared at the approaching threat.

At about twenty feet one of the girls yelled, "Shit. It's not him." They ground to a stop, glared at me, and then stalked off.

"Who the hell is Elvis?" I asked the driver.

"Beats me, kid."

The Marine sergeant that checked me into the cadet battalion confiscated the guitar and shipped it right back home.

That night, lying on my rack after lights out, I felt elated. Here I was. Not only was I going to be an officer and a gentleman by act of Congress, I was going to fly.

Two racks away, a classmate entertained the rest of the group. He'd stripped off his under shorts, picked up his Zippo, and lit his farts with spectacular effect.

2

I gave the instructor a thumbs up, then glanced yet again at the water some twenty feet below.

He leaned into the cut-off airplane cockpit, double-checked my shoulder harness and lap belt, then stepped back and pulled a large lever.

The open cockpit tipped forward off the platform, raced down a set of tracks set into the pool at a steep angle, and crashed into the water. I was flung against the straps, and then felt the cockpit rotate forward and go upside down as it sank. I was surrounded by air bubbles in the dark water and couldn't see a thing.

I fumbled with the lap belt latch long enough to feel the first twinges of panic . . . and then it came loose. Struggling to hold my breath, I reached down for the bow of the cockpit windscreen and pulled myself down, deeper into the water.

When clear of the metal, I pushed sideways and emerged from the bubbles to see the scuba-clad safety observer watching me from a few feet away. I gave another thumbs up and swam towards the light above.

Okay, I had passed the Dilbert Dunker test. Naval aviation pre-flight training is designed to prepare you to crash as well as to fly. That's probably a good idea.

The United States Navy has always used the Marine Corps to do its dirty work. Marines storm the beaches, protect the embassies, and guard naval prisoners. They also trained naval aviation cadets. We had two sergeants assigned to shepherd our class, Class 10-56 (the tenth class of 1956), through the sixteen weeks of pre-flight training. One of the sergeants spoke understandable English. The other spoke only Marine Corps. It worked.

Our days were occupied with flight academics, military stuff, and physical development. Of prime importance was learning to eat meals in less than five minutes. That gave us more time to march.

The cadet corps was made up of both NAVCAD and AOC (Aviation Officer Candidate) classes. We were all cadets, but the AOC's were college graduates who would receive their commissions at the end of pre-flight. We NAVCADs would stay cadets until we earned our wings and commission after about eighteen months of training.

Each cadet regiment was organized into four battalions, with each battalion divided into companies and squads. (Remember that Marines ran this show.) We had cadet officers at the head of each unit. As we progressed through pre-flight, the Marines selected various cadets, both NAVCAD and AOC, for promotion up the cadet officer ranks. These cadet officers were not always admired and appreciated by the non-selected.

One day my duties separated me from my class, and I wound up at stragglers lunch. This meant that I had the great luxury of half an hour to chow down. While I ate, I pulled out an unread letter from Pat, my girlfriend back in Tucson, and began to read it.

Cadet Lieutenant Smith appeared at my side. He berated me for reading in the mess hall and ordered me to proceed back to my barracks. We had words.

When I did return to my barracks, the sergeant who spoke Marine Corps indicated in words and signs that I was to report to the Marine captain who owned our particular battalion. This was a big deal. It looked very much like step one of a short trip to a sailor hat, bell-bottom trousers, and a destroyer in the Aleutians.

I snapped to attention in the captain's doorway, beat the doorframe three times with my knuckles, and belted out, "Cadet Bryans reporting as ordered, *sir!*"

The captain ripped into me for disobeying the orders of a cadet officer. Then he paused and said, "Cadet Lieutenant Smith has made a very serious charge against you. He says that you told him to go to hell. Is that true?"

"Captain," I blurted out, "I don't remember whether I told him to go to hell or not. But if I didn't, I sure wish I had."

The captain choked and gurgled as he tried to strangle a laugh. When he could talk again, he snapped, "Get the hell out of here, Cadet, and don't get into any more trouble."

I found out later that the captain then ripped Cadet Lieutenant Smith a new one. That episode is one of my many fond memories of Marines.

* * *

The program devoted a lot of effort to our physical conditioning. Running the obstacle course was an almost daily routine, as were workouts at the gym. And to graduate we had to pass the dreaded step test, which required you to step up on a tall bench and back down a hundred times in three minutes.

Swimming was also a priority. Besides the Dilbert Dunker drill, we had to do fun things like jump off tall towers into the pool to simulate abandoning ship, get out of a parachute harness while being dragged across the water at high speed, and survive the fully-clothed endurance swim.

I approached many of these challenges with a fair amount of dread, so I adopted a "get it over with" attitude. When we were told to line up for events such as the Dilbert Dunker or the tower jump, I clenched my teeth and stepped right up. The Marine observers seem to have confused this attempt to conquer my fear as leadership potential.

Class 10-56 graduated from pre-flight training on June 22, 1956—my 19th birthday. I stood with my back to the wooden reviewing stand, the four battalions of cadets arrayed across the parade field before me. I was the cadet regimental commander, top cadet.

Time dragged. Finally, the Marine sergeant, the one who spoke real English, stepped away from the reviewing stand twenty yards behind me and walked up to within speaking distance. "The admiral's late," he said. "I'll give you a signal when it's time to start the parade."

"Aye, aye, Sergeant."

We all stood in our places at attention while the minutes ticked by. Then I heard the sergeant call out something. There it was: the signal.

Taking a deep breath, I called out, "Regiment!"

Roaring back at me as the respective cadet commanders sounded off came four separate yells of "Battalion!"

Their shouts drowned out most of a strangled cry from behind me. *Somebody fall off the platform?*

I yelled, "Pass in review!"

Four hundred cadets went into motion, wheeling to march around the perimeter of the field and pass in front of the reviewing stand.

Turning, I saluted the admiral at the podium . . . but there was no admiral at the podium. His sedan, two-star flag snapping in the wind, was still coming down the street.

With a sinking feeling, I looked for the Marine sergeant at his post next to the reviewing stand. I can still picture him today, just as I saw him then.

The sergeant tore his expensive cover (hat) off his head, threw it onto the grass, and jumped up and down on it.

He told me later that his call to me, the one I'd misinterpreted, had been to advise me that the admiral would arrive in three minutes. Nobody except the sergeant and I seemed to care that the parade had started without the admiral.

After the ceremony, we cadet graduates piled into a bus and headed north for the short trip to NAAS (Naval Auxiliary Air Station) Whiting Field. At last, we were about to fly.

Our bus slowed as it approached the main gate at Whiting Field. We could see a bright yellow SNJ training plane crumpled on the ground about two hundred yards away; it was in flames. Two red fire trucks stood by while their crews watched the plane burn.

SNJs were the U.S. Navy version of the Air Force T-6 Texan. They were old (WW-II Army Air Corps pilot trainees got seventy-five hours in them), and they were cheap; the Navy sold them in flyaway condition for a thousand dollars apiece.

The firemen finally shot some foam on the downed bird to put out the flames. Nobody asked about the plane's pilot.

Goleta Air & Space Museum Photo

SNJ / T-6

Good news. We were to be the first class to get our primary flight training in the new Beechcraft T-34B instead of the SNJ. The T-34B was powered by a six-piston, 225-hp Continental engine and had a top speed of almost two hundred miles an hour. That was a little slower than the SNJ but fast enough for us. The real advantage was that, while the SNJ was a tail-dragger that required some special skill to land and taxi, the newer T-34 had tricycle landing gear (two main mounts and a nose wheel) that made these operations easier. We figured that the odds of making the grade were now somewhat improved.

Goleta Air & Space Museum Photo

T-34B

Maybe not.

I came out of the loop and reached for the barf bag tucked into the pocket of my tan flight suit.

"Are you throwing up again, Mister Bryans?"

"Yes . . . *raaalph* . . . sir."

"This is your fifth hop, Cadet, and you've barfed on every one of them. If you do it tomorrow, you're gone. Understand?"

"Yes, sir."

Thus motivated, I didn't throw up anymore. But the time I'd spent with my head in a paper bag hurt me. I had to fly eleven flights instead of the standard nine before my instructor turned me over to a check pilot for my safe-for-solo test.

The check pilot graded me while I flew around for an hour and did all the required maneuvers. Then he directed me over to a grassy field I'd never noticed before. Tall pine trees surrounded it. We did three touch-and-go landings on the little meadow before the instructor told me to land and taxi back to the edge of the grass.

Smiling, the instructor got out and waved me away. I was about to solo.

I took off and came around for my first solo landing. The field. Where was the damn field? All I saw was treetops. *Oh, shit. I'm too low. Power . . . power. There's the field, right where it's supposed to be. Whew!*

After the touch-and-go, I came around again, higher this time, so I could keep the field in sight, and landed.

The instructor shook his head as he crawled into the rear cockpit, but he gave me a thumbs up. I'd passed.

Classmate Tony Tambini was a sandbagger. He had over a hundred hours of flight time in light planes before he came into the program, and he never told anyone.

On his first flight, the instructor flew the plane around, did a few acrobatics, and then said, "Okay Tony, you have the aircraft."

Tony took the stick and gave the standard response, "I have the aircraft, sir." Then he flew straight and level. After about thirty seconds, Tony asked, "Can I do something, sir?"

"Sure," came the answer.

So Tony whipped the T-34 upside down, put in forward stick, and flew inverted.

The instructor went berserk when urine flew all over the rear cockpit. He'd been using the relief tube (a primitive funnel and hose arrangement), and inverted flight reversed the flow in the tube.

Our flight gear consisted of a tan coverall and a ribbed hard hat that looked like it belonged on some coal miner instead of a pilot. Old rubber-and-plastic goggles on an elastic band came with the hard hat. All of us, student and instructor alike, lusted for the smooth helmets with the flick-up visor that the Air Force had started to issue to its pilots.

Our other key piece of equipment was the parachute. Before every flight we went to the parachute riggers and checked out a

WW-II-era parachute, the kind that hung off your butt while you walked to the plane. Then you sat on it while you flew.

There were some bad days there at Whiting Field. A student in another class had engine failure on a solo flight and bailed out. His parachute didn't open.

The base CO (Commanding Officer) had ten chutes popped in a test: eight out of the ten didn't open. Riggers were imported from another base to re-rig all our chutes.

A few days later I watched a student and instructor make an emergency landing in an SNJ. A fire broke out in the cockpit right after the plane touched down. The base fire truck chased the plane down the runway, but the truck ran out of gas and rolled to a stop too far away to save the crew.

Primary training in the T-34 was all about the rudimentary flight skills: landing, stall and spin recovery, basic navigation, and some acrobatics to build confidence.

One of the first basics learned was the standard field entry and landing procedure. This started at an initial point some distance from the field. All returning aircraft came in over the designated point and requested clearance to enter the traffic pattern. The chatter went something like this:

You'd call, "Whiting tower, this is Bearpaw One-Niner, Initial Point for landing."

The tower would respond. "Roger, Bearpaw One-Niner. Cleared inbound. Call the break."

Flying up the duty runway at eight hundred feet you called, "Bearpaw One-Niner in the break."

"Cleared to break, One-Niner. Traffic is a T-34 on downwind."

When clear of the other traffic, you *broke* with a hard, level turn to the left, and then you pulled the power back. When the plane was slow enough, you dropped the landing gear and flaps, then ran the power back up.

You rolled out of your turn on the *downwind* heading (opposite to the landing direction) and ran through your landing checklist. You read each checklist item off a metal placard on the instrument panel.

The *one-eighty* was a point abeam the intended touchdown spot. When you got there you called for landing with, "Bearpaw One-Niner, one-eighty, gear down and locked."

"Roger, One-Niner. Cleared to land."

Throttling back, you started a 180-degree descending turn to line up with the runway. Halfway through that turn was the *ninety*, a good place to check your altitude. Then you rolled out wings level over the approach end of the runway, corrected for any crosswind, and landed.

Historical Note: In the late 1970s the Navy started individual call signs to, among other things, help differentiate between the "Sam" that referred to Sam Smith and the "SAM" that referred to a surface-to-air missile. (Radio calls like "Hey, you got a SAM at your six" could get confusing.) That's why Tom Cruise is known as Maverick throughout the movie *Top Gun*. But back in my day, call signs belonged to squadrons and individual flights, with radio calls like Bearpaw One-Niner or Rover Lead.

I had fifty-eight hours of flight time before we moved a few miles down the road to NAAS Corry Field in mid-September for Basic Training. As the bus drove through the gate at Corry Field, we could see another crashed trainer on fire.

Wow! Now we got to fly Navy T-28s. And this was the "B" model, not the wussie T-28A that the Air Force flew. The USAF version had an 800-hp engine and a two-bladed prop. Our planes had a 1,425-hp engine and a three-bladed prop. (We weren't going into combat against the Air Force version, but it was nice to know that our birds were superior.) As a matter of fact, the T-28B could perform right alongside the better WW-II fighter planes.

We got five dual transition hops before we were turned loose to solo the T-28. I remember that I was more than a little nervous when I cobbed the power to that mighty engine and roared down the runway all on my own.

Goleta Air & Space Museum Photo

T-28B

It was a mighty engine, indeed. A friend managed to stall out his T-28B at a thousand feet in the landing pattern; the plane fell off on a wing and rolled inverted. All he could do was jam the throttle full open. That three-bladed prop clawed air like a helicopter and pulled him, upside down, out of the incipient spin.

After the transition phase, we went into basic instrument training. We sat in the back seat of the T-28 under a cloth hood in order to simulate the inside of a cloud. We had to make the aircraft perform precise three-dimensional figures in the sky using only the instrument panel.

To do one of the easier maneuvers, we had to fly a precise figure eight while we lost and then regained exactly a thousand feet on each loop of the eight.

You had to develop a good instrument scan: attitude, altitude, airspeed, rate-of-turn, rate-of-climb; then attitude, altitude, airspeed, rate-of-turn, rate-of-climb; over and over.

I became pretty proficient at this, so instructors had a tendency to give me a break every now and then; they'd take control of the airplane and do acrobatics for a few minutes. This brought on bouts of queasiness that I managed to hide; I carried a barf bag just in case.

Then we moved on to NAAS Saufley Field for formation flying.

Yes, there it was, for the third time: a crash to welcome us. But this time all we could see was the column of smoke.

Formation was much more fun than flying on instruments, but it could get pretty scary at times. Two, and then four, novice formation flyers in close proximity can make your knuckles hurt. When four of us were all solo, the instructor's chase plane always stayed a healthy distance away.

A humorous tape floated around naval aviation for years that contained the screams of an instructor pilot as he tried to control a formation flight of four inept solo students. What he didn't know was that four instructors had switched with the students just before the flight, and they were wringing him out.

We got our first taste of night flying at Saufley Field. On one of the flights, we were supposed to fly a long racetrack pattern (there were eight of us) that ended in a touch-and-go landing. The navigation was pretty easy: you followed the lights of the plane ahead of you.

Halfway through the hop, I was doing just that when I realized that it was a lot darker below me than it had been. I swiveled my head and realized that I was about five miles north of where I should have been. I looked ahead for the aircraft lights I'd been following . . . and they were gone. I turned and headed back towards the field. The planes behind me stayed there until we were all back in the correct pattern.

Later, Tony confessed. He was the one who had led us astray. When he realized what he'd done, he turned off his lights, raced back into the traffic pattern, and then turned his lights back on.

At this point we were far enough along that our weekends were free, but there wasn't much for a young man to do in town. Almost every girl in the Pensacola area was married by the time she turned sixteen, so there weren't many prospective dates around. This was good news for all the sweethearts back home.

Stag beer parties at the beach were popular. Not with Ron Pickett, however. Ten of us were stuffed into a car headed back from the beach late one night when the right-hand rear door opened and Ron fell out. We must have been doing about forty miles an hour at the time, so Ron was lucky to only lose the skin on his back. We'd been on a dirt road, so Ron also had a lot of debris embedded in his back. He had to lie on his stomach in the cadet barracks for the next six weeks while the rest of us moved on to Barin Field.

As 1956 drew to a close, the Soviets had invaded Hungary, and Ike had defeated Adlai Stevenson to win a second term. Two new Navy planes from the Douglas Aircraft Company had entered service: the A3D Skywarrior and the F4D Skyray. *High Society* had been the biggest movie moneymaker of the year. And I now knew who Elvis was. He had two big hits out: "Love Me Tender" and "Don't Be Cruel."

U.S. Navy Photo

Naval Aviation Cadet at Barin Field, Alabama

April 1957

3

In February of 1957, my group transferred to NAAS Barin Field near Foley, Alabama, about twenty miles west of Pensacola. (There was no welcoming crash at the gate this time, but Barin Field's high student loss rate in an earlier era had earned it the title, Bloody Barin.) Ron Pickett stayed behind at Saufley, flat on his belly.

We were there for the last and best phase of basic training: gunnery and carrier qualification (CQ). I had 119 hours in the cockpit at this point, and I felt ready.

Goleta Air & Space Museum Photo

SNJ / T-6 (Again)

Bad news. The T-28s were all needed back at Saufley Field, so we had to transition into the Navy's few remaining SNJs. The SNJ was a lower-powered airplane, with a 550-hp Pratt & Whitney radial engine, and we would have to learn how to land with a tail-wheel after all. Worse, this would slow down our progress through the program by about six weeks.

It was wonderful. We loved the SNJs and the remoteness of Barin Field. The instructors were so loose it was almost like the good old days of WW-I, or at least our image of those days. We flew real low, landed in cow pastures, did formation take offs, and had mock dogfights.

We sometimes landed at a small strip away from Barin Field to refuel before flying a second hop. We parked the planes along the side of the crumbling asphalt runway while a fuel truck moved down the line to gas us up.

While I strolled back to my plane one day, parachute bumping me on the butt, I heard a whistling sound. I looked up in time to see an SNJ flying down the runway straight at me, its prop within a few feet of the ground. I belly-flopped, and the plane pulled up into a victory roll. It was an instructor, showing off.

Landing the SNJ turned out to be not quite the bugaboo we'd expected. Yes, it had a tail wheel instead of a nose wheel, and it did require more skill to achieve a smooth landing, but it was doable.

In a tricycle gear plane, you could touch down on the main mounts and let the nose fall through when you slowed down. With a tail wheel, you had to fly all three wheels onto the runway. The trick was to get the plane into a slight nose high posture just before touchdown, which meant you almost stalled it onto the runway.

The instructors preached three different techniques for landing a tail-wheel aircraft: the three-point landing, the whipstall, and landing on the rear of the front tires. You had to be an aficionado to tell them apart in practice. The three-point placed all three wheels on the deck at the same instant, the tail wheel hit first in the whipstall, and it was darn hard to put the backside of the front tires on the deck without having the tail wheel touch down.

Taxiing the SNJ was also a bit different because you couldn't see straight ahead: the nose of the aircraft was in the way. So, you had to do shallow S-turns as you went.

On March 2, 1957, I was on a solo flight southeast of Barin Field when the UHF (Ultra High Frequency) radio squawked. "All Barin Field aircraft return to base. High wind advisory. Repeat. All Barin Field aircraft return to base. We have high cross winds developing."

Returning home, I flew up the runway and broke left. At the one-eighty position abeam the landing spot, I started my turn to final and made my call. "Barin Tower, this is Boxcar One-Six, one-eighty, gear down, final."

"Roger, Boxcar One-Six. Be advised we have three crashed aircraft off the runway. You have seventy-degree crosswinds from the left at twenty knots with gusts to forty."

"Understand, gusts to forty." *Holy shit.*

Coming through the ninety, I could see three yellow SNJs off the runway on the grass near the touchdown point. I rolled out on final and tweaked the speed down to fifty-five knots. I used cross controls (left stick and right rudder) to keep the upwind wing down and the airplane over the center of the runway.

I brought the plane into a normal three-point attitude just before touchdown, chopped the throttle, and rolled out right down the middle of the runway. I never felt the touchdown. That was the best landing I ever made in the SNJ. I felt ready for gunnery, but that was still a month away.

April 24, 1957, was a beautiful spring day. I was on my third gunnery flight. I hadn't hit the target on my first two hops, and I was antsy as I sat on the *perch*, the roll-in point, and waited to start my firing runs. The tow plane was ahead and to the left. A towline about five hundred feet long trailed behind the tow plane and pulled a six-foot by thirty-foot, white banner. The perch was abeam the banner and a thousand feet above it.

The sliding canopy of my SNJ was open to clear the cordite smoke that would soon fly in my face when I pulled the trigger. My long white scarf was tucked into my leather flight jacket so the ends wouldn't fly out of the cockpit and strangle me.

The radio finally came alive. "Pineapple One, you're cleared in hot."

Keying the UHF, I responded. "Roger. Pineapple One is rolling in hot."

I rolled into a descending left turn and watched the lighted *pipper* (aiming point) on my gun sight sweep back as it followed the towline. When the pipper approached the banner, I flipped on the master-arm switch and reversed into a right turn, still diving. I set the pipper a bit ahead of the banner's nose and squeezed the trigger.

The nose-mounted machine gun chattered and a thick cloud of cordite smoke flew back past my face. Tracer rounds flashed out and appeared to die away in the banner's vicinity. Fresh paint on the bullets would smear onto the white banner—if I hit it—so I could tally my score after the flight.

As the banner filled my windscreen, I released the trigger, rolled wings level, and pulled up into a steep climb for the perch on the left side of the banner. I switched the master-arm off on the way up.

Then I waited my next turn.

When cleared, I rolled in from that side and made another gun run. I did four firing passes, but felt that the first one was the best.

Taxiing in to the line after I landed, I pushed my goggles up, then pulled my scarf free and flipped it out the open cockpit. It whipped and snapped in the backwash from the propeller. Like most of our SNJs, the prop made a whistling sound due to old bullet holes in it where the synchronization between gun and rotating prop had gone awry. As my grandkids might say, that was "so cool." And I found nine blue-tinged holes in the banner; that was my color. I felt like an ace.

About this time, Dad sold me his 1954 Buick Super, the model with eight ventaports (air holes in the side of the hood), and he even drove it out to Florida for me. Now I had wheels and could cruise into Mobile, Alabama, on liberty. Tony Tambini usually went with me. He found his future wife Angie there, and he owes it all to that '54 Buick Super.

Back during Pre-Flight, Tony and I had joined the NAVCAD Choir. Our motivation at the time was simple: the word on the street was that choir members were valuable to the program and were far less likely to be canned. Rumor had it that the choir's last star tenor had survived six crashes and still gone on to win his wings.

Throughout the year we spent in the Pensacola area, Tony and I went on one or two weekend choir trips a month. We sang at the Miss America Pageant in New York City where I escorted Miss Arizona, a young woman who had turned up her nose at the smell of my boots the previous year.

While we were there, we went on the *Ed Sullivan Show* out of Rockefeller Center and accompanied Kirk Douglas as he sang his "Whale of a Tale" number from the movie *Twenty Thousand Leagues Under the Sea*. (I actually got fan mail from Tucson out of that gig.)

We sang at the Miss Universe Pageant in Los Angeles, where I escorted Miss British Guiana. And we sang at Disneyland. Tough duty.

Tony and I frequently paired up for liberty on these trips, and I quickly learned more about my sandbagging friend. He claimed to have been an Arthur Murray dance instructor before he joined the Navy, but that was not his line when we were looking for dates at one of the many after-performance dances arranged by our host groups.

I'd talk a girl into joining us at our table, and Tony would go into his "Gee, I wish I knew how to dance" routine. Invariably, "my" date would volunteer to teach him, and off they'd go. I soon learned to pick up a date for Tony before finding one for me.

Then came carrier qualification. Unless you were going into some special program like helicopters or blimps, you didn't get out of naval aviation basic training without landing on an aircraft carrier six times. I can't think of any reason why one would have wanted to avoid it. I hope it's the same today.

Preparation consisted of eleven FCLP (Field Carrier Landing Practice) hops where we logged four to eight landings per flight. We flew our SNJs in a low, slow, racetrack pattern that ended with a touch-and-go landing on a runway marked with the painted outline of a carrier deck. When I say "slow," I mean fifty-five knots, only five knots above the SNJ's stall speed.

As we flew our final approach, we were guided by the LSO (Landing Signal Officer) who stood at the edge of the runway next to the touchdown area. LSOs are pilots who watch aircraft landing approaches from a platform alongside the touchdown area. They have specialized training: they can tell, using nothing but their eyes, whether the approaching plane is above or below glide path, accelerating or decelerating, or in danger. It's an art.

In those days, LSOs used two large paddles to instruct the pilot. These were a little bigger than ping-pong paddles, and the face was made up of ribbons of cloth to let the wind blow through. LSOs were referred to by the nickname *Paddles*.

As long as the approach was a good one (graded as OK), the LSO held the paddles straight out, shoulder high, one on each side. If both paddles went low, then you were low. If the paddles were held high, then you were high. To move you left or right, the LSOs tilted their arms, and you banked to mimic them. If the LSO clapped the paddles together in front of him, you added power. The more violent the claps, the more power you needed to add.

If the LSO wanted you to *wave off*—add full power and take it around—then he'd wave the paddles in a criss-cross pattern over his head, sometimes frantically.

The *cut* was a signal to chop power and land. The LSO held the left paddle out and brought the right paddle in to his chest in a sort of salute. At that point, you brought the throttle back to idle, assumed the three-point landing attitude, and plopped down on the deck.

During the first few FCLP flights, we got to see the LSOs go through a lot of frantic motions as we went from too high to too low and from too fast to too slow, or we did the opposite. This was often followed by a wave-off. Toward the end we saw a lot of steady OK signals followed by the cut sign. Then one day we were deemed ready.

Eight of us launched in two flights of four and headed out to sea. An instructor followed each flight in a chase plane. It was May 22, 1957, exactly eleven months after our graduation from pre-flight. Up ahead, a hundred miles out on the Gulf of Mexico, the aircraft carrier *Antietem* cruised on a beautiful blue sea dotted here and there with tiny flecks of white foam.

We had trained for the older, straight-deck carriers where you flew into a net barricade if you landed and didn't catch a wire (cable) with your tail hook. *Antietem* was now an angled-deck carrier, however. This meant that the port side had been extended out, and the landing area was now at a slight angle to the left of the main deck. Aircraft could be parked on the bow without interfering with the landing area. So, if you failed to catch a wire, you merely added power and went around for another try.

To *trap* is to catch one of the four steel cables attached at each end to big hydraulic engines. Each of the engines has to be set for the relative speed and gross weight of the aircraft about to be arrested. The cables and engines together are called the *arresting gear*. (The term *wire* is just a nickname for the cables; each one is really a *cross-deck pendant* connected at each end to a *purchase cable* attached to an *arresting engine*.)

If you land but don't catch a wire, for any one of several reasons, it's called a *bolter*. Of course, if you do a practice landing with the hook deliberately left up, then it's logged as a *touch-and-go*.

Unfortunately, I earned a wave off on my first try at the deck.

Like a dope, I forgot to drop my tail hook, and the LSO waved me off. But the next six passes resulted in six traps, and I was qualified.

The ship was equipped with two hydraulic catapults, but we didn't need them; the little SNJs could *deck launch.* Each time we trapped, the wire tugged us backward a few feet, and the hook came free during the rollback.

As we rolled back, a yellow-shirted *director* gave us the hook-up signal: a palm held flat in front of his chest with a thumb up beneath it. Once the hook started up, he waved his right arm in a big circle to signal the arresting gear crew to pull back the wire. Then he crossed his arms over his head and clenched his fists to tell us to hold the brakes.

From that, the director looked forward to make sure that the deck was clear, and then he went right to the two-finger twirl over his head that signaled us to go to full power.

We pushed the throttle forward, checked our instruments, and gave him a salute. When the director dropped to one knee and pointed up the angle deck, we released the brakes and commenced our take-off roll. We were airborne again before we reached the end of the deck.

This all happened very fast but very smoothly. It had to; the ship expected a plane to trap every thirty seconds.

Carrier deck operations are a fiesta of colors. The flight deck crew that directs the movement of aircraft, including the catapult crew, wears yellow jerseys. The ordnance crews wear red, the fueling personnel are dressed in purple, and the mechanics wear green. The safety personnel, including the LSOs, wear white jerseys.

At least in those days, the *flight deck officer* plotted the movement and parking of the aircraft from a cramped space in the base of the ships *island.* He used a steel, to-scale model of the carrier's flight deck set up as a work counter and little to-scale metal airplane outlines. The *hangar deck officer* did the same thing down on the hangar deck. (They may still do it that way today.) The *air boss* runs the whole show from a small control tower built into one of the upper levels of the island.

The entire operation has been described as a ballet. I wouldn't argue the point.

* * *

My celebration the night after I carrier qualified was dimmed when I found out my instructor had lost a bottle of scotch to another instructor on a bet that I'd need only six passes to get six traps. I let him down when I forgot to lower my hook on that first pass.

I had to check out at NAS Pensacola before I headed off to advanced training, and there I found out about Ron Pickett, he of the skinless back. As it turned out, when he crawled out of his bed at Saufley Field, the base was overflowing with T-28s, and a push was on. He flew two or three flights a day, qualified in gunnery and CQ from there, and beat me to advanced training by several weeks.

The detour to fly SNJs had cost me extra time in the training command, but I've never regretted it. If you haven't flown a "tail dragger," then you haven't flown. Just ask anyone who has.

The Marines had one more surprise for me when I tried to check out. It seems that, eight months prior, I had been placed on report for some minor infraction and had never paid the price.

Now I had to do penance before I could depart. For the next four hours I marched up and down the muster field in front of the cadet barracks with an M-1 rifle on my shoulder. Every time I did my about-face at the end of the path, I could see my suitcases sitting on the HQ steps.

As I neared the end of this embarrassment, a group of pre-flight cadets came out of HQ, sat on the steps, and heckled me.

The Marine sergeant stormed out of his office and ripped them a new one. "You know," he screamed, "that man marching out there has landed on an aircraft carrier. What the hell have you ever done?"

U.S. Navy Photo

Home

4

Advanced training was spread out across the country. Jet training was done at NAS Corpus Christi and NAAS Chase Field, both in Texas. If you were ordered to fly anti-submarine aircraft, then you went to multi-engine prop training at NAS Olathe, Kansas, or to seaplane training at NAS Corpus Christi. Single-engine prop training for the AD-4 *Spad* (not to be confused with the A4D) was done at NAAS Cabiness Field, a short drive outside Corpus Christi.

Blimp training was handled at NAS Lakehurst, New Jersey, but no one cared. The blimp program tried to recruit some of us. They offered a short curriculum with early promotion to ensign. Nobody in my group went for it. We made up jokes about the poopy bag acrobatic phase consisting of poopyloops and bagovers.

Ron Pickett had taken his new skin to Cabiness Field to train on the AD (later designated the A-1). It didn't make any difference what the aircraft's official designation was; the plane was always referred to as the Spad.

This was the most powerful carrier-based dive-bomber ever built. With three ordnance stations on the fuselage and six under each wing, it could carry more tonnage than a WW-II, four-engine B-17. Its Wright R-3350 radial engine with eighteen cylinders provided 2,700 horsepower, and the torque it generated tended to roll the aircraft. The joke was that AD pilots had oversize right legs because they had to counter all that torque with right rudder.

It was during this period that Ron married Kay. I was best man at the wedding, which was held clandestinely because the Navy vowed that any NAVCAD who married would be kicked out of the program. Ron figured it was a bluff, and I hoped that he was right. At any rate, the Navy never confronted him over the event.

But Ron had one more training-command episode. At the end of what was supposed to be his last syllabus flight, Ron arrived back at Cabaniss Field. In his landing approach, he got too close to the plane ahead and had to wave off. When the plane's engine began to backfire and miss during climbout, he decided to make a quick turn and land downwind.

He touched down long and fast, then stood on the brakes as the end of the runway grew closer. The brakes smoked. Suddenly the airplane's tail went up as the nose came down, and the propeller started biting into the runway. Sparks and dust flew everywhere.

The Spad finally stopped, nose down, at the very end of the runway. After a moment, the plane's tail fell back down and bounced a couple of times.

Taking off off the seat belt and shoulder harness, Ron leapt out of the cockpit and got out of the way of the arriving fire trucks.

Someone ran up to Kay, waiting in the nearby parking lot, and said "I don't think he's hurt!" That was the first indication that she'd been watching Ron make the colorful landing.

As an aside, Ron went on to fly some 250 combat missions in the Vietnam War and retire as a Navy captain.

U.S. Navy Photo

Spads

I had signed a two-year extension to guarantee that I got jets, and get them I did. I would have preferred NAS Corpus Christi near the water, but I was sent to NAAS Chase Field near Beeville, Texas. Beeville is a dry dot on the map about half way between San Antonio and Corpus Christi.

U.S. Navy Photo

TV-2 / T-33

Jet advanced training started in the TV-2, the Navy version of the USAF T-33. Both aircraft were a two-place outgrowth of the 1940's Lockheed F-80 fighter and cruised at a sedate 450 miles an hour. The TV-2's single Allison J-33 engine produced 5,400 pounds of thrust. That's not a lot of thrust for a fifteen thousand pound airplane, and it had lousy climb characteristics. It was all right to about thirty thousand feet, but if you wanted to get to its service ceiling of forty-five thousand, you were out of gas and needed to start your descent by the time you got there.

The TV-2s at Chase Field sported the Navy's new orange and white paint scheme for training planes. It screamed, "Out of the way, student pilot." But its tandem seats, straight wings, and poor thrust-to-weight ratio made the TV-2 a boring jet, especially when you were in the back seat under the long white hood that blocked out the sky.

Of course the TV-2 wasn't always dull. It had a 230-gallon fuel tank on each wing tip. One day two Chase Field instructors came back from a flight to the Caribbean and saw several squad cars from "Customs" sitting at the end of the runway. They took a wave off, hit the wing-tip fuel dump switch, and sprayed 460 gallons of rum onto the Texas scrub.

It was easier to fly a jet than a prop aircraft. The reciprocating engine needed a throttle, a mixture control, an rpm control, and a carburetor air temperature control. A jet engine just had a throttle.

On the flip side, things came at you a lot faster in a jet, and the early ones couldn't accelerate like a plane powered by a reciprocating engine. If you were in a prop plane and had to wave-off in close to the ship, you could jam the throttle forward, and the plane would likely claw its way to safety. If that happened in a jet, the engine would still be revving up when you hit the ramp. To fly a jet you had to think and plan well ahead of the game. (With due respect, this is what made flying jets different from flying Corsairs.) The transition syllabus was geared to make us do that.

After five jet fam and two solo hops, there were ten transition flights focused on navigation and formation flying, but these were folded in with the instrument curriculum. There were twenty-six dual instrument flights *under the bag*.

Primary IFR (Instrument Flight Rules) navigation methods in those days used ADF (Automatic Direction Finding). Powerful low frequency beacons were set up every two hundred miles along airways. You used the beacon behind you for a hundred miles and then switched to the beacon ahead of you. The beam width was three degrees, so at a hundred miles you could get an *on-course* signal up to 2.5 miles off center.

The beacons broadcast Morse code letters in four quadrants, alternating the letters A (dot dash) and N (dash dot). The quadrant borders were aligned along the airway. When you were on the airway, the A and N blended together to make a solid tone. If you were on one side of the airway you heard "dot dash"; if you were on the other, you heard "dash dot." When you passed over the station, there was a cone of silence (no tone), and then the A and the N reversed sides.

We did more than navigate along airways this way; we shot instrument penetrations and approaches with the system. Since there was no distance indication, most of the penetrations were teardrops.

A typical one went like this. You came into the cone of silence, turned to an outbound heading and started down. At some given altitude you started a teardrop-shaped turn and came back at the beacon. When you crossed the cone of silence at the new, low altitude, you turned to a final heading and descended to *minimums*, the lowest legal altitude. (This wasn't bad in a slow prop plane; it could get very interesting in a fast-moving jet.)

This A and N method had been in use since the 1940s, and we used it a lot in the advanced instrument phase. But a newer twist, the ADF needle, was much easier to use: the needle pointed at the station. It was mounted over a compass card, so you could maneuver to get yourself on a specific radial, inbound or outbound.

The next improvement widely used by the military was TACAN (Tactical Air Navigation). It came along about the time I got my wings. In this UHF system, the aircraft transmitted an electronic signal that was received and transmitted back by a TACAN station. An ADF-like needle pointed at the station, and DME (Distance Measuring Equipment) measured the time it took for the signal to make the round trip. That told you how far you were from the station. It was good up to 199 nautical miles and made straight-in instrument penetrations common.

Meanwhile, civil aviation went with the VOR (VHF Omnidirectional Range) system. Equipment aboard the aircraft interpreted two different signals sent out by the station to determine which radial *from* the station it was on. VOR did not include DME; that had to be purchased separately, sort of like "batteries not included."

Prior to 1957, you had to complete all of advanced training before you got your wings and commission. But the Air Force had started to award those at the end of basic training, so the Navy, in an effort to stay competitive, changed policy. We would get our wings and become ensigns in the United States Naval Reserve once we completed jet transition and the advanced instrument course.

And there was more good news: our date of rank would be backdated to the date we'd finished basic training. This would make us eligible for promotion sooner.

On September 27, 1957, I emerged from the cadet barracks in the uniform of a United States Navy ensign, and the base commanding officer pinned gold wings on my chest.

That afternoon I drove to San Antonio and flew commercial to Tucson. The next day, September 28, 1957, a Saturday, I married my hometown sweetheart, Pat. Dad had to sign a permission form; I wasn't twenty-one yet.

After the ceremony and reception, Pat and I flew to San Antonio, Texas, and right into an incredible infestation of crickets. There were so many crickets on the streets that not even the mighty 1954 Buick Super with the eight ventaports could get through to the honeymoon hotel I had planned. We slid all over the road out of the airport and pulled into the first No-Tell Motel along the way.

The next day we drove to Sinton, Texas, the only place within fifty miles of Chase Field where I could find an apartment to rent. I've seen Pat cry three times; the second time was when she saw the hovel I'd rented.

That was on a Sunday. On Monday I started advanced tactics in the swept-wing Grumman F9F-8. The leading F in F9F-8 meant that it was a fighter plane. The next two characters (the 9F) meant that it was the 9th aircraft line built by Grumman, and the -8 indicated this was the 8th version.

Earlier, straight-wing versions of the F9F had distinguished themselves in Korea as the Panther, but when the experimental F9F–6 version came along, it sported swept wings and a new name: Cougar.

The Marine Corps flew an underpowered F9F-7 while the Navy kept the best of breed, the F9F–8, for itself. One indicator of the airplane's beauty and prowess is that the Navy's Blue Angels flight demonstration team flew Cougars from 1955 to 1958.

The Cougar looked like a shark. It had a long, rounded snout, so some squadrons painted shark eyes and teeth on the airplane's nose to emphasize that appearance. Navy planes were painted a dark (Navy) blue in those days to make them difficult to see from above when they were flying over water, but a new paint scheme came along in the late 1950s that made the aircraft gray with a bright white belly to reflect the heat and radiation from nuclear blasts. (A signal that the Air Force's Strategic Air Command was not the only nuclear strike force.)

NASA Photo

F9F-8 Cougar

The F9F-8's big J48-P-8A jet engine put out 7,200 pounds of thrust, and it could push the twenty-two thousand pound airplane around pretty well, but the Cougar did go downhill much better than it went uphill.

There were two versions of the plane: the single-seat F9F-8 and the two-seat F9F-8T. Advanced tactics started with one flight in the T version, with an instructor in the back seat, followed by two solo flights in the single-seat bird. I remember that first solo.

October 3, 1957, was a crisp autumn day in east Texas. I was about to solo in a single-place, swept-wing jet. *Hot damn.* Two of us were to fly solo, with a chase plane behind so an instructor could keep an eye on us. The three of us taxied to the end of the duty runway and did our engine checks.

That day I was Banjo One, the other student was Banjo Two, and the instructor in the chase plane was Banjo Chase. We kept our radios on squadron tactical frequency while we did our final pre-flight checks. I had just finished my checks when I heard, "Banjo Chase, this is Banjo Two. My EGT is running hot."

There was a short pause and then, "Banjo Two, this is Banjo Chase. Go back to the line and get another aircraft. Hurry. I'll wait here for you. Banjo One, go ahead. We'll join you in the tactics area."

"Banjo Two Wilco," came from my fellow student.

"Banjo One Wilco," I added. *I'll be darned; I've been let off the leash.* "Banjo One switching." I changed the UHF radio to tower frequency. "Chase Tower, this is Banjo One, ready for take off."

"Roger, Banjo One. Cleared for take off."

Out on the duty runway, I ran the power up to a hundred percent, checked the gauges one last time, and released the brakes. Thirty seconds later I was a *real* jet pilot.

I flipped the landing gear handle up, sucked up the flaps, and put that beautiful dark blue bird into a climb for the tactics area. The sun sparkled off the star-and-bars insignia painted on the wing. I had to swivel my head to see it because it was on a swept wing. God was in the heavens, and I was climbing to join him.

After leveling off at twenty-five thousand feet, I looked around. A few thousand feet below, a flight of four TV-2s on a formation hop cruised by. I ignored them, but a couple of minutes later here they came again. This was too much. I swung right to put myself on the perch, and then rolled in on them. I had over two hundred knots of closure as I came up behind the placid flight. I was like a bobcat racing into a covey of quail.

When I was in range of the last TV-2, I imagined shooting my guns and then broke it off before I got too close. I soared skyward and reversed. The formation flight obliged me and turned away. Then I was down on them again.

"Check your six," came over the UHF. It was a very stern voice.

Could that be for me?

I looked over my left shoulder as I headed the Cougar up again. Nothing there. I looked over my right shoulder. *Oh shit.* The instructor was tucked in tight under my starboard wing.

"Take us home," the voice said.

"Wilco." I took us home, as smoothly as I could. The instructor waited for me while I crawled down the side of my plane and stepped onto the hot tarmac.

He ripped me a new one, started to walk away, then came back and ripped it again. After he stomped off towards the hangar, I stood still for a long time. I could visualize the drill: my new gold wings would be torn from my chest and thrown away.

After a while I walked, head down, across the ramp and into the hangar. I had to pass the instructor's ready room to get to the locker room. Their door was closed, but loud guffaws of laughter made it through the thin wood. I stopped and moved a little closer. I recognized my instructor's voice.

"You should've seen the look on the kid's face when he finally saw me." Much laughter.

"Well," a strange voice said, "what are you going to do? Write him up?"

"Hell no. The kids gonna make a fighter pilot."

The duplex apartment I'd rented in Sinton was ancient: the toilet had a water closet seven feet up in the air, and the bathtub had lion's feet for legs.

The bachelor who rented the other half of the duplex repossessed cars for a living. One night as Pat and I left for a rare dinner out, we found a man with a shotgun crouched behind one of the bushes in the front yard; he was after the man who'd repossessed his pickup truck. We went down the street and phoned the bachelor to warn him.

I made marital mistakes as well as flying ones. One afternoon I returned from a formal inspection attired in my service dress whites (the ones with the high collar).

Pat was sweaty and grimy, but she was obviously pleased with herself. "I spent the entire day cleaning this pig sty," she said. "You won't be able to find dust or dirt anywhere."

Still standing in the doorway, I pulled an old Marine trick; I slipped on one of my white gloves, reached over my head, and swept my forefinger along the top of the lintel. It came away with a streak of gray on it: dust. When I held it up to show Pat, I learned a valuable lesson about marriage.

There were forty-one flights in the advanced tactics phase. They included a few dual flights with an instructor whenever some new wrinkle was introduced; the rest were solo flights. We practiced formation flying followed by one-on-one, and then two-on-two, aerial combat. We flew over to Padre Island, just off the coast, to strafe with guns, fire rockets, and drop practice bombs. Some of that was at night when we attacked flare pots on the sand.

Many of the flights were remarkable in some way, but the one event from that period etched into my mind more than the others took place on October 27th. Two of us, with an instructor chase, were on a round robin, cross-country flight, and we stopped for fuel at NAS Jacksonville, Florida.

It was a hot day, we were taking off from there with full fuel loads, there was no wind, and I was the third to take off. I realized that, given the weight and heat, I'd chew up a lot of runway before I got airborne. What I didn't count on was the effect of the hot exhaust gases that lay over the runway from the two F9s that launched ahead of me.

The runway jutted out into the bay, so the end of it was above a rock jetty and water. I was about a thousand feet from the end of the runway, accelerating but still glued to the ground, when it dawned on me that I was in terrible doo-doo. It was too late to abort the take off, and it looked like the runway would end a little too soon.

When I crossed the last foot of runway, still not quite airborne, I did the only thing I could think of: I raised the landing gear.

She flew. My jet exhaust left a wake in the water, but that beautiful blue bird flew. I even managed to clear the trees across the bay by several feet.

On November 5, 1957, I flew two day hops followed by a solo night navigation flight around east Texas. It was a beautiful, clear night, and I was struck by how few lights there were down below. And all those illuminated oil rigs in the gulf made it hard to tell where the coastline lay. I gave up any idea of navigating visually and relied on old faithful: dead-reckoning navigation (heading, speed, and elapsed time). I arrived back home on time and had finished my training.

A fellow NAVCAD at Beeville flew his night navigation flight the following evening. The lights confused him, and he wound up lost over the gulf. He landed safely at an Air Force base out of state, but he never flew for the Navy again; he was dropped from the program.

It was easy to get dropped from the jet program in those days because the powers that be had decided there were too many jet students in the pipeline. But those in the seaplane program were in worse shape. A friend we nicknamed IBM Machine Sheen because his flying was so precise was the only cadet to make it through that training course.

But I was done. I checked out of naval aviation flight training with 310 flight hours, 10 of them at night.

I wound up with the second highest grade of the graduates that week. (I'd been number one before the wedding.) Grades were important because they determined who got first and second pick of the (very few) available squadron slots, and I wanted a squadron at San Diego.

It turned out that the guy ahead of me wanted the East Coast, and he picked a squadron there. That left a slot open in VA-56 (Attack Squadron Fifty-Six) flying out of NAS Miramar just north of San Diego.

Pat and I packed up and headed the Buick Super with the eight ventaports west.

Elvis was on a roll in 1957 with "Jailhouse Rock," "Your Teddy Bear," and "Treat Me Nice." Marty Robbins had a hit with "A White Sport Coat and a Pink Carnation." *Bridge on the River Kwai* was big at the box office. The Soviet Union had launched two Sputnik satellites, while our first try had blown up on the pad. But the Navy had two more new fighters in service: the Grumman F11F Tiger and the Chance Vought F8U Crusader.

Pat Richards - 1956

One can see why I married this girl.

U.S. Navy Photo

Ensign Brian K Bryans, USNR

I was twenty years old. Does it show?

5

Pat and I arrived in San Diego in early December and settled into a dinky little ground-floor apartment three blocks from the ocean in Pacific Beach. The building was a two-story, white stucco creation with an L-shape that faced the tiny manager's office situated on the street corner. I'm pretty sure that the word "nondescript" was coined just to describe the place.

Tony and his new bride Angie lived above us. (Tony was also headed for VA-56.) Since they beat us to San Diego by a week, they took the available (and cooler) upstairs unit and reserved the lower (no breeze) one for us.

In retaliation, I kept a broom handle by my nightstand and banged on the ceiling with great gusto whenever their bed squeaked.

Today Pacific Beach is a crowded bend in the coast road that runs from San Diego up to La Jolla. In 1957 it was a relaxed outpost away from the raucous civilization being packed into the area below Mission Bay. It had sort of a Bohemian atmosphere where going formal meant that you kept your shoes on. It was just the place for an infant ensign and his teenage bride. (The current generation of local dwellers looks like they share the same philosophy, but I bet that all that new asphalt burns their feet when they go shoeless.)

Back in those days, there were four major Navy airfields on the West Coast: NAS North Island on the Coronado Strand next to San Diego, NAS Miramar a short drive north of San Diego, NAS Alameda across the bay from San Francisco, and NAS Whidbey Island, Washington, near Seattle. (Nobody ever said that the Navy didn't know how to live.)

NAS Miramar sat astride Kearney Mesa, seven miles east of La Jolla Cove; its two long, parallel runways pointed west-northwest towards Torrey Pines. We junior birdmen clustered in three different convenient commute areas that depended upon factors I don't think any of us thought about at the time.

Those of us who were newly married and wanted to celebrate our youth and good fortune nested in Pacific Beach, about a twenty-minute drive to the southwest.

Our bachelors, driven by mating instincts of a much different flavor, homed in on "snake ranches" in the Del Mar and Del Mar Beach areas up the coast a ways. The drive was longer, but that gave them more time to sober up before the first launch.

Second-tour guys, at least those who were still married, bought starter homes in a new tract called Claremont Village that had opened up atop the mesa a bit south of the airfield.

The NAS Miramar of 1957 locked in my memory was a majestic creature. It was monarch of the mesa and owned all of it west of what is now I-15. Its junior partner across the highway to the east was a Marine Corps grunt base. People didn't want to move too close because of the jet noise, and the Navy liked it that way.

There were a couple of new big-box hangars on the base where the home guard hunkered down, but we of the transient squadron element were assigned to ancient Quonset huts set on a grassy field near the west end of the runways. I loved it. It felt like we were in one of those WW-I aerodromes in France. I unpacked my white silk scarf.

Seven of us *nuggets* fresh out of the training command were assigned to Attack Squadron 56. I happened to be senior among our bunch. (This is sort of like maturity among teenagers.) I owed this dubious distinction to the fact that my last name started with the letter B. Since all seven of us had the same date of rank, we were placed in the naval officers' *Blue Book* in alphabetical order.

Now seniority in the Navy can be a big deal. There are pages and pages of *Naval Regulations* devoted to the responsibilities of the *Senior Officer Present Afloat* and the *Senior Officer Present Ashore* (the SOPA in either case). If something goes awry and you are the SOPA, you are in deep doo doo. (I don't remember that exact result being described in the regs, but the intent is there.)

I dwell on this a little here because, since I was the senior ensign that arrived that day, I wound up as the air group duty officer for the rest of the day. (Air Group Five was made up of six squadrons, including VA-56.) In turn, that led the air group commander to order my immediate court martial.

When Tony and I checked into the squadron's Quonset hut that morning so long ago, we found that VA-56 was in the process of flying in from the aircraft carrier *Bonhomme Richard* after a five-month cruise. Those flinty-eyed warriors ripped off their survival gear, shook our hands, and raced off to their women.

The squadron skipper welcomed us aboard and assigned me (since I was the senior ensign present) to be the squadron duty officer for the day. Then he left, presumably for the same reason as his pilots.

A few minutes later I received a call from the air group office; I was to also be the air group duty officer. This meant that I had to watch out for the interests not only of VA-56, but also the other five squadrons that comprised the air group. *Oh joy.*

After all the cars tore out of the parking lot, a sailor from the base communications office popped in and asked for the air group duty officer. When I confessed to that honor, he gave me a stack of naval messages about six inches high. When I asked what I was supposed to do with them, the sailor gave me one of those looks reserved for ignorant ensigns. He did, however, advise me to read them and make sure that any required action was taken. *Piece of cake.*

At the top of each message was about four inches of absolute unintelligible garble, something along the lines of RUBUDWA, RUHBBDU, etc. Now, I had never in my life seen a naval message. (The Navy expects you to pick up a lot on your own.) I tried to decode these mystical phrases but got bogged down. Almost plain English did appear down at the bottom of some pages, but the few I looked at seemed routine. I was sure the important stuff was up in the code, and I focused on that.

After a couple of hours of frustration—the other ensigns around couldn't figure them out either—the problem was resolved.

The air group commander himself, an awesome presence, stormed into our hut and punctuated the air with his fists as well as his tongue. He wanted to know why the hell I hadn't notified two of the squadrons in the group that their aircraft had been grounded for safety inspections; the message must be right there in the stack.

While my mouth moved and nothing very intelligent came out, he grabbed the stack of messages, riffed through them, and yanked out a page sprinkled with RUBUDWAs. He held the bottom of the page under my nose. It was indeed possible to see words near the bottom that spoke of grounded fighter planes. The commander screamed that I was relieved of duty, and he was ordering my court martial. He stormed out as he had entered. I remember that the door hit him in the ass on his way out. I didn't laugh.

To say that I had a miserable evening would be an understatement. The next morning the VA-56 squadron commanding officer called me into his office. I expected the worst.

Now our CO had achieved some fame as one of only two reserve (instead of regular Navy) officers to make squadron command, and to celebrate this distinction he wore red and green argyle socks with his blue uniform. They were on display for me as he sat with his feet propped up on the desktop.

I did not salute since naval officers, unlike their brethren in the other services, do not salute when uncovered (no hat). I came to attention in front of his desk and stated, "Reporting as ordered, sir."

The man gave me a cold stare.

Grimly, I awaited the skipper's condemnation.

He let me sweat for about ten long seconds and then allowed a grin to creep across his face. He shifted his considerable weight forward, and the colorful socks disappeared as he stood.

"Son," he said, "I think you better relax before you split a gut. I convinced the group commander that you weren't derelict; you're merely stupid. He's cancelled your court martial."

Then he then gave me a one-minute course in how to read a naval message. It was not very hard to grasp the key element: you ignored all the RUBUDWAs.

Ever since Pearl Harbor, the Navy has been built around the aircraft carrier. Today, of course, this has been aggrandized to Carrier Battle Group, which generally means one aircraft carrier surrounded by cruisers, destroyers, and other support ships. Submarines scurry around unseen below.

In the 1950s, at least in the limited vision of us junior birdmen, the end of the world was the aircraft carrier. We could expect to rotate between sea duty and shore duty every three or four years and to spend about half of our sea duty time on an aircraft carrier. Back then, the commanding officer of an aircraft carrier held the rank of captain and was always an experienced naval aviator. Today he (or she) is apt to be a rear admiral and may or may not be an aviator. *Ah, progress.*

An aircraft carrier's airplane complement was designated an *air group*. It was made up of five or six squadrons plus some odds and ends such as tanker aircraft and photo recon birds.

The commander of the Carrier Air Group (CAG) reported to the captain of the aircraft carrier to which the air group was assigned. Thus, when aboard, CAG was a department head on the carrier. When the air group was not assigned to a carrier, CAG was pretty much God. The CAG was a senior commander (nowadays a captain). Squadron commanders reported to the CAG whether aboard or ashore.

A typical carrier-based squadron had twelve aircraft, eighteen pilots, a couple of warrant officers (who made everything work), and about 120 enlisted men. The squadron CO, almost always a junior commander, was the senior pilot in the squadron, screened and selected by special personnel boards for his aviation and leadership skills. (It should be noted that some boards did a better job of selection than others.) These fearless leaders were called Skipper if they were liked, Captain if they were not, and other things (behind their back) if they were hated.

So, you had a Navy commander called Skipper or Captain who reported to another, more senior commander called CAG, who reported to a real Navy captain, called Captain. (Lest you think that the carrier's captain had it knocked, he frequently had a guest residing aboard his carrier: his boss, Rear Admiral So-and-So, commander of Task Force Such-and-Such.)

About 1958, the Navy decided that the Air Force had received too much publicity and budget dollars with its talk of *Air Wings*, so they changed the Navy's Carrier Air Group to Carrier Air Wing. Some of us waited breathlessly to see if any CAG would tolerate being called CAW. No way, Jose. To this day, the carrier air wing commander is still called CAG. (The Carrier Air Wing designation is now CVW.)

Life in VA-56 turned out to be a young pilot's dream. We had good airplanes and good times. When I checked in, the squadron was equipped with Grumman F9F-8 Cougars, the same swept-wing jet that some of us nuggets had flown back at Chase Field in Texas. The guys from Corpus Christi had flown the straight-wing F9s, but now we were all young studs strapped into sleek, swept-wing aircraft.

U.S. Navy Photo

VA-56 F9F-8 Cougar

There were several other reasons why our life in VA-56 was good:

First, we were between carriers and had no WESTPAC (Western Pacific) cruise on our schedule. Our next carrier, *Ticonderoga*, had gone into the "yard" for overhaul, so there we were, stuck in San Diego. *Drat.*

Second, we were scheduled to transition to a newer aircraft soon, so the formal training schedule was held in abeyance. We pretty much had free rein to do whatever we wished in the air.

Third, we drew one of the great CAGs of the era, Commander Butch Voorhis, the fighter pilot who'd started up the Navy's famed Blue Angels flight demonstration team.

And finally, we had a squadron skipper who was a reserve officer instead of a regular. (Remember the red and green argyle socks.) As it turned out, some of us youngsters needed his rather relaxed approach to things.

Besides the skipper, our squadron pilot roster started out with two lieutenant commanders (the executive officer and the operations officer); three lieutenants on their second tour of sea duty; four lieutenants junior grade who had just completed their first WESTPAC cruise; and eight ensigns. (The eight ensigns were we seven nuggets plus a slightly senior officer who transferred in.) I was the youngest of the lot, not yet 21.

FYI: Standard naval officer abbreviations used in this book are

CAPT for Captain, CDR for Commander, LCDR for Lieutenant Commander, LT for Lieutenant, LTJG for Lieutenant Junior Grade (commonly referred to as "j.g.'s",) and ENS for Ensign.

A typical day started at 0800 hours (8:00 A.M.) with coffee and doughnuts in the squadron *ready room*. This was the morning AOM (All Officers Meeting), but that terminology seems a little too dignified to describe what actually occurred.

If the skipper had any important news to pass on, it was done there. He usually let the operations officer talk.

On occasion the air wing flight surgeon would come over and lecture us about flight physiology. (For example, he advised us that we should drink lots of coffee in the morning so that we'd have a bowel movement before we pulled more than one g. That was to prevent hemorrhoids.)

The bachelor fliers usually looked like death warmed over at these meetings, but their smiles showed through.

Once the AOM ended, most of us tried to get into the air. The scramble for an airplane was sometimes intense. Although there was a flight schedule, it was flexible, and whoever wanted to fly the most could usually get on it. It worked out that at about 0900 we would call *Maintenance* to find out how many airplanes were up (flyable). The fastest movers got them. I never saw a fist fight over an airplane, but I did see rank pulled on occasion.

Usually we briefed the flight like we were supposed to, but sometimes it was: "We'll all meet at eighteen thousand feet over Ramona. Dogfight."

Naval aviation was still pretty casual in those days, and we had the accident rate to prove it. (Things are different now that airplanes cost real money.) The only jets in the sky then were military, and pretty girls still asked, "Do you fly jets, mister?"

Commercial and private aviation stayed under ten thousand feet, where cabin oxygen wasn't required, so the high-altitude radar coverage was minimal. We'd head for the territory above ten thousand feet and "bounce" anybody we found up there who looked like they wanted to play.

What we usually found up there was . . . us. I fondly remember some eight-plane, intra-squadron dogfights that used playground rule number one: every man for himself.

There was, however, an Air National Guard guy flying an F-86 (a plane that earned fame in the skies over North Korea) who taught us lessons in air-to-air combat. He was very, very good.

He'd announce his arrival with a "Rat a tat tat" over the UHF Guard Channel (243.0 MHz) that everyone monitored. If we looked in our mirrors quickly enough, we could see him coming up fast in our six o'clock position (behind us); we had already lost.

Sometimes he would flash by underneath with about two hundred knots excess airspeed and then pull up right in front of us so that his slipstream flipped us upside down. Needless to say, we vowed to get this guy. We never did.

These days you would never hear a fighter pilot say anything corny like "Rat a tat tat" over the radio. Today they'd say something cool like "Guns, guns, guns," to indicate they had fired theoretical guns at you, or they might cry "Fox one" or "Fox two" to indicate that they'd fired a hypothetical air-to-air missile.

FYI: Fox-1 indicates launch of a semi-active, radar-guided missile such as the Sparrow. Fox-2 refers to launch of an infrared missile like the Sidewinder. Fox-3 is reserved for an active radar-guided missile such as the Phoenix.

But dogfights were still up close and personal back then. The players used guns, and they used them at close range. If you wanted a gun kill, you got on the victim's six o'clock, got in range, and blasted away when you could keep the other fellow in your gun sight for a few seconds.

As the planes grew faster, it became more and more difficult to arrange a good gunfight, so missiles came into play. You could fire a missile at the enemy from a little farther away, the missile could do some of the tracking, and it could outrun that sucker as he fled for his life. But, until the 1980s, you still pretty much had to be behind the bugger to give the missile a good chance.

Nowadays, fighter pilots can fire a batch of long-range missiles against multiple targets that are still over the horizon, and the aircraft's on-board computer guides all the missiles to separate kills. Modern fighter planes have Intel inside.

Things were pretty lax in those days, but you could still get into trouble. One day early in 1958, seven of us were mixing it up at about twenty thousand feet over the Santa Ana Mountains of southern California when a shiny Air Force T-33 jet trainer cruised through.

Like dogs that size up a stranger, we stopped and looked him over. Since he didn't make any aggressive moves, we left him alone and went back at each other. A couple of minutes later, here he came again. Once more, we broke off our engagements and watched the interloper move through our airspace. Again, we let him pass unmolested. Then he turned and came back.

That was enough. I went for him, and so did the others. For about ten minutes we turned him every which way but loose and flipped him with our jet wash several times.

When one of our guys called "Bingo" (low fuel, time to land), we broke it off and streamed for home. I found out later that the T-33 pilot followed us home and got our tail numbers from the tower.

The skipper was on the phone when we strolled into the ready room. His end of the conversation changed our mood. He spoke about "His boys" and said "Yes, sir" and "No, sir" a lot. A lot. At one point he yelled, "Dammit, Colonel, I'm raising fighter pilots here, not a bunch of pussy cats, and I won't do that." Eventually, he thanked the colonel, hung up the phone, and ripped us a new one.

It turned out that March Air Force Base had recently been assigned a new TACAN initial point for instrument approaches. The B-47 bomber crews that used it had reported several near misses with other aircraft.

Their base safety officer had taken off in a T-33 to look for aircraft messing about their new initial point. He found us—and how.

All that saved us was the fact that their new IP didn't show up yet in the aviation manuals, so we couldn't know about it. (That, and the fact that our skipper raised fighter pilots instead of pussy cats.)

U.S. Navy Photo

F9F-8 Cougars from VA-56 in *Echelon*

This formation is used when entering the *break*. The leader *kisses off* and makes a hard left turn. The number two pilot flies ahead for a few seconds (half the interval desired) then kisses off and breaks left also, and so on.

U.S. Navy Photo

F9F-8 Cougars from VA-56 in *Balanced Formation*

The leader's wingman is the far aircraft. The two near aircraft comprise the second section.

6

I bought a book called *The Naval Officer's Guide*. One Sunday I scanned through it while eating lunch; I needed to know what to do with the calling cards I'd recently purchased. The book said you left two cards in the silver tray by the door when you called upon your commanding officer. *You were supposed to call on your commanding officer?*

Concerned, I took the book upstairs and showed it to Tony. We decided that we'd been derelict in our duties and needed to call on our CO as soon as possible. Well, it was a Sunday. We alerted the wives.

At two o'clock that afternoon the four of us pulled up in front of the skipper's house. He was on his knees in a flowerbed that ran along the edge of his front yard, in overalls. He looked a bit surprised to see us.

"Well, hello," he said, still on his knees. "What brings you all out here?"

"We're calling on our commanding officer," Tony said.

Our commanding officer stood up. "You are what?"

"Yes, sir. Brian here bought a book on how to be a naval officer, and it said we should call on our commanding officer."

"Huh?"

"Sorry we didn't do it earlier, but we didn't know."

The CO grinned, turned, and called his wife out of the back yard. She arrived with dirt and a puzzled look on her face.

"They've come to call on their commanding officer," our CO explained.

Navy wives are resilient. She smiled and wiped her face with the back of a gloved hand. "Well then," she said, come on inside. I'll make us some coffee, and I think we have some fairly fresh cookies in the jar."

We had a pleasant visit, said our thank-you's, and left. There was indeed a silver tray on a side table by the front door, and we left our cards in it, as was proper.

The next morning, after the AOM, the skipper called Tony and me into his office and explained how "calls" were supposed to work:

the CO announced a time, like from 5:00 to 6:00 on a certain Sunday afternoon, and then every officer and his lady showed up during that period. *Oh.*

Tactical aircraft almost always operate in pairs: a leader and a wingman. If there are four aircraft, they operate as two pairs: a lead *section* and a *wing element.* Hold out your right hand palm down and fold away the thumb. This is the *finger-four* formation. The lead is the longest finger, the section lead is the next finger to the right, and the section leader's wingman is the little pinkie. The forefinger on the left of the leader is his wingman. This is called a *balanced formation.*

If the aircraft are then tucked in close together, it is called *parade formation.* (Two planes can also be in parade formation if the wingman is tucked in tight.) When the leader's wingman moves over to the right and slips in between the lead and the section lead, they are in a right *echelon.*

Since it's not very maneuverable, parade formation is used for (what else) parades. It's also used to enter a traffic pattern. As the flight approaches the landing pattern, the leader will signal his wingman (or sometimes the second element) to cross under to the right. The flight will then become staggered from left to right in a right echelon.

Over the runway or ship, the leader will break left to the downwind leg, chop power, pop the speed brakes, and then drop his landing gear and flaps when he is slow enough. The rest of the aircraft will fly straight ahead.

Each new leader will time for half the landing interval desired and then break left in turn. (Every now and then, an inattentive leader will put his flight in a left echelon and then break into the flight. The results vary from comical to tragic.)

Free cruise is a loose finger-four where each aircraft owns an arc of airspace behind the plane ahead. This allows them to drift inside a turn to catch up, or slip outside a turn to stop from overrunning the plane ahead. It minimizes throttle movement, which can be almost constant in parade formation.

A *combat spread* has the finger-four formation stretched out over a several hundred yards or more. If an enemy sneaks up behind either section, the other element can spot it, call for a turn away, and wind up on the enemy's rear.

The most important job we nuggets had was that of wingman. Fellow nugget Ed Luetschwager set the standard early on. He was wingman to one of our second-tour pilots when they did a section take off in parade formation.

Just prior to lift off, the leader's engine flamed out. His Cougar ran off the end of the runway, left its landing gear in a ditch, and wound up lying on its belly about a hundred yards into the sagebrush.

Lying next to it, also on its belly, was Ed's Cougar, still in perfect parade position on his leader's wing. Not one soul in the chain of command questioned Ed's decision to shut his bird down and stay in position. He was, after all, the wingman.

My test came a few days later. The new CAG, Butch Voorhis, came over to check out a Cougar, and the skipper assigned me to be CAG's wingman. We did a section take off in parade formation. As our wheels left the runway, CAG's landing gear started to retract, and I slapped my gear handle up. His flaps moved, and I raised mine. Then CAG rolled hard right into me and pulled about three g's.

We were instantly in an eighty-degree banked turn. I was tucked in tight under CAG's starboard wing, his wingtip about three feet from my head. Out of the corner of my eye I could see the sagebrush as it rushed by in a blur about ten or twenty feet below my starboard wing. We stayed in that hard turn for six years . . . or at least it felt that way. After about 120 degrees of turn, CAG rolled out and pulled us up into a steep climb. I was already damp with sweat.

After a routine hop while CAG checked out the airplane, he led me back over Miramar at twenty thousand feet. Since I knew we were headed home, this seemed a little strange to me; he hadn't followed the standard entry path over the town of Ramona. CAG gave me the free cruise signal (a hitch-hike motion with the thumb over alternating shoulders), and then he rolled away from me and pulled us into another high-g turn. I stayed tucked in under his belly while we spiraled down.

The cutaway g-suits we wore were like a pair of cowboy chaps with inflatable bladders across the lower abdomen, around the thighs, and around the calves of the legs. When you put more than the normal one-g on the aircraft, a valve opened automatically and pushed air into the g-suit to inflate the bladders. This was supposed to keep blood from draining out of your head and into your feet. The more g, the more air pressure.

I don't know how many g we had on. Despite the g-suit, enough blood had drained from my head that all I could see through my tunnel vision was the blurry image of the belly of CAG's airplane. It felt like my bulging g-suit would cut me into pieces.

Then here came CAG's cheery voice over our tactical frequency, "How you doing, Brian?"

Grunting out the syllables, I said, "Just . . . fine . . . CAG."

We abruptly snapped into level flight. The blood returned to my head, and I saw that we were over the duty runway. We switched to tower frequency, CAG called for landing clearance, and then he broke.

Relaxing, I timed upwind for a few seconds to get my interval on CAG and breathed a sigh of relief. I was pretty sure that I had been tested, and had passed.

About this time, the Navy issued new hard hats. They were smooth and looked sharp, but they still weren't quite as nifty as the Air Force version. The USAF hard hats had big flip-up visors that sat on your forehead when they weren't in use. This looked pretty sexy. The Navy version had a visor that slid up into a covered recess above the face opening. This wasn't as neat as the USAF version, but we were delighted to get rid of our miner's hats. (The Air Force eventually phased out the hard hats we admired so much and went with the same ones that the Navy settled on.)

VA-56 was an attack squadron; so mock dogfights were practice for our secondary mission. Our primary job was to attack ground targets. Conversely, the fighter squadrons, with primary responsibility for air-to-air, had a backup air-to-ground mission. The distinction was blurry; we were flying F9F-8 fighter planes in an attack role. (The Navy has now awkwardly resolved the issue with the F/A-18 fighter/attack aircraft.)

So, the Miramar-based attack squadrons periodically deployed to three Naval Auxiliary Air Fields for air-to-ground weapons training:

NAAF El Centro, in southern California near Yuma, NAAF China Lake in northern California, and NAAF Fallon, Nevada. All three places had miles of desert set aside for such ordnance practice.

In March 1958, VA-56 deployed to NAAF Fallon, Nevada to fire guns, shoot rockets, and drop bombs. (The attack mission was actually a lot more fun than the fighter mission. Besides using all that ordnance against the earth, you got to fly real low.)

The Cougar had four twenty-millimeter (20-mm) cannon set in that slick nose, could mount 2.75-inch rockets under the wings, and could carry up to four 500-pound general purpose bombs. We got to do a little low-level strafing with the 20-mm cannons and fire rockets into ground targets at close range. We also dropped a whole lot of Mk-76 practice bombs.

I was eager to fire the Cougar's guns again. Four of us orbited in a racetrack pattern about five hundred feet above the sagebrush-covered desert. We kept our speed around 360 knots (a knot—nautical mile/hour—is about 1.15 statute miles/hour).

A bulldozed strip blazed a trail across the sand leading to the target banner set between two poles. The banner resembled a large tennis net, except made of cloth. A blue twenty-gallon barrel sat every hundred feet before and after the target for five hundred feet in either direction.

Impatiently, we waited for the range officer (a sailor in a shack) to give us radio clearance to roll in. I was number three in the flight, the section lead.

We finally received our go-ahead signal. "Champion Lead, you're cleared in hot." (Our squadron call sign was "Champion.")

The flight leader, one of our second-tour pilots, turned in down the run-in line and called, "Roger that. Champ One in hot."

I followed number two around and then rolled into a shallow dive down the run-in line. I moved the master arm switch to *on* and called, "Three's in hot." My airspeed passed four hundred knots as I leveled the wings and roared down the dirt strip towards the target.

Leaning forward, I watched the lighted pipper of my gunsight race toward the target as I descended through two hundred feet. Within seconds the target filled my windscreen, the pipper slid up on the banner, and I fired.

The noise startled me, as usual. I saw dirt geysers a bit beyond the banner as I pulled up hard and broke left to avoid being hit by one of my own rounds in a *ricochet*. (All the real great aviation words seem to be French.)

Turning the master arm switch *off*, I called, "Three's off." Then I pulled back up into the pattern, established interval behind number two, and waited to do it again.

We each got six passes before it was time to *rendezvous* (the French again) and head for home. NAAF Fallon was a mere five miles away.

As in the training command, the bullets had different color paint on them so that someone could look at the bullet holes in the banner (preferably after we had left the area) and count each pilot's hits by the paint color smudged around the holes. I don't recall that we pilots worried much about counting holes. Shredding the banner, now that was a decent goal. Lord, was that ever fun.

Firing rockets was even better. The flight pattern around and into the target was about the same as for strafing with guns, but your dive was a little steeper, and you fired farther out to give the rockets time to fly. The targets were usually stacks of old oil drums painted blue. (Why always blue?)

When the rocket ran straight and true, it was a great sight to behold. When the rocket went crazy due to a bent fin or a bad burn, it was spectacular. (Years later, in an A-6, I had a renegade rocket fly rolls around me until its burn ended and I outran the sucker.)

If you pressed the target, rockets were pretty darn accurate. We pressed, and we put most of the rockets within thirty feet of the bull's-eye. On one flight I had a nine-foot average, and the other three pilots in the flight beat me. Rockets were much more accurate than bombing.

A bomb rack was either a TER (Triple Ejector Rack) that carried three bombs, or a MER (Multiple Ejector Rack) that held up to six weapons. We usually used MERs to carry six MK-76 bombs under each wing.

Mk-76 practice bombs are about eighteen inches long and shaped like a teardrop with fins at the skinny end. They weigh about twenty pounds. The nose is hollow and carries a smoke charge (about the size of a twelve-gauge shotgun shell) secured in place by a cotter key. When the bomb hits, the jarring impact ignites the smoke charge, and the target *spotters* can mark the hit.

The technique used to spot our hits in those days was basic but effective. Sailors were posted in three wooden shacks (that resembled out-houses) positioned several hundred yards away from the bull's-eye. The shacks were situated such that they made three points of a triangle. When the smoke went off, all three crews took a bearing on it using a fixed compass dial and then called that bearing in to the main spotter. He did a quick triangulation using the three spotter bearings, plotted the hit on an overlay chart, and called the hit up to the fliers above. For example, "Champ One, your last hit was a hundred feet at four o'clock."

Every so often the Mk-76s strewn about the target range were picked up by the ordnance crew, reloaded with fresh smoke charges, and used again. This was one of the military's more cost-effective operations.

Ever since the Navy started dropping bombs, the standard way to drop conventional (non-nuclear) weapons has been the dive-bombing attack. In a typical dive attack, you fly your airplane to a point about a mile abeam and thirteen thousand feet above the target, set your power to give you the desired airspeed at weapon release, and then roll into a 30-degree dive towards the target. (If closer abeam, you use a steeper, 45-degree dive.)

The gunsight/bombsight is a marvelous little box that uses lights, mirrors, and a glass plate to show you the pipper, a white spot that moves across the target area. The pilot pre-sets the sight to account for the intended dive angle and airspeed at release. When you roll in on an attack, you point the aircraft so that the pipper is short of the target. As you dive, the pipper moves steadily toward where you want it to be when the bomb comes off the rack.

You correct for windage with the sight. For example, if you expect the wind to move the bomb a hundred feet from right-to-left while it falls, you want the pipper to be a hundred feet to the right of the target when you pass through *pickle* altitude with the proper dive angle and airspeed.

So, you are trying to make four parameters all come together at one instant in time: dive angle, airspeed, altitude, and pipper placement. If you achieve this happy state, you'll get a good hit.

This is especially important in combat where, if you miss, you'll have to come back again or, worse, the target may get you. (It's also more difficult in combat because the other guys are shooting at you.)

Since the Navy was part of the U.S. nuclear war plan, the SIOP (Single Integrated Operations Plan), our squadron had a nuclear mission as well. Our typical pre-planned mission in case of a nuclear war was to strap on a single nuke, launch from the carrier, fly deep into enemy territory, and then flip the weapon onto the target using what was called an *idiot loop*.

I was about to do my first idiot loop. It was March 10, 1958, Pat's 20th birthday, and I was once again in a racetrack pattern a few miles west of Fallon. This time the graded trail led to a huge bull's-eye marked on the desert floor with boulders painted white. There were three rings that marked one hundred, five hundred, and a thousand feet. Billboards were set alongside the run-in line every five thousand feet out to twenty thousand feet indicating distance to the target.

"Champion flight, you're cleared in hot."

"Roger," called our leader. "Champ One in hot."

I was the leader's wingman that day, so I was number two. I flew straight ahead for thirty seconds to give myself a one-minute interval on the leader and then turned in.

"Champ Two is in hot."

I leveled off about forty feet above the bulldozed trace, shoved the throttle forward, switched on the master arm, and then eased the plane down to about twenty feet. When I passed my planned IP (Initial Point), the billboard labeled 10,000 FT, I depressed the red bomb pickle on top of the control stick and held it down with my thumb.

The pre-set timer started to count down. Fourteen seconds later a tone went off in my headset and I started a smooth pull up to put four g on the aircraft in four seconds.

Before I got to that point, however, the tone went off, and the practice bomb was released. I continued my pull-up, went over the top to complete the first part of a loop, and then rolled upright to make it a half-Cuban-eight. I was then in a dive pointed back from whence I came. The object now was to run like hell.

In the meantime, the little bomb flew down range in an arc to impact in the target area. This was called a *low-angle loft*.

After calling "Two's off," I switched off the master arm, and turned away to set up for the next run.

My UHF radio sputtered. "Champ Two, your hit is four hundred feet at eight o'clock."

Not too good, but like horseshoes, close counts in nukes.

This low-angle loft maneuver was good if you wanted a ground burst or low-altitude detonation. If you needed a higher-altitude burst or didn't have a good initial point from which to time for a loft, you went for the *over-the-shoulder* option.

On this one, the target itself was your initial point, and the weapon stayed with you on your half-Cuban-eight until you were somewhere a bit past straight up, depending on various factors. System release occurred at a set angle above level flight. The bomb then stayed on its upward trajectory while you pulled over the top and commenced your escape dive. The bomb's flight soon peaked, and the weapon fell back down to its detonation level above the target.

The over-the-shoulder method was also a back up option if you missed a planned IP for a low-angle loft or if the timer was out of whack.

If the automatic system that kicked off the bomb wasn't working, you could always use the over-the-shoulder method as a backup. You started your four-g pull-up at the target and went, "One potato, two potato, three potato, four potato, pickle."

We got to drop a *shape* every now and then. This was a fake bomb the size and weight of a real nuclear weapon. My first shape drop was exciting.

I was doing an over-the-shoulder delivery with a big, blue shape hung under my port wing. I roared low over the target and pulled up into my four-g idiot loop.

Everything was normal as I went over the top and started downhill inverted. Then I tried to roll out. Nothing happened. The plane wouldn't roll. Down and down I went, inverted, while I tried to roll right side up. The plane wouldn't roll. In desperation, I tried to roll the other way, and did two and a half snap rolls before I brought the bird under control and right side up.

As I pulled out of the dive, not very far above the sand, the problem became clear: the shape hadn't released. That damn fake bomb still clung to my wing. My initial attempts to roll upright had been unsuccessful because I was trying to lift that heavy shape. When I reversed the roll direction, the extra weight threw me into snap rolls.

The Navy had practiced the loft and over-the-shoulder deliveries for over two years at this point. So I was more than a little surprised when *Life* magazine came out with a big article about how the United States Air Force had just invented this slick new way to drop nuclear weapons using a loft maneuver.

7

The Cougar could go supersonic, but barely, and then only in a steep dive. One day when we were back at Miramar, Tony and I decided to go out over the Pacific and become *Mach Busters*. (Breaking the sound barrier was still new and unusual in those days. I was given a North American Aviation Company certificate when I finally did it in an FJ-4B. The certificate still hangs on my study wall.)

There are numerous restricted areas off the coast of California reserved for certain aircraft maneuvers, naval gunfire, etc. To the best of my knowledge, we weren't in one of them when we commenced our dives from about thirty thousand feet.

Tony went first. I climbed a little higher before I rolled in. Tony called "Mach 1" about the time I passed through twenty thousand feet in a vertical dive.

Then three puffs of AA (anti-aircraft) flak blossomed next to my starboard wing. Close!

That got my attention. I broke off the dive and pulled away from the smoke puffs, jinking as I went.

Down below, a destroyer churned up green water as she turned; little wisps of smoke rose from her guns.

We didn't make Mach 1 as we left the scene, but we went about as fast as our Cougars would go right then.

I wanted to hang the destroyer crew that had fired at me, but it turned out that all of us were right on the edge of a restricted area reserved for the destroyer to shoot at drone aircraft, and it had expected one to arrive about the time that I appeared. It was hard to tell who was in the wrong, them or us. I shut up. At least they'd missed.

The Cougar would fall backward quite well, like a big blue brick. It was quite common in our mock dogfights to run out of airspeed whenever we went straight up. You either let the nose fall through on its own, or you did a *hammerhead stall* out of it.

To do the hammerhead maneuver, you hit full rudder one way or the other just before you ran out of airspeed. At that point, the aircraft was about to quit flying and become the brick, but you still had enough air flow over the rudder to kick the nose over sideways and swivel into a dive.

If you missed the point where a rudder kick was effective, nothing bad happened; the airplane fell tail first for a while before it righted itself. (Unlike what happened to me in the A4D.)

One long-remembered moment in my life occurred when two of us ran out of airspeed at the same time and place. As usual, we were in a multi-plane dogfight somewhere in the neighborhood of twenty-five thousand feet. After many high-g turns, I followed my opponent straight up. It had been darn hard to get on his tail, and now that I was there, I wasn't about to give up my position.

I was a hundred feet behind him when it dawned on me that he was falling . . . right down onto me. I yanked on the control stick and kicked the hell out of the rudder pedals. Nothing happened. By then I was falling backwards also. But he had started earlier, so he fell faster and was gaining on me.

We did this graceful *pas de deux* down through space for about ten of the longest seconds of my young life. I don't think my colleague had any idea how close we were until we rolled canopy to canopy as he slipped past me about six feet away.

Naval aviators have regular jobs in addition to flying; I was the squadron's navigation officer. As such, I was responsible for the unit's supply of charts and other navigation items, and I had to keep them current. One of the more demanding aspects of this dull job was to make sure that our *sandblower* low-level training routes were up to date. These were approved routes across America's Southwest (and adjacent Pacific Ocean areas) where we could fly low. I mean really low. I think the rules may have required that we stay at least five hundred feet away from people, but I was always a little fuzzy about that number.

One day I conceived the idea of a sandblower route that would run from San Diego to Tucson and back. That way I could visit my parents and rack up approved training at the same time. In due course I managed to have the new route approved.

Jim Jennings was a second-tour lieutenant j.g. and a friend. On April 28, 1958, Jim and I headed to Tucson on the new sandblower route.

I led on the trip over, and it was pretty uneventful, almost boring. My special route took us right along the railroad tracks, so navigation was not a chore.

It was dusk as we approached Casa Grande, and there, headed towards us through the gloom, was the single headlight of a train. I couldn't resist. I slowed below 250 knots, dropped to about ten feet above the tracks, and lowered my landing gear.

Jim, on my wing, probably thought I was nuts.

When the train was about a mile away, I turned on the big white taxi light attached to the nose-wheel strut. I have no idea what went on in the mind of that engineer.

After an enjoyable night with my parents, Jim and I headed back to San Diego. This time Jim led. The sandblower route ended at the edge of the desert near Plaster City, but we stayed low when we turned northwest and climbed the eastern slope of the mountains that separate the desert from the coast. We were in sort of a combat spread, with Jim a ways ahead of me and off to the north.

Within minutes I had a serious problem. I'd started up the slope at too slow an airspeed and waited too long to jam on the power. *Oh oh.* I traded airspeed for altitude, but it became apparent I might not clear the ridge ahead. I wanted to turn and run downhill, but I was flanked on either side by higher terrain.

About then I remembered the story about a student who found himself in a similar situation in a T-28 and used a hammerhead stall to reverse course and go back down the ravine he was in. I considered trying that, but things began to look up; I decided I'd just make it over the ridge ahead.

My cougar was almost in a stall as it staggered over the treetops that crested the ridgeline, but we'd made it. But my sigh of relief was interrupted when all I could see in front of me was the big white dome of what turned out to be the Palomar Observatory. (God's revenge for tricking the train engineer?)

In what had to be instinctive reaction, I hit the flap handle to the full down position. The flaps rotated down, the airplane ballooned up . . . and we sailed over the dome.

Soon after that, VA-56 vacated the Quonset hut and moved into new digs in one of Miramar's two huge, cement-and-steel hangars. The maintenance crew worked out of first floor shops; we officers had second-deck spaces. I was sorry we had to move. I missed the feel of the Quonset out on the grass.

After we moved into the hangar, we set up a little snack bar in the ready room. All we had was a refrigerator with sodas in it and some candy bars. There was a jar for money, and we operated on the honor system. I was soon designated the squadron's mess officer, which put me in charge of the snack bar. (In the Navy, "mess" refers to food. You have to eat the chow to understand this.)

At the time, we had three options for lunch: brown bag from home, eat at the roach coach parked next to the hangar, or change into uniform and go to the Miramar Officer's Club. (The Air Force allowed fliers in flight gear into separate rooms at their officer's clubs, but the Navy held out for full uniforms in the clubs until the 1970s.)

Brown bags didn't work well for the bachelors; the food at the roach coach was edible but mysterious; and it was a pain to swap a sweaty flight suit for khaki in order to eat, especially if you had another flight in the afternoon. This situation led to one of my brainstorms.

I talked the skipper into assigning a sailor to work at our snack bar (now to be a lunch counter) during the middle of the day. I bought food at the base commissary on Friday and sent a roast and a ham home with two designated husbands. Their wives, always volunteers, cooked the meat over the weekend and sent it back to the ready room on Monday morning, where it was placed in the fridge.

Come lunchtime, we could have roast beef or ham sandwiches with lettuce, tomato, and mayonnaise, along with pickles and chips. The sailor on duty made the sandwiches to order right there in the ready room, and he collected the money. The food was great, and the price was even better. Everyone in the squadron was delighted with the arrangement.

Then word leaked out to the other squadrons, and their pilots started to come by for lunch. This led to some inter-squadron camaraderie in our ready room and huge profits for our lunch counter.

Soon the base commanding officer came to call. Seems he'd been flooded with complaints of lost business from the owner of the roach coach. The base CO had been able to sidestep those, but when the manager of his officer's club bitched about lost revenue, he folded. He ordered us to shut down our little restaurant.

Along about this time, the Navy started to use a British invention called the *mirror landing system* to help the LSO get planes safely aboard aircraft carriers. A bank of bright lights was placed on the port side of the carrier's flight deck, aft near the stern. The lights pointed forward and were focused on a large mirror that sat on the port side up near the end of the landing area. Two arms covered with green lights stuck out from the sides of the mirror. (If you look hard at the carrier pictured on Page 30, you can see the mirror on the port side.)

What the pilot saw on his landing approach was a blob of light on the mirror (called the *ball*) and the two green-lit arms. If the ball was even with the green arms, he was on glide path (OK). If the ball was above the green, then he was high; when the ball was lower than the green arms, he was low.

If the pilot got too low, the LSO hit a button that made a vertical bank of red lights along each side of the mirror flash. That was the wave-off signal.

Lineup and aircraft speed were separate issues for the pilot to control.

There's been a lot of talk about this system, but I'd never seen it until I cruised past NAAF El Centro one day on my way back from a navigation hop. The sun was setting over the mountains to the west, and the lights on the mirror system that sat next to the main east-west runway stood out.

Not being in any hurry, I decided to try it. I switched my radio to El Centro's tower frequency and got clearance for a touch-and-go landing on that runway. I throttled back, dropped my landing gear and flaps, and set up a long straight-in approach for a touchdown next to the mirror. *This was great.*

Leaving the power alone, I used the stick to control my approach. (Big mistake.) I experimented with a high and a low, and then centered the ball on the mirror. Using the stick, I kept that orange ball dead even with the green arms.

Wham. I slammed onto the runway doing about twenty knots faster than normal; I'd neglected to control my airspeed. And I'd also forgotten to latch my shoulder harness.

The impact threw my head forward and down, over the stick and under the instrument panel. And my hard hat stuck there. My head was trapped under the instrument panel, my chin between my knees. I was rolling down the runway at about 150 knots, and all I could see was my feet.

I almost strangled myself while I tore at the chinstrap, but I managed to rip my hard hat off and raise my head. I was almost out of runway. I jammed the throttle forward and managed to get airborne again before the asphalt turned to sand.

My cougar had climbed through two thousand feet before I got my hard hat back on and checked out with El Centro tower. If they thought my behavior on their runway was a bit odd, they didn't comment on it.

In July I went to instrument refresher training at NAS North Island. This meant nine flights under the bag in the TV-2 again. Since almost all of our flying in VA-56 was daytime VFR (Visual Flight Rules), this refresher course was a good idea. When I got back to Miramar, we had new airplanes to fly: the North American Aviation FJ-4B Fury.

8

The FJ-4 Fury saw active squadron duty for only four years, 1956 through 1959. Aviation writers of the day, however, considered her to be the best jet day-fighter in the world without an afterburner. I couldn't agree more. She was one sweet airplane, and she had an interesting pedigree.

U.S. Navy Photo

FJ-4 Fury

In 1947, North American Aviation sold the Navy a jet follow-on to the company's famous P-51 Mustang. This straight-wing aircraft was designated the FJ-1. The Air Force bought a swept-wing version designated the F-86 that was to gain fame in the skies over Korea.

The Navy soon recognized its mistake, bought the Air Force version, and designated it the FJ-2. That bird had problems around the carrier, so fixes were installed to make a newer version, the FJ-3.

That bird didn't pan out well either.

Then the Navy did a major rework on the FJ-3. It enlarged the plane's fuselage, put in a bigger engine (the J-65-W-16A with 7,700 pounds of thrust), and gave it a *wet wing* by milling the wing out of a single piece of aluminum. (Thus, the wing doubled as a fuel tank.)

This new bird, the FJ-4 Fury, entered service in 1956. In 1958, 222 of these fighters were modified so they could carry bombs and air-to-ground missiles. These became the FJ-4Bs.

I found twelve of them waiting for me in August when I returned to Miramar from instrument refresher training.

Our free-for-alls in the sky continued. And since we now had the better fighter plane, we went looking for that Air National Guard guy in his F-86. We never found him. I think he was on the prowl for people still flying Cougars.

Now that I've said all these nice things about the Fury, I should add that she was a mobile hydraulic leak. When you go out to pre-flight most planes, if you see a pool of hydraulic fluid under it, you aren't going to fly. With the FJ-4B, if you could jump across the puddle, you flew it.

In August I finally broke the sound barrier, and I did it accidentally while in a shallow dive. The plane went through Mach 1 so smoothly that I doubted my airspeed indicator for a moment.

That September I made a deliberate try at a low-level Mach-1 *boom* and almost got in serious trouble (again). I was leading a section of two FJ-4Bs with Ed Luetschwager flying my wing.

As we cruised around east of Los Angeles, I spotted a small mountain lake. We were on squadron tactical frequency when I called my wingman. "Ed, hang on. I'm going to make a supersonic pass low over that little lake to the north. We'll boom the fish."

"Roger that."

I pushed the throttle up and went into a shallow dive towards the mountaintop that cradled the lake.

Ed came up. "Keep her subsonic, Brian. One of my drop tanks is loose and vibrating."

"Wilco." I throttled back and settled in for a low altitude run at 0.97 Mach, barely under the speed of sound.

Treetops flashed beneath my wings, and I noticed that Ed had stepped up; he was now above me. (This was standard practice when the leader was flying close to the surface.)

It was beautiful. The lake was hidden behind the trees now but would come into sight in a few seconds. There were houses in the trees. Houses? I glanced in my starboard rear-view mirror and saw a yellow school bus pull off the road into a ditch. I looked ahead and glimpsed a real street . . . with buildings.

Holy shit, this is Big Bear. I had a clear vision of some admiral ripping the wings off my chest. But they had to catch us first.

We flashed past main street and then over the near shore of the lake. I went down, right on the water. The lower we were, the harder it would be for someone on the ground (or the water) to get the side number painted on our planes.

"Ed, when we clear that lip up ahead, I'm going down."

"Roger that."

The lake is in a crater. Up ahead there was a low lip of crater edge followed by a sheer drop off of several thousand feet. We skimmed over the edge. I rolled inverted and pulled for the desert below.

My wingman stuck like he was welded onto me.

Bottoming out a few hundred feet above the ground, I led us south, just under Mach 1. I wanted to be high enough to talk to Miramar but low enough that radar couldn't pull us out of the ground clutter.

"Ed, I'm switching to Miramar Approach Control."

"Roger."

I changed frequency and lied like hell; I wanted to establish an alibi. "Miramar Approach, this is Champion Four-Zero-Three, flight of two approaching the TACAN fix at twenty thousand. Request a TACAN penetration and straight-in to a section landing."

The fix I referenced was forty miles east of Miramar. We were a hundred miles north of that position and about nineteen thousand feet lower.

"Roger Champ Four-Zero-Three. You are cleared. Squawk Mode Three, Code Twenty-three-hundred. We do not have you on radar." The *squawk* was a setting for my IFF (Identification, Friend or Foe) radar responder.

"Wilco, Approach. Squawking."

But I wasn't squawking. We were now about fifty miles from

the TACAN approach fix, racing south along the east edge of the mountains. Still low.

"Champion Four-Zero-Three, check your squawk. We still don't have you on radar."

"Wilco, Approach. Maybe your radar is out."

"We'll check it, Champ Four-Zero-Three. What's your position?"

"We're at the TACAN fix, twenty thousand, commencing our descent."

Actually, we were thirty miles from there, wending our way up through the mountains, still at high speed and low altitude.

"Champion Four-Zero-Three. Our radar appears to be functioning normally, but we still don't paint you. Say your position."

"Five miles out, descending through one thousand feet. Request clearance to land."

We really were about five miles out now, but we were still on the deck and still at high speed. I gave the signal to Ed, popped the speed brakes, and ballooned up to a thousand feet.

Approach saw us. "Roger, Four-Zero-Three. We have you now. You are cleared to land. Sorry about our radar. Don't understand the problem."

"No sweat, Approach. Thanks."

I signaled Ed again, dropped the landing gear, lowered the flaps, and landed. Ed stayed right on my wing through touchdown and roll out.

Pushing my oxygen mask out of the way, I gave Ed a big grin and thumbs up. We'd pulled it off. When we cleared the runway, I signaled Ed and switched to Ground Control frequency.

The radio growled. "Champion Four-Zero-Three, this is Ground Control. The base operations officer wants you to report to him as soon as you shut down. Understood?"

Oh shit. "Wilco, Ground." I looked over at Ed.

He made a face.

Twenty minutes later I snapped to attention in the doorway of the NAS Miramar operations officer and did the knuckle rap on the doorframe. The ops boss looked up from his papers and glowered at me.

"You Ensign Bryans?"

"Yes, sir."

"Get in here."

"Aye aye, sir." I stepped up to his desk.

"Mister, you've flown your last flight. I'm going to make an example of you. We're about to yank your wings so fast you won't know you ever had them."

"Sir . . . why?"

"Why? For killing chickens that's why. Over a thousand of them."

"Chickens, sir? Where?"

"Over by Yuma, that's where. As you damn well know. You and your wingman did a supersonic pass so low over this farmer's chicken coop that over a thousand chickens dropped dead."

"Yuma? Sir, we weren't anywhere near Yuma." (This was true.)

"Oh yeah? Well, Mister, where were you?"

"Umm . . ." Buzzing Big Bear might be worse than the crime of which I was now accused, and the fake instrument penetration was no help. So, lie again. "We were doing high work over the Salton Sea, sir."

"Can you prove that, mister?"

"Guess not, sir. But you have my word of honor that we did not kill any chickens near Yuma."

"We'll see about that. I have a call in to your commanding officer, and I'm about to start an investigation. You're grounded until I get to the bottom of this."

When I got to the squadron ready room, the skipper was hanging up the phone on the duty officer's desk. Ed was next to him, looking poorly.

The skipper shook his head and went into his office.

Ed and I sat and waited.

An hour later the phone rang. The duty officer answered it, listened, and then handed the receiver to me.

Swallowing hard I said, "Ensign Bryans."

"This is the operations officer. I have good news for you. You're in the clear."

I glanced at Ed and gave him a thumbs up. "Yes, sir. Thank you, sir."

"Yeah, well, sorry I ripped into you like that. It turns out that a witness in Yuma got the tail number of one of the chicken killers. They were two National Guard types in F-86s."

Seems Ed wasn't satisfied with his ride across the desert floor on the belly of his Cougar. He now did it at high speed in an FJ-4B. After a maintenance test flight, he broke to land, and when he retarded the throttle, the engine flamed out. He figured he was too low to eject, so he rode it into the *malpais* behind the Marine base next door. He safed his ejection seat, opened the canopy, and landed wheels up at about a hundred and forty knots on a little stretch of level ground.

His plane then skidded in a fishhook-shaped path through a field of automobile-size boulders, shedding parts as it went. Ed wound up with the forward third of his bird stuck out over the lip of a deep wash.

When the plane stopped, Ed unlatched his lap belt and tried to climb out onto the port wing. A sheet of flame came up in his face, so he leapt onto the starboard wing and fell down the side of the wash. But he walked away.

Back at the hangar, several of us clustered at the window and watched the column of black smoke rise from behind a low ridge about a mile away. Someone said, "I wonder how Ed is."

"Just fine," said a voice from astern. We spun around. Ed had come up behind us while we gawked. He was dirty, scratched, and singed, but he was all smiles.

We practiced carrier landings at Miramar for a big chunk of October. We flew a left-hand racetrack pattern at five hundred feet that led to the left runway, while normal traffic stayed above us and used the right runway.

Then, on October 28, I flew aboard *Kearsarge* (CVA 33) off San Diego. The FJ-4 came aboard at 130 plus knots, a whole lot faster than the old SNJ, but the plane was a sweetheart around the ship, and our day traps were no big deal. Not so my first catapult shot.

Kearsarge was equipped with two of the old H-8 hydraulic catapults. To prepare for launch, you taxied onto the start of a 225-foot slot in the carrier's deck that was the catapult track. A *bridle* made up of inch-thick steel wires was hooked to one point on each side of the plane's fuselage (near the main mounts) and into the curved mouth on the front of the *shuttle* plate that rode the slot in the carrier's deck.

Each shuttle was attached to a piston situated in a long tube under the cat track. (Imagine a slingshot with the ends of the band attached to the plane instead of the arms of the wood handle, and the rock holder slipped over the shuttle. In its own way, the bridle actually was a slingshot.)

A *holdback fitting*, a piece of ceramic that looked very much like a weight lifter's dumbbell, was slipped into a slot under the plane's tail and attached to the deck with another steel cable.

The shuttle was then tensioned: hydraulics moved it forward until the bridle was taut. At this point, the plane squatted from the forward pressure of the shuttle fighting against the strength of the holdback fitting. A huge, steel jet-blast deflector (always referred to merely as the JBD) located a few feet behind the plane was then raised up at a steep angle.

When the crew was ready to shoot you off the bow, the yellow-shirted catapult officer stepped over in front of your wing to prove that you wouldn't be fired off until both of you were ready. He then raised one arm over his head and twirled two fingers.

You shoved the throttle forward to a hundred percent power and grabbed a small metal rod that stuck out of the cockpit wall slightly ahead of the throttle. You held the throttle head and that metal rod together in your left hand to make sure that your hand, and the throttle, didn't fly backwards when the cat fired.

After a quick check of the engine instruments, you gave the cat officer a salute with your right hand. Then you tucked your right elbow into your gut and set your hand behind the stick; you didn't want it to come back in your lap on the cat shot.

At this point, the cat officer stepped away from in front of your wing and, fingers still twirling over his head, did a quick check of your path to make sure it was clear. Then he did a fencing move, a thrusting motion that took him down on one knee, face and arm towards the bow. His outstretched fingers touched the deck, and the cat fired.

It was in that instant that the hydraulic catapult distinguished itself from the more modern steam catapult. The *slug* that caught the shuttle and pushed you down the catapult started from a point about twenty feet behind your plane. It had accelerated to full bore by the time it picked up the shuttle and you on its way to the end of the track and a final speed of about 165 mph. When this force hit you, the holdback fitting snapped in two; it didn't even slow the shuttle down.

The first time this happened, I blacked out. I came to about sixty feet in the air . . . flying. I was so thrilled by this unexpected and wild event that I keyed the UHF radio button and yelled, "Yah-hoo!"

And I blacked out the next time. It didn't affect everyone like that, but I blacked out momentarily almost every time that I was fired from a hydraulic cat. This was even more of a thrill at night, but that was still in the future.

On November 16, 1958, we seven nugget ensigns were promoted to lieutenants, junior grade. We replaced our single gold bars ("butter bars") with single silver ones. Then we celebrated. (Of course these were temporary promotions; we were on probation. Permanent promotions lagged several years behind.)

Earlier in 1958, the People's Liberation Army of China had fomented the Quemoy-Matsu Crisis. The F-104 Starfighter and the F-105 Thunder Chief were now in service with the U.S. Air Force, and Pan American Airlines had begun to fly the Boeing 707. Sayonara, with Marlon Brando and James Garner, was in theatres across the land, and Elvis was in the Army.

U.S. Navy Photo

FJ-4B Fury - 1958

Note the *dorsal fin* along the aircraft's spine. This marks the 4 and 4B models. The 4B had beefed up *hard points* on the wings that permitted the aircraft to carry bombs in an attack role.

9

To celebrate the New Year, 1959, the squadron welcomed another new airplane in January. Twelve brand new Douglas A4D-1s arrived to replace our FJ-4Bs. As great as the FJs were, they weren't really compatible with our nuclear mission. So, we were to be the first West Coast A4D squadron.

A4D-2 Skyhawk

The A in A4D stood for Attack. This made it clear that our prime mission was air-to-ground. The 4D meant that it was the Navy's fourth model from the Douglas Aircraft Company. The A4D's official name was the Skyhawk, but it was often called Heinemann's Hot Rod after Edward H. Heinemann, the plane's designer at Douglas Aircraft. It has also been called the Bantam Bomber and the Scooter. It was a very small jet aircraft.

The A4D had swept back *delta* wings with a wingspan of only twenty-seven feet. (The FJ-4B had a span of thirty-nine feet.) This meant that the A4D didn't need the ability to fold its wings like every other carrier-based aircraft.

Its other unique feature was stilt-like legs. The landing gear struts were extra long so that a nuclear weapon could be hung below the fuselage. (The A4D could carry a single Mk-28 nuclear weapon a thousand miles.)

A Wright J65-W-2 turbojet engine that had been boosted to provide 8,500 pounds of thrust powered the plane. That was a lot, considering that the A4D's empty weight was a mere 9,146 pounds. The A4Ds top speed was 660 mph, about twenty mph slower than the FJ-4B.

Another innovation that came with the A4D was the *torso harness*. To get ready to fly, you put on a cutaway g-suit over the flight suit. Then you put on the torso harness. As its name inferred, this was an armless and legless coverall that zipped up the front. Your lap belt and shoulder harness were built into the torso harness.

Sewn-in straps ended at four *Koch fittings*, one on each shoulder and one on each hip. You pulled the short hose connected to your g-suit through a slit in the left side of the torso harness, grabbed your helmet, and you were ready to go.

When you slid into your seat in the A4D cockpit, you sat on your survival pack (raft, etc.) and leaned back against your parachute. The two male Koch fittings on the shoulder clipped into two corresponding female fittings at the top of the parachute, and the Koch fittings on your hips attached to your survival pack. All four fittings also attached you to the aircraft (until ejection).

And the cockpit was tiny. You didn't really get into the A4D; you strapped it on.

U.S. Navy Photo

The A4D Cockpit

Preparation to fly the A4D for the first time was pretty casual in VA-56. I was headed out the door for home one evening when the skipper handed me a copy of a half-inch-thick document titled the *A4D Pilot's Manual*. "Read this tonight," he said. "You're scheduled to fly one on the first launch tomorrow." (Things are a bit different today.)

The next morning I had my ground crew help me get one of the A4Ds started. I taxied out, took off, and fell in love with another airplane. She was a sweetheart. The A4D looped and rolled with the best of them, and she was responsive to a very light touch.

I got a shock when I came in to land, however. I flew over the runway at eight hundred feet, broke hard left, and popped the speed brakes. The A4D slowed down smoothly and I dropped the gear and flaps. I put in a little nose-up trim as the plane slowed.

Then, as I neared the one-eighty position abeam the landing point, the nose started to drop. Odd characteristic, I thought. I pulled back on the stick, but the nose continued to fall, and the airplane lost altitude. I added power and more back stick, but the plane still seemed hell bent on going into a dive.

My next move would have to be an ejection. In desperation, I searched for a clue on the instrument panel. There it was. The nose trim tab showed full down. *Damn.*

It took less than a second to discover that part of my leather flight glove had wedged under the little trim button on top of the control stick and had run the nose trim to full down. Three seconds later I had normal trim, followed by a salvaged landing. I changed the way I gripped the control stick.

Some of us got to fly both the FJ-4B and the A4D that month, and we spent the time testing them against each other. We had many fine dogfights over southern California. Our informal comparative study concluded that the FJ-4B was a superior fighter above fifteen thousand feet, but that delta wing on the A4D made it the better one at low altitude. And low was where we intended to operate.

On January 27, 1959, several of us went to the FAA (Federal Aviation Administration) building down at Lindbergh Field (the San Diego airport) to take our tests for a commercial pilot license. That piece of paper would allow us to fly commercial aircraft. (Some planned to use it for that purpose; I just wanted it for insurance.)

We emerged from the building as Convair's first commercial jet airliner thundered down the runway and climbed out into a cloudless sky. I watched it disappear, and it occurred to me that we had just witnessed the end of an era. No longer would we jet flyboys own the sky above ten thousand feet. Civilization had come to the Wild West.

The A4D's nuclear mission required us to be able to fly long distances at low altitude to escape enemy radar. This meant we had to practice low-level, DR (Dead-Reckoning) navigation over California, Nevada, Arizona, and the Pacific Ocean. *Aw shucks.*

The over-water part consisted of a low-level drive straight out to sea for a hundred miles or more, then a run north for a couple of hundred miles followed by a turn to the east. The objective was to hit a precise coast-in point after you'd crossed several hundred miles of water. We did this alone and low on the water, and we learned to judge the wind that affected our flight. We watched the swells and the spray that came off the waves and adjusted our navigation.

Our over-land routes took us far into the deserts of Nevada and northwestern Arizona. There's a rancher up there in Arizona that is probably still gunning for me. One beautiful clear day I came boiling along at 360 knots, about twenty feet above the ground, headed for a checkpoint in the Grand Canyon. I topped a low ridge and found myself crossing over a huge pole corral full of cattle and cowboys. When the corral appeared in my rear-view mirrors, I saw about a thousand head of cattle stampede right through one side of the corral, the cowboys in hot pursuit.

As an ex-cowboy myself, I felt pretty bad about the stampede. But it didn't stop me from flying low. Ten minutes later I sailed over the lip of the Grand Canyon and dropped down into it. When you come up on the canyon low and fast like that, its beauty leaps out at you like a birthday surprise.

I went up that canyon on several flights before I found out there was a cable strung across it that sagged down to about where I usually flew. It pays to be lucky.

In early March, we took our A4Ds to NAAF Fallon, Nevada, for weapons training, and I stuck my head in another noose. The squadron sent an advance detachment up in a transport plane on Sunday morning, and I led a flight of four A4Ds up that afternoon.

The plan was that we'd handle the Monday morning target times while the rest of the squadron came up. We four pilots had settled in at the BOQ (Bachelor Officer Quarters) when I got a phone call from the skipper. He said that the rest of the squadron had been delayed and wouldn't arrive until Tuesday or Wednesday.

Well, that meant we had to sit on our hands for a day or two and lose valuable training time. *Aha.* Since I was the senior officer present (remember SOPA?), I called out the troops and explained that we were going to fly even if the rest of the squadron wasn't there.

In all fairness to the other junior officers with me, they thought I was nuts. I had to get a little testy with them (I pulled rank) to get them to cooperate.

Early Monday, we had four airplanes working the target times while our small cadre of enlisted men kept our birds turning and burning. We did that all day Monday and were still at it when the skipper arrived with the rest of the squadron on Tuesday.

To say that the CO was surprised to see his planes in the air would be a bit of an understatement. He came right over to me. "Brian, what in hell is going on here?"

"We're flying, Skipper. We had good target times, and we've used them." I was proud of what we'd done.

"Shit. Whose idea was this? Yours?"

"Yes, sir." Pride had ebbed; concern had grown.

"What did I tell you that gave you the idea I wanted you to do this?"

"Nothing, sir. I just thought it was a good idea."

There was a long pause. "Brian, the reason we couldn't fly up here on Monday was because we found out that the squadron was broke. We didn't have money to pay for gas until we got a *supplemental* approved last night."

Now it was my turn. "Oh shit."

"Indeed," the skipper said. "Get out of here, I'll call CAG and ask him to get some money from somewhere to cover your flying."

I left.

Twenty minutes later the skipper called me into his room. "You're off the hook, Brian. CAG pulled some money from VF-51. And he agreed with me that initiative in young officers shouldn't be punished." He winked. "Now get back into the air."

After we returned to Miramar, I spent four days at the Nuclear Weapons School on NAS North Island where I learned about *Mach-y stems* and other elements of mass destruction. My training there was interrupted on Saint Patrick's Day.

That very memorable day, I was in an auditorium on the base, along with about two hundred other naval aviators, listening to a speech by the local admiral. The admiral paused, took a note from a messenger, read it, and asked, "Is there a Lieutenant Junior Grade Bryans in the audience?"

Stunned, I rose and said, "Here, sir."

"Well, son," the admiral said, "you better get on home. Your wife is having a baby."

"Yes, sir." I trotted out of the auditorium and was in my car before I remembered my hat; it was still under my seat in the auditorium. It was an expensive part of the officer's uniform, and I really couldn't afford a new one. So, I went back into the building to retrieve my hat.

"What in the hell are you doing back here?" the admiral asked. All hands stared at me.

"I forgot my cover, sir."

I have chosen to forget the words the admiral mumbled next as he shook his head. I grabbed my hat and retreated from the room.

I picked Pat up at the apartment and rushed her to the La Jolla Hospital. A few hours later, Kathleen Kelly Bryans was born.

A nurse escorted me to the incubator room to see my first child. She was covered with black, curly hair. For the second time that day I was stunned; she looked like a baby monkey.

When I was allowed in to see Pat, she gave me a quizzical look. "Have you seen her?"

"Yes," I admitted. "I think we got a lemon."

The day after Pat and the baby came home, Tony and Angie Tambini came by to see our first child. Angie went in first and was polite, but when Tony looked into the crib he paused and said, "That is the ugliest baby I have ever seen."

Fortunately, over the next few weeks, she turned into a cute-as-a-button, blue-eyed blonde.

Shortly thereafter, I was transferred from the Naval Reserve to the regular Navy. I was now USN instead of USNR and could plan on a full naval career. This was no small achievement; I was the only junior officer in the air wing accepted that year.

Naval aviation changed. A stack of manuals was delivered that altered our lives. Stamped across the top of each document were the words *Naval Air Training and Operating Procedures Standardization (NATOPS) Program.* The letter that accompanied the manuals explained that, in order to reduce the Navy's high accident rate, we would now be expected to operate our aircraft in a standard manner; everybody was to fly any particular plane the same way.

"This is bullshit," I declared. "We all do things the same way now. We all break, pop the speed brakes, lower the landing gear, and then lower the flaps. What more do they want?"

Tony looked up. "You lower the landing gear before the flaps?"

"Yeah," I said. "Don't you?"

"No. I always put the flaps down first."

Well, maybe we *could* use a little more standardization.

In May we swapped out our planes for a newer version of the A4D, the A4D-2. The modified birds had a strengthened fuselage and a single-skin rudder that reduced vibration and the concomitant skin cracks. The most noticeable addition was a non-retractable refueling probe attached to the starboard side that stuck out ahead of the nose fairing. It looked like a six-foot ballpoint pen. (See the photo on Page 83.)

The most important addition from the pilot's point of view was the new Escapac rocket-boosted ejection seat. At least in theory, it gave us the ability to eject at ground level (as long as we weren't in a descent at the time).

Since we now had air-to-air refueling capability, we practiced a little of that. The tanker was an A4D with a *buddy store* mounted below the fuselage. The buddy store was a contraption that looked like a large bomb, but it contained a fuel tank forward and a hose reel aft. The reel held about thirty feet of two-inch hose with a *drogue* at the end. The drogue looked like an enlarged badminton shuttlecock. We called it the "basket." When it was time to refuel somebody, the tanker pilot flipped a switch that unlocked the reel, and air pressure against the basket pulled the hose out.

A pilot who needed fuel would fly behind and below the tanker, then ease forward to drive the tip of his refueling probe into the basket. At the center of the basket, and about two feet into it, was a receptacle the size of a cereal bowl. When the tip of the receiving aircraft's probe locked into the receptacle and pushed the hose forward, fuel started to flow from tanker to receiver. The tanker pilot could transfer fuel from his own plane down into the buddy store, if needed.

This was like trying to thread a needle. At least that was how it seemed at first. The airflow around the tanker sometimes made the basket dance around the approaching probe. If your probe passed the basket without engaging it, the darn thing whipped around outside your cockpit. Then there was always the case where your probe got stuck in the "feathers"; this twisted the basket sideways and put a kink in the hose. That could get exciting. More than a few planes returned home with a cracked canopy from a botched pass at the basket. Of course, since we were all young males talking on our squadron's private tactical frequency while we did this, there were many ribald comments passed along with the gas.

The ship was about a hundred miles off San Diego, and it was a black night. I was out there to trap aboard, and I was in trouble: I'd made four attempts, gone low in close each time, and been waved off. This was try number five.

I turned downwind and set up for another pass. There was no moon and no horizon. A high, thin layer of clouds hid even the stars. The only way to tell which way was up was the instrument panel. A single red light at the carrier's masthead was the sole clue to the carrier's location. I seemed to be the center of a black universe.

In those days, the Navy still suffered from a WW-II fear that an enemy sub or scout plane might spot a lighted warship, so carrier night ops were done with a minimum of lights. There was that single red masthead light, of course, and when you rolled into the groove astern the ship, three tiny, shielded, white lights became visible along the centerline of the landing area. Except for the lights on the mirror, that was it.

Words cannot describe how hairy night carrier ops were on a black night with no horizon. This was especially true in the A4D. You couldn't see any piece of your airplane outside the cockpit. There was just you and the pale red glow of your instrument panel alone in that big, dark, dangerous world.

On the downwind leg, I flew on instruments at five hundred feet on the reverse of the ships course. Four wave offs had me sweating. I was not accustomed to night flying, and I wasn't used to failure.

As the red masthead light went by my port wing, I keyed the UHF. "Champ Four-Zero-Four, one-eighty."

"Roger Four-Zero-Four. Cleared to land. The wind is still calm, twenty-four knots across the deck."

Easing the throttle back, I tweaked the trim again. Trim was key to a smooth pass. I monitored my angle of bank, airspeed, and altitude while I flew instruments around the turn. At the ninety-degree position, the altimeter read three hundred feet.

I slid into the groove behind the ship and saw the faint phosphorescence where the ship's screws had churned the water. I leveled the wings and transferred to semi-visual flight. There were the three centerline lights. There was the mirror. I was a little right of course and a tad high. I eased power and called the ball. "Four-Zero-Four, Skyhawk ball, nineteen hundred."

That confirmed to the ship that I was an A4 with nineteen hundred pounds of fuel aboard. The arresting gear crew would make sure the four arresting wires were set for the correct gross weight about to trap.

Back on centerline now and the ball of light on the mirror eased down to an on-glide-path indication. This was a good one. Then the ball dropped.

The LSO screamed: "Power . . . Power! . . . POWER!

I pushed the throttle far forward.

The red lights on both sides of the mirror flashed, and the LSO shouted into his mic: "Wave off! Wave off!"

Damn. I slammed the throttle against the stop, brought in the speed brakes, and pulled the nose up until the little airplane on the attitude gyro indicated best climb attitude. I had about two seconds not knowing if I would clear the fantail . . . then I was across the deck and back into the black void. The hand on the stick trembled.

"Champion Four-Zero-Four, your signal is Bingo." The ship had sent me home. *Thank God.*

"Wilco, Panther. Switching." I cleaned up the bird, turned east, and switched to Miramar approach. I had just enough fuel to make it home. The coast lights appeared, and I had a horizon again.

The next day, CAG caught up to me at Miramar. He looked grumpy. "Where were you last night, Brian? I looked for you on the ship."

"I didn't make it, CAG. I was Bingoed."

"That was *you* out there?"

"Yes, sir. I can't understand it. Every damn time I got in close, the bottom fell out on me."

"They told you the wind was calm, didn't they?"

"Yes, sir. Why?"

CAG snorted. "Well, when the air is calm, the ship has to make its own wind across the deck to reduce your touch down speed. That puts the hot stack gas right across the fantail and creates a downdraft there. If you don't squeeze on a little extra power in close, the bottom falls out. I thought you young studs knew that."

As part of our readiness training, we pilots had to go to survival school. This was a one-week course in survival, escape, and evasion. There are several scattered around the world; we got to go to the one near San Diego.

It started with a bus ride up into the mountains. There, we received instruction on survival. We were shown how to kill and eat snakes, find bird's eggs, etc. None of us would volunteer to kill the little bunny they had, so we didn't learn how to skin him. (I already knew that from my cowboy days.)

We were then expected to starve while we camped out on the mountain and lived off the land. I wound up with a couple of helicopter drivers who had a surprise for me. They had choppered up the day before class started and buried tins of food. After the instructors went to sleep, we dug up the stash and dined on Dinty Moore's Spaghetti and Meat Balls.

Then came the evasion phase. We were to traverse an area comprised of several square miles of brush and trees without being caught by the instructors. None of us made it.

They dragged us POWs into a compound that looked like a cattle corral, and then "tortured" us. We each had a session in the horizontal box and the vertical box. The difference between them is obvious. Each box was so small that it took several interrogators to fold me up and stuff me inside. The vertical box was the more painful of the two because my weight crushed my knees against a wooden brace.

I forgot about that pain when one of my oppressors fired a rifle just on the other side of the slab of wood jammed against my ear. The ringing didn't end until the next day.

Now that we'd mastered mountain survival and resistance to torture (?), we were bussed down to a remote strip of ocean beach on NAS North Island. There we were to learn seaside survival.

That night we pooled our money, and two strong swimmers

volunteered to swim up the coast to fetch cheeseburgers and milk shakes. They'd been gone for about half an hour when someone discovered that the crabs were out. One crew started a fire and got a big (conveniently located) pot of water to boil; another crew caught crabs.

By the time the two swimmers returned with plastic bags full of food in tow, we were too stuffed to eat the burgers. The swimmers were pissed. Then, when they discovered that all the crabs had been eaten, they were *really* pissed.

When I got back home, I weighed myself. I had gained two pounds while at survival school.

Much of southwestern Arizona contains restricted areas designated for military training flights, and the area includes several gunnery and bombing ranges. One bright summer day, I was blessed with the opportunity to race through that piece of desert on another low-level navigation mission.

Once again I was able to enjoy the combination of high speed and low altitude while I followed the marks on the strip chart clipped to my kneeboard. I was at 360 knots again because that translated to one nautical mile every ten seconds—six miles a minute—and it made navigation a bit easier.

The chart indicated that several old, abandoned airfields left over from WW-II were in the restricted area, and my flight plan used one of them for a checkpoint on my route. Two large metal hangars appeared up ahead, right on schedule, and I changed course a few degrees to pass between them.

They both were two-story structures, open at each end, and I toyed with the idea of flying right through one of them. Those big open hangar doors were inviting, but after a moment my common sense took charge.

As I zipped through the narrow gap between the two hangars, I received another of those surprises I seemed to encounter with great regularity: the airfield wasn't abandoned. There were planes all over the place, and people too.

I blasted away across the sand dunes and hoped that, once again, I'd been too low and too fast for them to get my number. It must have worked out that way because I never got any feedback from the stunt. (I wonder what would have happened if I'd flown *through* one of those hangars.)

Tom Cruise's movie *Top Gun* made a lot of people aware of the Navy's fighter weapons school by that name. In 1959, however, the school was not in existence, and the title *Top Gun* went to the Navy's best fighter and best attack squadrons.

That year, VA-56 won the Kane Trophy as the Light Jet Attack *Top Guns* at the fourth Naval Air Weapons Meet. (I have a Top Gun patch on my leather flight jacket to prove it.) Our little squadron also won the Pacific Fleet Battle Excellence Award and the Chief of Naval Operations Aviation Safety Award. It was quite an outfit.

As the rest of 1959 passed by, we concentrated on our primary mission: daylight attack with conventional and nuclear weapons. We did very little instrument work and almost no night flying. Until December, that is. We were required to have ten hours of night flying each year, and about December 1 we tallied our hours and got serious about it. For all of 1959, I had 10.4 hours at night, 7.4 of it in December. I had fifty-four daylight carrier landings, but none at night. Well, I'd tried.

The year 1959 saw Lee Petty win the first Daytona 500 and Castro's troops enter Havana. Alaska and Hawaii became states. The People's Republic of China invaded Tibet, and the Barbie Doll debuted. The Douglas DC-8 went to work for Delta Airlines and United Airlines. *Ben Hur* was the hot movie as the year ended, while Bobby Darin sang "Beyond the Sea."

U.S. Navy Photo

A4Ds over the Pacific – 1959

AP Photo - 1959

The only time I made the Tucson newspaper. The plane captain and I were both Arizona boys.

10

On January 2, 1960, hung over or not, the squadron got serious about going to sea. Our two-year lolly-gag was over. During the next two months, we did a lot of FCLP and spent some time at sea.

Our work aboard ship usually came in the form of a five-day mini-cruise. The carrier would leave San Diego Monday morning and return Friday evening or Saturday morning. That kind of schedule was good for the crew's morale. When the ship sailed, our enlisted men and some of our pilots had to be on the carrier; the rest flew aboard when the ship was ready.

One bright morning I was part of the crew that *manned the rail* in our dress white uniforms while we cruised up the channel, rounded Point Loma, and headed out to sea. There was no wind to consider, so the bullhorn sounded as soon as we turned west. "Secure from parade formation. Flight Quarters. Flight Quarters. Stand by to recover a flight of F3H Demons."

As the LSO crew trotted past me, I asked our guy, Spence Thomas, if I could go with them and watch the recovery from the LSO Platform.

"Sure," he said.

So I tagged along. The LSOs stood on a platform about ten feet by ten feet that jutted out over the port side of the ship, aft near the fantail. A canvas-and-rope net was rigged below to catch anyone that fell or was blown over the side. I stood on the outboard corner so I wouldn't get in the way.

The ship settled onto a steady course, and the flight of four Demons broke overhead. Since the wind was calm, the captain revved up turns to make the necessary wind across the deck. I watched the first F3H turn through the ninety and then noticed that flecks of black soot from the ship's stack had settled onto my newly laundered dress white uniform. I decided to bail out of there to save the cost of another trip to the laundry.

I dropped down into the safety net, opened the steel hatch there, and stepped inside the ship. Just then the first Demon landed and caught a wire. But that wire was set for an A-1 Spad, a lighter airplane. The wire snapped and whipped back across the deck. The

Demon managed to get airborne again, but the wire wiped out everyone on the LSO platform.

The toll was one dead and three critical. Spence had been almost cut in half, but he was still alive.

Our on-board doctors earned my respect that day and night; they kept the wounded alive until they could be stabilized and choppered into the Balboa Naval Hospital.

Spence lived to fly again a little over a year later. He may have had second thoughts about it later. His first catapult shot after his recovery was a *cold cat*; the catapult malfunctioned and dribbled his A4D off the bow well below flying speed.

The plane splashed into the water ahead of the ship, and the carrier's bow cut the A4D in half just behind the cockpit. The two pieces tumbled over and over along the bottom of the ship, missed the whirling screws, and then sank at the standard rate of seventeen feet per second.

Having lost his oxygen supply when the plane was cut in two, Spence found himself out of air and trapped in the cockpit. By the time he fought his way out of the cockpit, he was on the verge of passing out. His last conscious effort was to pull the toggle on one side of his life preserver.

He regained consciousness bobbing about in the ship's wake. He'd been underwater without air for three minutes.

And he still went back to flying.

Ticonderoga ("Tico Maru" as we future Asian fliers liked to call her) sailed for WESTPAC with Air Wing Five aboard on March 5, 1960.

Launched in 1944, *Ticonderoga* (CVA 14) was the sixth *Essex*-class carrier and the fourth U.S. warship to bear that name. She carried a crew of 3,448 officers and men, and could do thirty-three knots. She was 888 feet long, with a flight deck that measured 192 feet at its widest, and was equipped with two steam catapults.

Each catapult had two bullet-shaped pistons that sat inside two parallel cylinders set under the flight deck. An inverted T bar connected the two pistons, and the leg protruded up through a slot in the deck. The plane was hooked up to that leg.

To launch you, the catapult officer allowed steam pressure to build up in the cylinders behind the pistons. When the pressure built to the level necessary for the aircraft's weight and launch conditions (temperature, humidity, wind across the deck), he fired you.

The added pressure of the released steam broke the holdback fitting and shoved the pistons, aircraft attached, down the cylinders. Water brakes stopped the pistons at the end of their run while the plane continued on into the air. A mechanical device pulled the pistons back for another shot.

Even though the steam cats accelerated planes from zero to 160 knots in two seconds, the steam made for a hell of a lot smoother ride than the old hydraulic cats, and I never blacked out on a steam shot.

(Note: *Ticonderoga* was decommissioned in November, 1973.)

Air Wing Five was made up of VA-52 with A-1 Spads, VF-51 flying F4D Skyrays, VF-53 with F3H Demons, VA-55 and VA-56 flying A4D-2 Skyhawks, and VAH-4 with twin-engine A3D Skywarriors. (The A3D carried a crew of three. It was so difficult for the crew to exit the airplane in an emergency that the men who flew her said that A3D stood for All three dead.)

Our schedule called for five days of fun and frolic in Hawaii before we continued west. Not so fast.

As we pulled into Pearl Harbor, our skipper was called to the bridge. The Navy needed a night nuclear attack capability to counter the U.S. Air Force's claim that only they could strike around the clock. Budget dollars were at stake, and VA-56 had been designated the Navy's first night, all-weather, nuclear-attack squadron. *Holy shit.*

While the rest of the air wing enjoyed the nightlife along Waikiki, we did night FCLP at USMC Air Station Kaneohe Bay on the north side of Oahu. It was black out that week, but at least we had a horizon lit by the glow of our comrades' nightlife on the other side of the island. The bad part was the downwind turn. It was just inside an unlit butte a little higher than our pattern altitude. If you went long, you hit the butte.

When we put back out to sea, I got ten night landings right away, six traps and four bolters. (Not very impressive.) Then, after that initial spurt, our night flying became pretty sporadic. This made it worse. Not only was night flying in the A4D unnatural; you were rusty every time you went up.

The Navy's attitude back then was that, unless you were flying in the soup, one set of procedures was enough. So, we flew at night like we did in the daytime. It was common practice to launch a two-plane section off the two bow cats simultaneously, so we were in parade formation when we came off the ship. When we came back, we entered the landing pattern in formation at eight hundred feet, just like daytime. If our landing was to be delayed, our signal was *Delta*, and we stayed in a racetrack pattern at eight hundred feet. If our signal was *Charlie* (cleared to land), then we did the standard left-hand break and descended to five hundred feet, just like daytime.

As wingman on a night flight, you came off the cat already on the wing on your leader. (The leader's aircraft was strapped to the port cat, the wingman's aircraft was on the starboard one, and both catapults were fired at the same time.)

You stayed glued to the leader's side for an hour and a half and then lost him when he blinked his formation lights (goodbye) and broke away to land. Suddenly, there you were, all alone in the black void. Frequently, you got a good look at your instrument panel for the first time since you did your engine run up prior to the cat shot, and now you had to shift into instrument-flying mode at eight hundred feet.

If there was a horizon, it wasn't too bad. When there was no horizon, words cannot describe how hairy this could be.

Just as a precaution, the Navy almost always had a *plane guard* on station during carrier operations. This was either a destroyer astern of the carrier, or a helicopter that hovered nearby, ready to pluck a downed flier out of the water.

It was also SOP (Standard Operating Procedure) to have an airborne tanker (or a plane with a buddy store) in an orbit above the carrier's traffic pattern. If a plane boltered and went low-state, the tanker could drop down and provide fuel to the emergency aircraft while it turned down wind and set up for another pass at the deck. There weren't any Bingo fields in the middle of the Pacific Ocean.

The F3H Demon pilots routinely *downed* their aircraft if their radar altimeter was not working. We couldn't do that; we didn't have a radar altimeter.

And our regular altimeter, a WW-II model, couldn't be trusted; it stuck. We commenced our instrument-weather TACAN approaches from twenty thousand feet or so and leveled off at two thousand feet. It was not unusual to see the altimeter unwind down to five or six thousand feet and then sit there while we continued downward.

Prudence required that we time our descent. The standard penetration called for a four thousand foot-per-minute rate of descent. So, if we pushed over from twenty thousand feet, we'd punch the timer on our clock and level off four and a half minutes later. (This in what the Pentagon Navy considered a night, all-weather, attack aircraft.)

As part of our preparation for a possible nuclear mission, a team of experts flew out to the ship to grill us on our pre-flight planning. Each of us had several different missions prepared in detail since the carrier could be anywhere in the western Pacific when the balloon went up. This was all Top Secret and very serious. So I was all business when I was called in for my session.

And the Navy captain I faced was all business too. He picked one of my target folders, scanned it, and then looked at me. "After you drop your weapon, how far away can you get before you run out of fuel."

"From twenty to a hundred miles, sir. It depends on the winds."

"What do you plan to do after you eject? You'll be deep in enemy territory, and everybody around you is going to be pretty pissed off. They'll connect you to that big mushroom cloud right away."

"Ah, I plan to hunker down, survive, and wait for possible rescue, sir."

"Yeah, right." He paused. "Okay, it's the next morning. You wake up, and there's a pretty little eight-year-old girl from the village down in the valley standing about ten feet away looking at you. What would you do?"

I knew what was expected of me: she couldn't be allowed to tell where I was. "I'd kill her, sir."

The captain looked pleased, so I dropped the other shoe. "Then I'd cook her and eat her, sir."

* * *

On May 1, 1960, Gary Powers flew his U-2 spy plane over the Soviet Union and got shot down. Ten days later, President Eisenhower took responsibility for ordering the U-2 flights. Five days after that, Nikita Sergeyevich Krushchev interrupted a Big-Four meeting in Paris to demand an apology from Ike. That ended the conference.

Out in the western Pacific, the skipper took me aside and said the balloon was going up. The ship had orders to launch two nuclear strikes that night: an A3D twinjet bomber—and me.

We all knew there was a crisis, but ... *this? Me?*

I went through denial for several minutes, but that ended when the A3D pilot came in and said that we needed to get some coordination done. I would fly wing on him until we reached the coast, then we'd split. He had a nearby target; mine was way inland, a one-way trip.

He was all serious, and I couldn't deny it any more. *This is real.* I spent the next two hours reviewing my mission.

Then we got the call, suited up, and went on deck to pre-flight our airplanes—and our weapons. My nuke was on the A4's centerline, right where it was supposed to be. Armed Marine guards stood on each side of the airplane.

Moving as if in a daze, I went through the detailed weapons checklist, preflighted my plane, and strapped in. Another black night. No problem, I wasn't coming back. I wouldn't have to make another night carrier landing. *Whoopee.*

The yellow-shirted director came up and gave the signal to start engines. The A3D was taxied onto the port catapult, and I was put on the starboard cat. We'd be launched in parade formation, standard procedure.

There was still some hope that this was only a test, but then the cat officer gave us the turn-up signal.

At full power, the A3D squatted against the holdback fitting.

I ran my power up to a hundred percent, grabbed the bar in front of the throttle, checked my gauges, and waited.

The A3D's formation lights flicked on; he was ready to launch.

Ramming my head back against the headrest, I flicked my exterior lights on. I was ready to go; denial had already left.

One very long minute passed while our two birds quivered at full power on the catapults.

Then the cat officer stepped in front of my port wing and gave the throttle-back signal.

The plane and I relaxed together. So it *had* been a test: to see if we were well trained, and to see if we would go. There is not a doubt in my mind that a certain captain picked me to be a test subject because of that, "cook her and eat her," crack. I wondered, however, if he did it because he thought I was a smart-ass or a hard-ass.

We were a couple hundred miles east of Tokyo when the skipper ordered me to fly in to NAS Atsugi, a Navy airfield about thirty miles southwest of Tokyo, to see if I could scrounge up an attitude gyro for one of our planes; there were none left in the ship's supply system. The skipper warned me that I might have a problem with the NAS Atsugi supply people since we were a fleet squadron.

Soon as I landed at Atsugi I caught a ride up to the main hangar. My ride waited while I trekked to the aviation supply office, a window that opened onto the hangar bay. A steel mesh grid protected the goodies and the sourpuss chief petty officer behind the counter.

Putting on a broad smile, I said, "Good morning, Chief."

"Whaddya want?"

"I need an attitude gyro for an A4D-2. Got one?"

"Lemme see the papers."

I handed across the requisition and waited while he scanned it.

"Don't know any Attack Squadron Fifty-Six. We don't give stuff to fleet outfits, yah know. You ain't from one of those boats, are yah?"

"No, Chief. We're moving here from Okinawa. I'm part of the advance detachment. We need one more attitude gyro to get all our birds up here tomorrow."

"Okay. I got one. Been sitting on the shelf back there for a year now, but I reckon it's still good. I'll get it."

He got it. I handed him the rest of the paperwork, took the boxed gyro, and beat feet back to my ride.

I filed my flight plan to *Ticonderoga,* cranked up my A4D and taxied to the duty runway. I keyed the UHF and called the tower. "Atsugi tower, this is November Foxtrot Four-One-One for take off."

"November Foxtrot Four-One-One, hold your position, base security wants to talk to you. They're on the way."

I looked towards the tower. Two Shore Patrol squad cars were headed down the taxiway towards me, their lights flashing.

"Roger Atsugi tower, understand I am cleared for take off." Cobbing the power to the A4D, I swung the plane onto the runway.

"Negative November Foxtrot Four-One-One, hold your position. Hold your position."

In response, I keyed the UHF and made noises like static as I ran up to a hundred percent and released the brakes.

The squad cars slid onto the runway behind me and chased me until I got airborne.

Back aboard the ship, the skipper was waiting for me. "Brian, we got a message here from Atsugi that says you stole an A4D attitude gyro from their base supply office."

"I didn't steal it, sir. I left them the requisition."

"Did you get the gyro?"

"Yes, sir. I gave it to the maintenance chief."

"Good going," the skipper said. "I better go help the captain draft a reply to Atsugi."

Tico Maru cycled up and down the western Pacific throughout our deployment and gave us a fair amount of liberty in Japan, Okinawa, Hong Kong, and the Philippines. Most of our in-port time was in Yokosuka (pronounced Yo-koos-kah), Japan. Yokosuka is a naval seaport a short train ride south of Tokyo. The major commercial port city of Yokohama is half way between them, and the coastal resort city of Kamakura is right next-door, so it should have been easy to play tourist.

But 1960 was a low year in U.S.-Japanese relations. We had a security treaty with Japan that dated from 1951, when the Korean War was on, and the treaty was up for renegotiation. It turned out to be controversial in Japan, and there were riots in Tokyo.

This unrest culminated on June 15th when seventy thousand very angry Japanese, spurred on (and ostensibly controlled) by the communist element, stormed the Diet, the Japanese Parliament. *Ticonderoga* was in Yokosuka while this storm was building, and liberty in Tokyo was forbidden.

Then a message came in that said Tokyo was now calm, and liberty there was allowed. Herb Foreman, one of the squadron's newer members, and I happened to be in the squadron ready room that morning when the message arrived. Although he and I had not hung out together very much, we both seized the opportunity to get off the ship before the others found out that Tokyo liberty was permitted and made it a game of who got to go and who had to stay aboard.

With Herb in tow, I showed the message to the skipper and got permission for the two of us to head for Tokyo. Twenty minutes later we were in a taxi headed for the Yokosuka train station.

We learned later that, about the time the taxi took us out the base gate, another message arrived onboard saying that the first one had been a terrible mistake. This one said that Tokyo was still in the midst of severe rioting.

The squadron tried to head us off at the gate, and again at the train station, but their efforts were a few minutes too late.

Herb and I began to get hints of trouble ahead when we got off the train at the main Tokyo train station. There were very few people around, and those who noticed us wore odd expressions.

As we went down the long set of stairs that led to the main street, we looked in vain for a taxi. It was very quiet. There was no traffic. There were no pedestrians. It occurred to us that we were now the only people on the street. Not for long.

A loud, rumbling noise came at us from two opposite directions. We looked at each other. What the hell is this?

Then a crowd of people turned the corner at the south end of the long block and headed towards us. Their heads were wrapped in red bandanas, and they carried huge banners.

There were many of them. They marched about twelve abreast, and we never saw the tail end of the procession. The noise swelled, and we looked north.

Another procession, similar to the first, came around that corner and headed towards us.

Then the leaders of both groups saw us. They screamed and pointed, then they all broke into a run—right at us.

Herb and I each carried new Japanese cameras with tripods. Herb ripped his tripod loose, I grabbed mine, and we stood back to back, the tripods held like clubs. We were about to go down, but we'd go down fighting.

Just then, against all laws of probability, a taxi sped out of an alley in front of the southern mob. It screeched to a stop at the curb next to us, the back door popped open, and an oriental face smiled at us.

In a beautiful American accent, the face asked, "You guys need a lift?"

We dove headfirst into the back of the taxi. I wound up on the floor while Herb sprawled on the seat.

The cab lurched forward while stones and bricks hit the pavement behind us. I don't know how we got out of there; by the time I sat up we were moving at high speed down a narrow alley.

"Wow," I said. "That was close. Thank you. *Domo arigato.*"

"No problem," our driver said. "Glad to help out a couple of Americans in trouble."

"Where did you learn to speak American so well?" Herb asked.

Grinning, the driver said, "I spent a year at USC." He spun his cab onto a major street. "Loved it there."

Our new friend took us to a small hotel in a quiet neighborhood across the street from a Papagayo's tourist restaurant.

After that little adventure, we spent the day holed up in our room and didn't go across to the restaurant until it got dark. We had a great meal and tremendous service; we were the only customers. The place even put on a hell of a floorshow, right at our table.

Next morning we caught another taxi and had it take us all the way back to Yokosuka. We didn't want to risk another train trip.

Herb's reprieve was temporary; a year later he flew a light plane into a cliff in Hawaii. His wife and two friends were also aboard. All four were killed.

Brenda Lee sang "I'm Sorry" that year, and Roy Orbison told us about "Only the Lonely." *Spartacus*, with Kirk Douglas and Laurence Olivier, was on the big screen.

U.S. Navy Photo

USS *Ticonderoga*, CVA-14

"Tico Maru" is taking on fuel from the *oiler* at left.

11

The A4D had a bothersome idiosyncrasy: you couldn't see out the front of the windscreen in heavy rain. The center panel of the windscreen was a thick, flat plate. There were curved corner pieces on either side, but the flat center plate pretty well accounted for your ability to see forward, and in a heavy rainfall it collected water forced there by the airflow.

Coming down the penetration chute one afternoon, I flew in and out of cloud layers all the way down from twenty thousand feet. I leveled off at two thousand feet, dirtied up (dropped gear and flaps), and bored in towards the ship.

CCA (Carrier Controlled Approach) picked me up on radar as I neared the final approach point.

At their call, I put out the speed brakes, reduced power, and started down. (We kept our speed brakes out on final so that we could carry a higher power setting: about eighty-five percent. This gave us better engine response if we had to take a wave off.)

Passing a quarter of a mile, CCA turned the approach back to me; I had to do the rest visually.

When I came up off instruments to call the ball, all I could see out the front of the windscreen was a wall of water pressed against the glass. And you didn't crane your neck around in an A4D; there wasn't room to move your head.

I keyed the UHF. "Champ Four-One-One, twenty two hundred. Skyhawk. No ball."

Our Puerto Rican LSO, Carlos Font, came up. "You lookin' good. Kip it coming."

In close now, I could see the ship's wake boil past under my port wing. "I can't see the ship," I cried.

"You chust a little high. Kip it coming."

The ship's island flashed past my starboard wing, and the landing gear kissed down just past the wires. I had almost landed, and I never saw the deck.

I executed a bolter, turned downwind, and found myself under the lowest cloud layer, in and out of rain. Now I could see the ship through the side panels. I flew a VFR pattern under the cloud layer and came in for another pass.

When I rolled out in the groove, I lost the ship again. "Champ Four-One-One, Skyhawk, seventeen hundred. No ball."

"Kip it coming. Kip it coming."

Enough of this. I squeezed on more power, dropped the port wing, and jammed the starboard rudder forward. The plane's nose slewed to starboard enough for me to see the deck through the small, curved part of the windscreen to the left of that center plate. I was flying crooked, but I could see the deck again.

"Kip it coming."

As I crossed the ramp, I neutralized the controls and trapped.

In today's Navy, e-mail, direct deposit, international banking, and other modern communication tools have made deployments easier on the logistics of maintaining a family back home while you are on cruise. Back in the 1960s this could be a real problem.

Take pay. The Navy paid in cash, on the ship. To get money home, you took the cash to the ship's post office, bought a money order, and mailed it home. A COD (Carrier Onboard Delivery) aircraft flew aboard every few days with inbound mail and then carried your letter to some overseas air base. From there the letter made its way into the U.S. postal system and then to your home. The process could take a couple of weeks or more.

An alternative was to take out an allotment. You went without part of your pay for a month, and then the Navy mailed a check for that amount straight to your dependent every month. This made sense, but many of us couldn't manage to go without a major part of our pay for an entire month in order to prime the system.

We had a rare port call at Kobe, Japan. (Kobe is sort of the San Francisco of Japan.) Our first night in port, about a dozen of us caught a tram to the top of one of the mountains that cradle the harbor. The view was spectacular, and the restaurant there had a reputation for serving the finest cuts of world-famous Kobe beef. We had a couple of drinks and ordered dinner.

Halfway through the salad course, a sailor with a shore patrol armband came in and told us we had to return to the ship right away; a typhoon was about to strike. We hustled down the mountain and barely made the ship.

The captain wasted no time; he beat feet out of the harbor and headed for deep water. Two hours later we were taking green water over the carrier's bow.

In June 1960, President Eisenhower visited Taiwan. *Ticonderoga* was part of a naval security force for the president's Asian visit, and we planned to put on an air show for him.

One afternoon while the air wing practiced for the big show, the pilot of one of our fighter planes flew over the ship at seven thousand feet, moved a switch, and an electrical malfunction released a weapons rack from his plane.

That rack fell over six thousand feet and hit the pilot of an A4D in our sister squadron on the head as he called the one-eighty for landing.

Smitten, the A4D rolled inverted and plunged into the ocean. *Fate.*

Our propensity to fly low and fast became almost an obsession while we operated near the Philippine Islands. One of our favorite sports was to fly low over Manila Bay, a huge expanse of water on the west coast of Luzon.

The bay was covered with small fishing boats that carried masts about eighteen feet tall. The fishermen would reef their sails while they fished, and the fleet looked to us like a giant slalom course. The water was usually smooth as glass, and it was difficult to judge altitude. So the lead aircraft would let down until the stepped-up wingman called "Rooster tail" as soon as the leader's jet exhaust left a wake in the water. Then, off through the sailboats we went, weaving in and out as if we were skiers.

Once in a while a frightened fisherman would bail out of his boat when we approached, but mostly they waved at us. They preferred us to the Japanese.

Maybe Lieutenant Commander John Harper, the XO (Executive Officer), wanted to show us young studs that he, too, could operate at low altitude. One beautiful summer day (and they were all like that), the XO led a flight of four of us around the hills at the entrance to Manila Bay. I was his wingman, in the number two slot off his starboard wing. The other two birds were staggered off his port wing.

Despite the low altitude, the XO put us in tight parade formation. When we flew in tight like that, I put the tip of my leader's wing about three feet from my head and looked right up the leading edge of his swept-back wing. The A4D was great for that. The wings were well overlapped, but the airflow around the planes seemed to want to keep you right there. Of course being that close meant you didn't look around; you didn't dare take your eyes off the leader.

I knew we were low because my peripheral vision saw browns and greens flit past close below. But, like any good wingman, I had complete faith in my leader.

After a minute, the XO turned towards me and made a motion with one hand that I took as a signal to move away from him a little.

Well, okay. I moved out a few feet.

The XO leaned forward and peered over the glare shield on his instrument panel. Then he looked at me again and made another of those flick motions to move away.

Fine. I moved out; there was now a good three or four feet between our wingtips.

This is not the way to fly formation, I grumbled to myself.

Then—*flash*—a telephone pole went between the XO and me.

After I blinked real hard, I stared at the XO.

His oxygen mask dangled from one side of his hard hat, unused. He pulled it aside so I could see his giant grin. I thought the XO was done for the day, but not so fast. He signaled me to move back in tight.

I could tell we were now over water by the deep blue with white chop that skimmed past underneath. Then the anchor of a large ship zipped past, almost over my head. The XO had taken us so close to a cruise liner in the entrance to Manila Bay that I darn near hit the anchor that hung below the raked bow. I wondered what the ship's passengers thought.

Ticonderoga sailed back into San Diego harbor on October eleventh, but Air Wing Five launched for home when the ship was still a hundred miles at sea.

We landed at NAS Miramar and expected our wives to meet us. No wives. An hour later, here they came, in a high-speed cavalcade of cars.

They had waited at NAS Miramar until they were told that we were flying into NAS North Island. They all took off for that airfield. When they got there, after a half-hour drive and a ferry ride to Coronado, they were told we were at Miramar after all.

There's an old Navy saying: "All those aft go forward; all those forward go aft. Those amidships direct traffic." It is often appropriate.

The West Coast A4D community had lost so many pilots in operational accidents that some deployed squadrons were short-handed. It was easy to cross-deck an aircraft from a carrier headed home to a deployed one, but pilots were another matter; most of them wanted to go home with their ship.

In response, the Navy created a RAG (Ready Replacement Air Group) at NAS Miramar that contained pilots who could be deployed to any A4D squadron that needed them.

RAGs also became type-training squadrons. This new approach meant that you learned to fly the appropriate type of airplane *before* you joined your fleet squadron.

So November brought decision time. At this point I had 143 traps, 22 of them at night, and was considered ready to deploy. My options were to stay in VA-56 for a six-month turnaround and another seven-month cruise or join the RAG (VA-126) and gamble. I might get sent out pretty quick, but I could expect a much shorter period of time on cruise. Ed Luetschwager, Tony Tambini, and I volunteered for the RAG.

On December 19, 1960, fire swept through the aircraft carrier *Constellation* under construction in the Brooklyn Navy Yard; fifty men were killed and another 150 injured.

By the end of January 1961, Tony, Ed, and I were back in WESTPAC, this time aboard *Coral Sea* (CVA 43), a ship more modern but quite similar to *Ticonderoga*. She'd been moved down to the South China Sea after Pathet Lao forces captured strategic positions in Laos. (The initial contingent of 3,500 American troops was now in South Vietnam.)

Squadron numbers tracked to the air wing's number back then.

Thus, the squadrons in Air Wing Fifteen (CVW-15) aboard *Coral Sea* were VF-151 flying F3H Demons, VA-152 flying A-1s, VA-153 and VA-155 flying A4Ds, and VF-154 flying F8U Crusaders. There was also a small detachment of RF-8 Crusader photo birds on board.

Tony and Ed went to VA-153; I was assigned to VA-155. My first duty was to attend a burial at sea. It had been a rugged cruise for the Coral Maru, and it didn't get any better.

We were soon back in Japan, where I managed to catch walking pneumonia while wandering around Yokohama on a cold and wet winter day. So for the next month I was grounded and couldn't fly.

Commander McElwee, the skipper of the VA-155 Silver Foxes, was not happy about this. Here he'd managed to get a replacement pilot from the states, and the damn replacement got sick.

But I was back in the saddle by March, and I logged sixteen flights that month.

When you fly at night, you hear and feel vibrations that you wouldn't notice in the daytime. It's probably for the same reason that we hear things that go bump in the night. But once in a while that feeling comes along on a bright, sunny day.

That afternoon I was out on a routine post-maintenance test flight when a strange sensation worked its way up from the deck of the cockpit into my consciousness. Something didn't feel right. There was a faint tremor that shouldn't have been there.

I throttled back to a mid-range power setting and cruised around for a few minutes trying to figure it out. Yes, there it was: a vibration I hadn't felt on previous flights. Something was wrong with the engine. There weren't many gauges to check, just the RPM and EGT. They both looked steady and normal. Then here it came again: a tiny, persistent twitch that shouldn't have been there.

Keying the UHF, I called the ship. "Mustang, this is Five-Zero-Seven."

"Five-Zero-Seven, go ahead."

"Mustang, request you turn into the wind. I have an engine vibration and I'm declaring an emergency."

"Stand by."

Three long minutes passed. Then, "Five-Zero-Seven, this is

Mustang. We are turning. Fox Corpen is two-two-zero. You're cleared to come aboard." (Fox Corpen is the ship's course.)

"Roger, Mustang. Estimate ramp in six minutes." *If I'm wrong about this, I'll never hear the end of it.*

As a precaution, I set the power at eighty-two percent; that put the least pressure on the bearings that supported the jet's spinning rotors. Then I put out the speed brakes and started down.

"Paddles, Paddles," I called, "this is Five-Zero-Seven. Do you read?"

"This is Paddles. Read you loud and clear. What's your problem?"

"I have a strange engine vibration. I'm coming aboard using speed brakes only."

"Copy that. A vibration?"

Was that a snicker?

"Yes," I said, "a vibration."

"Roger that. We have you in sight."

After dumping some fuel to get down to landing weight, I flew a long, straight-in approach using the stick to hold the airplane's angle of attack, and controlling the rate of descent by moving the speed brakes in and out.

At a quarter mile I called the ball. "This is Five-Zero-Seven. Skyhawk ball. Two thousand."

"Roger that. Looking good."

Using the stick, I kept the ball centered on the mirror. To control speed, my left thumb was busy with the speed brake switch on the throttle head. In and out. Flick. Flick. Flick.

I trapped and pulled the throttle back to idle as the wire dragged my plane to a stop.

The engine ran down and seized in a mere six seconds; compressor blades flew out the air intake and sprinkled the deck with twisted metal. (Normally, the engine took over a minute to spool down.)

Fire fighters rushed my plane, but there was no fire.

When I climbed out, I kissed the deck.

Back at the Pentagon, somebody was thinking again. They decided that we should temporarily be an *All-Attack Carrier*. This meant that the two fighter squadrons would be offloaded to NAS

Atsugi, Japan, and two Marine A4D squadrons stationed at MCAS (Marine Corps Air Station) Iwakuni, Japan, would come aboard. This would give *Coral Sea* one three-plane squadron of A3Ds and four twelve-plane squadrons of A4Ds, fifty-one strike aircraft.

Our fighter jocks roared off for extended liberty in Japan. We attack pukes stayed behind and watched the Marines fly aboard.

Their first flight of four came into the break and set up for landing. The first Marine at the ramp boltered and then spun out when he turned downwind.

At the same time, the second Marine spun out of his approach at the ninety-degree position.

It was confusing as hell. We were familiar with planes in the water by now, but two at a time was a brand new experience. (Just like the old saying: All those aft ran forward, while all those forward ran aft.)

In all fairness to the Marines, they went through the same flight training as we Navy types, but after those six traps at the end of basic training, they rarely saw an aircraft carrier again. They were game as hell, but this was not what they were used to.

A safety bulletin came out to alert us to a strange and deadly problem. Some A4Ds had come off the catapult, flipped upside down, and plunged into the sea. This had happened to half a dozen planes in three oceans, and nobody had figured out why.

We junior officers had quite a discussion about it after the movie that night. Theories abounded. I ventured that it had to be caused by asymmetric slats, and the cure was to kick top rudder to slew the nose up and shake the stuck slat free.

Slats are like flaps, except that they're on the leading edge of the wing instead of the back edge. They droop for slow-speed flight and channel the airflow through a slot between the slat and the wing. This keeps the boundary air closer to the wing and allows slower controlled flight.

The slats on an A4D floated free. At slow speeds, they drooped all on their own. When the airflow increased, it forced the slats up to their normal position as part of the wing's leading edge. But if one stuck ...?

I had the first launch the next morning. When I came off the catapult, my plane rolled sharply to port.

As it passed through ninety degrees of bank and the nose fell towards the water, I kicked the starboard rudder—hard.

My plane rolled back to the right.

Slapping the gear handle up, I put the plane in what I judged was its best climb attitude right then, and said, "Come on, God."

The little A4D flew. Witnesses on the bridge said that it left a wake in the water, but it flew.

Would I have done that if we hadn't talked about the problem the night before? Who knows?

A few days later another safety bulletin identified the cause. On the cat stroke, both slats were forced into the full up position. At the end of the stroke, both should have dropped to the down position. In the case of the accidents, one slat dropped; the other did not. Some grease solved the problem. (By kicking the rudder I had unstuck the jammed slat.)

Australia beckoned. We stopped air ops and headed south. We were to spend two weeks in port in Australia as part of a commemorative celebration of the allied victory in the WW-II Battle of the Coral Sea. Two glorious weeks in Australia, and then we were to proceed home. We couldn't have asked for a better end to the cruise. *Right.*

I went to bed one beautiful spring night while the ship steamed towards the Southern Cross. When I woke up and went out on deck, the morning sun was on our starboard side. Something was wrong here.

Yep, Australia had been cancelled. *Coral Sea* was now to take up a position off the coast of South Vietnam and fly photo recon missions over the various factions fighting in Laos.

The air wing's RF-8 Crusader photo birds would take the pictures; A4Ds with buddy stores would sit off the coast and tank the photo RF-8s as they went in and out. It was *not* Australia, and it was boring.

Coral Sea pulled into homeport in Alameda, California in June 1961. On its eight-month cruise, the ship had lost twenty-one aircraft and nineteen pilots/aircrew. This on a "peacetime" cruise.

VA-155 took up residence in one of the old blimp hangars on

NAS Moffitt Field at the south end of San Francisco bay. I remember two things about that place: the bird poop in the blimp hangars and the fighter pilot whose parachute didn't open.

This lucky fellow took off headed north over the mud flats and promptly flamed out. He ejected all right, but the chute didn't have time to open. When the rescue crew got there, they found him buried up to his neck in mud, but he was very much alive. He'd gone into the muck like a dart, feet first. *Fate.*

Pat and I rented a small apartment in Mountain View (now the heart of Silicon Valley) and waited for orders. They came. I was to attend the University of Washington at Navy expense for two years to obtain my bachelor's degree.

I'd requested the Navy's *Five-Term Program* for ex-NAVCADs, and I'd asked for the U of W. Both requests had been granted.

My glee was dampened by the rest of the orders: I was to major in chemistry. I hated chemistry.

I called BUPERS (the Navy Bureau of Personnel) and asked for a different major, any other major. Nope. My aggie background had done me in. Only in chemistry could I graduate in the five semesters allowed. I gave up. I would be a chemist if it killed me. It almost did.

John F. Kennedy was president. Patsy Cline sang "Crazy" like she meant it, and many of us went to see *Exodus* starring Kirk Douglas.

UNIVERSITY · OF · WASHINGTON
LVX · SIT
· 1861 ·

HUSKIES

12

We rented a small two-bedroom house in Lynwood, a northern suburb of Seattle. We were pretty crowded, so I set up a desk next to a space heater out in the garage. That was my den. (Our Opel station wagon remained out in the cold and wet.) I settled into the student life while Pat raised little Kelly. It was a major change from squadron life for both of us.

The University of Washington is a beautiful place. I asked to go there because it had impressed me when the NAVCAD Choir visited Seattle back in 1956. We five-termers had to attend universities with Naval ROTC units, and this was the only school in that category I'd ever visited.

About a dozen of us reported to the NROTC Commandant at any time. The NROTC staff handled all our paperwork and kept us in touch with Mother Navy. (Richard Nixon's brother was on the NROTC staff at the time.) We wore civvies and focused on our studies.

Our sole military activity was flying out of NAS Sand Point located a few miles up the west coast of Lake Washington. (Sand Point lost its aviation capability nine years later and became plain Naval Station Sand Point. It's now Warren G. Magnuson Park.)

I was delighted when I located my assigned parking lot on a map of the campus; it looked like it was about a hundred feet from the NROTC building where I was to start each day. What the map didn't show was the stairway from the parking lot up a steep cliff to the campus level, the stairway with 222 steps. (I counted them many times. I gave up cigarettes on day four.)

I'd been out of college for five years and had been an Aggie to boot. Now I was re-starting as a junior. That first semester smacked me right between the eyes.

The worst part was organic chemistry, the weeder course for everyone who wanted to go into the medical field. I worked my tail off to get a C-Minus in that course.

At the end of that first semester, I made an appointment to see the head of the mathematics department. Our conversation went something like this.

"Professor, I need your help."

"What's the problem, Mister Bryans?"

"I'm a Navy Five-Term student enrolled as a chemistry major because I used to be an Aggie. I'm told that it's the only major that can use most of my old credits to get me a degree in five semesters."

"So what's the problem?"

"Turns out I hate chemistry. And it hates me."

Laughing, he said, "And you want to switch to math?"

"Yes, sir," I said. "I enjoy math."

"Hmmm. Let me see your printouts."

Eagerly, I handed him my records from the University of Arizona and my first-semester University of Washington schedule.

He fussed with them for a few minutes, brow furrowed. "Well, you probably don't know this," he said, "but I worked with some of you fellows for a couple of years while I did a bit of research for the Navy. I like Navy pilots. I'll help if I can, and I think I have a solution for you."

"Good." I could hardly contain my enthusiasm. "What is it?"

"I'll set up a special two-semester math course focused on the mathematics of navigation, from dead-reckoning to celestial. If you carry a full load for the next four semesters, almost all math courses, that'll give you enough credits to get a bachelor's degree in math."

"That's great, sir. I'll—"

"Wait. It'll be a BA degree, not a BS. Do you care?"

"Hell no, sir. I mean—"

"I know exactly what you mean. Come see me next week. That'll give me time to fix up a curriculum and get it approved by the school."

That is what he did, and I became a math major.

The flying there wasn't bad either. It was pretty much like being a member of a flying club, a very good club. NAS Sand Point had T-28s and SNBs. They were well maintained, and it was easy to get on the schedule.

When we aviators were not engaged in operational flights, we were assigned to *proficiency flying*. Beyond the four hours of monthly flight time needed to earn our flight pay, we had to rack up at least a hundred hours a year (ten at night) in order to maintain our flight status. This was, in the Navy's view, the minimum number of flight hours needed to maintain proficiency. (I agree. Every time I read about some light airplane crash, I wonder how many hours the pilot had flown in the last year.)

Larry Renner, one of my colleagues, was an experienced fighter pilot, so we'd check out a couple of T-28s from time to time, fly out to sea, and have at one another. It made for a good workout for both the airplanes and us.

But most of my time in the air was spent in the mighty "Bug Smasher," the SNB (C-45). When that plane was born in 1937 as an outgrowth of the Model-18 Twin Beech, it was dubbed the Expeditor, but Navy pilots always called it the Bug Smasher. It had two 450-hp Pratt & Whitney R-985-B5 radial engines that could move the plane right along at 210 miles an hour. The plane carried a pilot, co-pilot, and two-to-five passengers. The Navy bought fifteen hundred of them over the years, and I bet there are darn few Navy pilots of that era who didn't have pilot time in them.

I gave one of my multi-engine cohorts a thrill one day; I rolled the SNB inverted and let the nose fall through in order to start a descent to the field.

He let out a yell and grabbed the glare shield. He hadn't been upside down since the training command.

Goleta Air & Space Museum Photo
SNB / C-45

Up to my neck in math courses, I was a twenty-four year old ex-Aggie in with a pack of smart youngsters. I not only didn't know what a *parabola* was, I didn't know how to pronounce it. I embarrassed the hell out of myself when I asked what it was, and the whole class tittered.

My revenge came in the third semester when I took a probability and statistics course. There were twenty students in the class, divided into three sets: a group of four super-smart young men, fifteen normal math students, and me.

I had no idea what was what. I sat in the back and looked confused.

Every so often the professor would stop, look back at me, and ask, "What don't you understand, Mister Bryans?"

Then the gang-of-four would turn around, look at me, and snicker.

The grade for the course was based on the final exam. One test, one grade. The night before the final, I realized it was hopeless; the only chapter in the entire book I sort of understood was Chapter Seven. So I studied that chapter, nothing else. There were practice problems at the end of it and answers in the back of the book. I worked those Chapter Seven problems over and over; then I prayed that at least one of the questions on the final would be from that chapter.

When the final exam was passed out I darn near whooped. The set of practice questions from Chapter Seven *was* the entire final exam; only the parameters had been changed.

The next day the professor walked into class with the graded tests and gave a little speech. "I like to grade on a curve," he said, "but I can't do it this time. The grades are too skewed."

One of the smart guys asked, "What do you mean?"

"There's one grade of ninety-six, four scores in the low eighty's, and the rest in the fifty's and sixty's. I have to give the ninety-six the single A and the four in the low eighty's all B's. The rest get C's.

The four smart ones looked at each other. One of them turned to the professor and asked, "Which of us got the A?"

"Mister Bryans there in the back of the room."

To this day, I treasure the look on their faces.

On October 22, 1961, President Kennedy announced to the world that the Soviet Union had ballistic missiles in Cuba.

Over the next few days, over half of the male students in my classes disappeared: their Reserve and National Guard units had called them up.

But I, who was on active duty, was allowed to stay in class. I didn't knock it, but it seemed strange.

Seattle socks in along about September, and we didn't see the sun again there until April. Every so often throughout the winter, we pilots felt the need to fly to San Diego for some sunshine. We'd dance around on the tarmac when we got out of the airplane and felt the sun on our faces.

One weekend, my multi-engine colleague needed a co-pilot for a trip to San Diego to attend a party. I volunteered to go, and he took me to the party. There I learned about martinis: two of them and I was knee-walking drunk.

The next day we crawled back into our SNB with super-sized hangovers. To make our trip more unpleasant, we discovered we'd be in some crappy weather once we passed Los Angeles.

We entered the soup right on schedule. About that time, my friend in the left-hand seat passed control over to me and went to sleep.

No problem, the concentration required to fly instruments would take my mind off a stomach that gurgled and a head that ached.

Suddenly, we were in a descent . . . and I couldn't get the SNB back up to my assigned altitude: ten thousand feet. A quick check showed that clear ice had formed along the leading edge of both wings. (This disrupts the airflow and reduces lift.)

Belatedly, I turned the wing deicer boots on, added carburetor heat, moved the mixtures to rich, ran the RPM up, and went to max power. We were still going down—slowly—but down.

The pneumatic wing deicer boots were made of heavy neoprene and flexed as air pressure inflated them and then bled off. But I'd waited too long, and the ice was too thick to crack. It continued to build. (Over six hundred aircraft were lost while flying "The Hump" between India and China in WW-II. More than half of them went down because of ice.)

If I'd recognized the problem sooner and used the deicer boots wisely, we might have avoided the problem. If ice had been mentioned in the weather report, we would have been more cautious. If we'd been alert instead of hung over. If . . .

We continued to descend through thick clouds. I tried to call ATC (Air Traffic Control), but we were over the Sierra Madre Mountains north of Santa Barbara, and were now too low for radio contact. Too low indeed. The TACAN needle no longer pointed at the next station, it spun around. The back-up ADF needle also rotated. We were now reduced to dead-reckoning navigation, in the soup, through mountains.

Yanking out the charts, I did some fast math. (Thanks, Professor.) The air navigation route we were on pointed at a narrow gap in the mountains. At our present true air speed and rate of descent, we'd clear the terrain in the gap by about five hundred feet. If, that is, we hit the center of the gap; it was only a few miles wide.

Compass heading now became critical. It would have been nice to know the winds down at our new altitudes, but I had to assume that the wind correction in place for ten thousand feet was still good at the lower altitudes.

I glanced at my partner, still asleep. Should I wake him?

He seemed to smile in his sleep.

No, I decided. We'd either make it together, or he would never know. All I had to do was hold my heading, keep our descent to a minimum, and wait.

Finally, the TACAN needle sprang to life and pointed dead ahead. The ADF needle homed in on something. I heard a radio transmission. We were through the gap.

I called ATC, told them of the ice and our new altitude. They cleared traffic away from beneath us. Then I heard a *crack*. Ice had broken off and rolled back over the wing. We had descended into warmer air, and life was good again. I woke up the pilot.

There were U.S. military advisers in South Vietnam, and Marilyn Monroe was dead. Chubby Checker did "The Twist," and Steve Lawrence sang "Go Away Little Girl." The Air Force needed a better combat aircraft and decided to buy the Navy's F-4 Phantom. (Historical Note: The USAF flew both the Navy A-1 and the Navy F-4 in Vietnam, and the Navy had developed every single air-to-ground weapon the Air Force used in that war.)

Navy SNB

Navy SNB Cockpit

This being a twin prop job, there are all sorts of engine controls and dials. Far more complicated than a jet.

13

In May 1962, Pat presented me with a brand new son, Stuart Alan. We had tried to prepare Kelly for the arrival of a little brother, but events proved that our efforts had been futile. The day after Pat came home from the hospital, our lunch in the kitchen was interrupted by screams from the baby in his bassinet in the living room.

Pat and I raced into the living room.

Little three-year-old Kelly stood next to the bassinet, a tree switch in her hand, beating the baby with it. She watched us run towards her, but she didn't stop hitting baby brother until we grabbed the switch.

Their enmity came to dominate much of our home life for years.

A year later we left Seattle with my bachelor's degree in mathematics and a set of full lieutenant's "railroad tracks" on my collar. I was on my way to become a jet flight instructor.

My orders said that I was to report to Training Squadron Nine (VT-9) based at the Navy's newest Naval Air Station, McCain Field, near Meridian, Mississippi. (The base was named for Admiral McCain, Arizona Senator John McCain's father. The Senator, a naval aviator at the time, flew there as an instructor shortly after I did.)

The Navy had purchased the property for the airfield from the Stennis family. At the time, Senator Stennis, of Mississippi, was Chairman of the Senate Armed Services Committee. (No comment; the event speaks for itself.)

Our first evening in Meridian was one of those wonderful southern postcards; jasmine and other sweet aromas were adrift in the soft breeze. We went for a walk to get away from the motel for a while.

A little old man that looked like Colonel Sanders, white goatee and all, tipped his hat to Pat and said, "Evenin' Ma'am." Pat loved it.

My welcome aboard VT-9 was also interesting. The

commanding officer (called "Hose Nose" behind his back) summoned me into his office. When I stood before his desk, he looked up at me and said, "You don't draw on the Lone Ranger, you don't piss into the wind, and you don't screw around with me. Got that?"

"Yes, sir."

"Dismissed."

I never did find out what that was all about. I think he mistook me for someone else. It was a large squadron.

We were lucky enough to draw base housing, so we moved into a tidy little home that fronted on a well-maintained street—and backed onto a swamp that separated the officers and enlisted housing areas. We were warned to be careful when we mowed the lawn. "Water moccasins, you know."

While I'd been away in school, the Navy had changed our aircraft designation scheme to fit better with the USAF. (I smelled the hand of Congress in this; it was difficult for them to keep track of two different systems.) The old AD-6 was now the A-1, the A4D-1 had become the A-4A, the A4D-2 was the A-4B, and so forth. This may have helped the senators, but it confused me.

So VT-9 flew what was now called the T-2A Buckeye. It was a straight-wing, two-seat trainer with a single Westinghouse J-34 jet engine. It was underpowered; the hottest thing about it was the bright orange-and-white paint job. The squadron had sixty of them. Our sister squadron, VT-7, also had sixty, so there were 120 of the little beasties parked on McCain Field. On a busy day it seemed like bees around a hive.

This was a basic training field, so our students had already been through primary in prop trainers. The syllabus here covered transition to jets, aerobatics, basic instruments, navigation, night familiarization, and basic formation flying.

The students also received 170 hours of ground training in aerodynamics, meteorology, leadership, and Navy organization. But we instructors in VT-7 and VT-9 didn't do the ground training; we flew 'em.

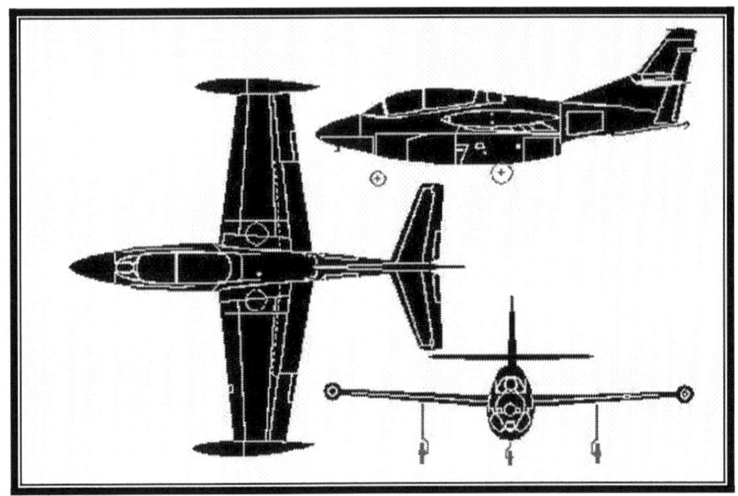

The T-2A

First I had to go through the eighteen-flight syllabus to make me a T-2A pilot and instructor. I finished that in August and started the grind.

We instructors flew two or three flights a day. Each one involved half an hour to brief, half an hour to pre-flight and get airborne, an hour and a half in the air, and a half hour to debrief. That's three hours per student. A three-student day was nine hours long, not counting meetings, slipped schedules, and collateral duty (our ground job).

Unlike the Air Force, Navy pilots have real jobs besides flying, like running the squadron. A typical junior officer job was personnel officer, responsible for the service record entries of everyone in the squadron.

Our first brief was at 0600 hours, and it was rare to leave the hangar much before 1700 (5:00 P.M.), so living on base was a distinct advantage over the guys who had a house in town and commuted. Still, I frequently fell asleep on the couch while Pat fixed dinner.

Pat hated my schedule there but enjoyed golf with some of the other wives. I used to tease her about Meridian golf: "Hit the ball, whack a snake."

* * *

The instructor cadre of both VT-7 and VT-9 included a lot of Marine aviators. They are different. They're related to naval aviators, but there is a distinct difference to their thought patterns. It would take a trained psychologist to explain it, so I won't try. And then there were the MARCADs: Marine Aviation Cadets.

When I was a NAVCAD, you didn't opt for one service or the other until it was time to determine your advanced training. (The Marine Corps didn't need seaplane pilots or blimp drivers.) By the 1960s, however, cadets entered flight training with the decision already made. This led to two distinct breeds of cadet in VT-9: normal and Marine. And I mean that exactly the way it sounds.

Despite pressure from the corps to get more of them through, the washout rate for MARCADS was much higher than for NAVCADs. There was a simple reason for this: many of them could not fly. I concluded at the time that quite a few of these fellows had been ordered to flight training primarily to get them away from bayonets.

Don't get me wrong. There were MARCADS that went on to be great pilots. There were also a lot of them whose lives we saved by booting them out of the program.

When faced with an airborne situation, there are three possible courses of action: do the right thing, do nothing, or do the wrong thing. Doing nothing was a popular student choice.

We were in the touch-and-go landing pattern. I had a MARCAD in the front seat; I was in the back. The kid had quite a few landings under his belt, but on this one he went too far past the one-eighty before he started his turn. That gave us an extra-long final approach. We were then slated to land short, right on the barbwire fence that surrounded the field.

I piped up on the ICS (intercom system). "We gonna make the runway?"

"No, sir." But there was no change, except that we got closer to the fence.

"Where do you figure we'll land?"

"On that fence, sir." Still nothing moved.

"Don't you think you should add power then?"

"Yes, sir." But he didn't.

Shaking my head, I took over. "I have the aircraft."

* * *

Of course once in a while a student would try to kill you. I was in this business only a few weeks before I learned to keep my left hand behind the throttle and my right hand behind the stick whenever we were low and slow.

One day we were in the landing pattern when the student up front got slow . . . real slow. I put my hands in position. At the first nibble of a stall, the kid did two wrong things simultaneously: he jerked both the throttle and the stick *back*. He darn near broke my hands, but I pushed both forward real hard and we recovered from the incipient stall.

My briefing with the first student of the day was interrupted one morning by an announcement on the hangar's speaker system: "If any of you own a small boy and a basset puppy, please contact base security."

The student and I laughed. Then I realized that *I* owned a small boy and a basset pup.

Yep. It turned out to be Stuart, who had been walking for only a few months. He'd snuck out of our house before dawn and, accompanied by our basset puppy, made it across about two hundred yards of swamp. (The swamp that was infested with water moccasins.) Boy and dog wound up in one of the back yards in the enlisted housing area.

There was a short course down at NAS Pensacola that taught instructors how to survive students, but it had a backlog, so I didn't get to go until November. The high point of the course was inverted-spin-recovery training. One of their guys took you up in a T-34, and you did inverted spins.

Now a regular upright spin can be pretty wild. You go down in a tight spiral that can bounce you around a bit. (Visualize a bran flake as it spins around the drain hole when you pull the sink plug.) At least the g forces are positive in a normal spin since the cockpit is on the inside of the spin.

In an inverted spin the cockpit faces out, and you experience negative-g. The spin throws you at the canopy. You strain against the lap belt and shoulder harness, your knees try to hit your chin, and worst of all, the blood rushes to your head, and you "red out."

(Your vision turns redder and redder as blood is driven into your eyeballs.)

The first one was enough for me, so naturally we did several. Those guys were sadists. (But *they* had to do this all the time. Tough guys.)

I guess that all of us alive back then remember where we were when President John F. Kennedy was assassinated. I was in the classroom at the instructor course in Pensacola, learning about inverted spins, when an officer interrupted the class with the announcement.

One day back at Meridian, my student finished some aerobatics at the far edge of the restricted area and set up a long, gentle descent for home. The T-2 was a very stable airplane, so I decided to demonstrate this to the kid, who had a tendency to manhandle the plane. "Trim this baby up as good as you can," I ordered.

"Yes, sir."

"Okay, take your hands off the controls."

"Sir?"

"I want to see both hands up on the canopy. Come on."

He put them up, and the airplane drifted into a left turn.

"Okay, fix your trim," I said.

He did; then he put his hands back over his head. The plane was steady.

"Good. Now, put a little pressure on the left rudder and do a slow left turn." The plane went into a gentle left turn. "Now straighten it out with right rudder."

He did.

"Okay. Now fly this bird all the way to the entry point with your hands up."

"Yes, sir."

And he did.

Years later, a pilot walked up to me in an officer's club and said, "Do you know when I learned to love flying?"

"I have no idea," I said. "Who are you?"

"I'm the guy you taught to fly with my hands above my head. And that's the day I started to love flying."

On June 21, 1964, James Cheney, Andrew Goodman, and

Michael Schwerner disappeared near Meridian, Mississippi. They were civil rights workers, and racial tensions in the South were raging. Foul play was suspected.

President Johnson ordered all hands at NAS Meridian to join the search effort. Almost everyone on the base spent the next three days in the boonies as we looked for ... we weren't sure what.

One student, an ensign out of the NROTC program, objected. "I came here to fly," he said, "not to search." He was flown to the Pentagon that afternoon and never seen again. We heard he'd been discharged before sunset.

We never did find anything. Years later, the bodies of the three young men were found buried near a stock tank a few miles from our base. (The movie *Mississippi Burning* depicted the events surrounding their murder.)

On the night of July 30, 1964, South Vietnamese patrol boats attacked two small North Vietnamese islands in the Tonkin Gulf.

The next morning, the U.S. destroyer *Maddox* steamed into the Gulf, well away from the islands.

Then, on August 2, 1964, two North Vietnamese gunboats reportedly attacked *Maddox* under cover of darkness.

Two nights later, a "possible" confrontation occurred when the destroyers *Maddox* and *Turner Joy* thought they were under further attack. Fighter aircraft were launched from the nearby aircraft carrier *Ticonderoga* to assist. This *Tonkin Gulf Incident* was the key that opened up the massive United States intervention in Vietnam that was to follow.

Every summer the Naval Academy sent midshipmen (students) to NAS Pensacola, Florida to experience naval aviation. This is supposed to help the kids decide which Navy they want to enter: surface warfare, submarines, or aviation. (Or the Marine Corps.)

In August 1964, I was one of several instructor pilots at Meridian tasked to spend a week in Pensacola and give the midshipmen orientation rides in our T-2A jets. We all took our wives and kids and camped out at a beachside park. Great fun. The flights were short, easy, and full of aerobatics. The middies were bright and eager, and only a few got airsick.

Then, while I got ready to leave the hangar for the beach at the end of the third day, I got a message to call a detailer at BUPERS. I called.

A commander who identified himself as the Aide Detailer answered. "Thanks for returning my call so promptly, Lieutenant. I understand that you're in Pensacola with the midshipmen. How's it going?"

"Great, sir. What can I do for you?"

"How would you like to be an aide, Brian?"

"You mean as in aide to an admiral?"

"Yeah. We've gone over your record and think that you would make a good aide. It'll help your career, you know."

"No thank you, sir."

He laughed. Well, hear me out before you make up your mind."

"I have made up my mind, sir. I've never even met an admiral. I'd have no idea what to do."

"Well, here's the plan. We don't normally tell prospective aides where they'll be assigned, but we'll make an exception in this case." (Alarm bells should have rung in my head. This was right out of a door-to-door sales class.) "You'll be Aide and Flag Lieutenant to the Commander, Middle East Forces in Bahrain, that's in the Persian Gulf."

"The Persian Gulf?"

"Yes, and it's just a six-month tour. You'll have the fact that you were an admiral's aide recorded in your personnel file after only six months. It'll be a hell of an experience and good for your career."

"I don't think—"

"Wait. There's more. We'll fly you and your family to New York. We'll give you a few days to see the town, and then we'll put you on an ocean liner for London. When you get there, we'll give you thirty days leave en route and travel expenses to get to Bahrain, any way you choose."

"Me and my wife . . . and two kids?"

"Yes. And after your six-month tour is up, we'll send you and the family to San Francisco on another ocean liner. Or you can fly, if you prefer. It'll be a round-the-world trip for you and your family, a once in a lifetime opportunity. Now, are you interested?"

"Where do I sign?"

When I got back to our camp on the beach, I took Pat aside and told her of my conversation with the detailer.

"Sounds too good to be true," she said. "Is there any guarantee they won't send you someplace else?"

"This is the Navy, hon, there are no guarantees."

"What's the worst place they could send you?"

"Hmmm. I guess that would be Korea."

They sent me to Korea on a six-month, no-family tour. In October I received orders to report for duty as Aide and Flag Lieutenant to the Senior Member, United Nations Military Armistice Commission, Panmunjom, South Korea.

T-2A Buckeye

The slight haze and puffy clouds were typical of a summer day around Meridian, Mississippi.

14

It was October 1964 when I met Rear Admiral Paul P. (Brick) Blackburn in Hawaii. I checked in at the CINCPACFLT (Commander in Chief, Pacific Fleet) headquarters to make sure they knew that "my" admiral would fly in on a commercial flight that evening. They knew.

Then I went to pick the admiral up in a rental jeep. I watched while a caravan of three black limos pulled up, cut me off, and whisked the admiral and his luggage away. I followed in my green-and-white, candy-striped jeep.

When the admiral disembarked at CINCPACFLT, he walked back to my jeep. "Are you my new aide?"

"Yes, sir."

"And did you come down to pick me up in this jeep?"

"Ah ... yes, sir."

"That was nice of you. But, as you can see, other arrangements had been made."

"Yes, sir."

"Lieutenant, do you know anything about being an admiral's aide?"

"No, sir."

"Why did BUPERS pick you to be my aide?"

"I have no idea, sir. I thought I was going to Bahrain."

"Uhuh, the old switcheroo," he said. "They did that to me too . . . when I was an aide."

South Korea was the U.S. Army's best-kept secret: life could be good there. The admiral and I lived in the Yongsan Compound, the Army's huge headquarters complex inside Seoul.

I moved into a *hooch* (house) already occupied by two other aides: Captain Bill Benoit, an Army pilot, and Captain Roger Gaines, an Army airborne ranger. The hooch had three bedrooms, one bath, and a living room. There was no kitchen; we ate in the commanding general's mess across the street. (Excellent food and inexpensive.)

Our living room was pretty sparse when I arrived, but we cadged a ten-foot, red-lacquer bar with a black-leather cushion from another hooch, and we made all of our stereo purchases right then instead of waiting until time to leave the country. With some Korean art on the wall, the place took on a unique atmosphere with good music.

Each of us aides had a jeep, so transportation was no problem. We chipped in and hired two Koreans, a laundress and a houseboy, to keep up the hooch and our uniforms. When we drove up in the evening, the hooch was clean, our uniforms were washed and pressed, Barbara Streisand was on the stereo, and the houseboy met us with our favorite drink.

The admiral got his own private house with a housekeeper, a sedan with driver, and offices with an American secretary (with U.S. security clearances). His office suite was in the Yongsan compound, but his real job was to meet with the North Koreans at Panmunjom, an hour's drive to the north.

A well-demarcated line ran east-and-west through the middle of the Panmunjom complex. The North Koreans had the north side (naturally), and the United Nations had the south. The U.S. soldiers that guarded our side had been specially screened for the job: they were all at least six feet tall and looked pretty darn efficient. The North Koreans were much shorter, but they glared a lot.

One Quonset hut straddled the boundary line. The line actually ran through the middle of the hut, like a belt, and right down the center of the conference table. The North Koreans sat on the north side; Admiral Blackburn and a few members of his UN staff sat on the other. Nobody ever smiled at the sessions held in there.

The North Koreans liked to play head games. We'd arrive to find that their little tabletop podium was now an inch higher than the UN podium, or their flag was now larger. The admiral reciprocated.

Everyone who visited the UN side was briefed never to cross the line. There was no doubt that anyone who did would be shot by the North Korean guards; it had already happened.

One day in early December, a busload of U.S. congressmen and senators arrived and were briefed to stay on the UN side of the line.

"That's bullshit," one senator snorted. "They wouldn't dare shoot a United States Senator." And he marched towards the line. One of our soldiers tackled the moron about one step before he became dead meat.

The legislators then carried out their real mission in South Korea: Christmas shopping at the Yongsan Compound Base Exchange.

There was a small officer's club on the UN side of Panmunjom that catered to the half-dozen or so Army officers stationed there. It looked and felt like a mountain chalet. This look was enhanced, of course, by the fact that it was winter, and we were at some altitude.

One of the best parts of that operation was the superb meals put out by Captain Tony Cataldi and his team of Army chefs. The admiral and I always enjoyed being invited to dinner there after a meeting. Tough duty.

The non-fighting element of the United Nations operation consisted of small teams of observers from four neutral nations. The Swiss and the Swedes lived on our side of the border; the Czechs and Poles lived on the North Korea side. They were uniformly a cheery, hard-drinking lot that also enjoyed the hospitality of the Panmunjom officer's club whenever they could.

A few weeks into our tour, the Czechs and Poles cleared it with the North Koreans and invited the admiral and me for dinner at their camp several miles across the border. We went. Talk about a strange feeling. Pushing midnight, several of us wound up singing along with a pretty good piano player. The other singers were all wearing green uniforms with red stars on them. I don't remember what we were drinking, but it was made from communist potatoes.

One day the admiral called me into his office. "Brian," he said, "I want you to get me a blue-and-white checked bedspread for my bed. I hate that green Army one I have now. Oh, and I'd like it on my bed when I get home tonight."

"Yes, sir. No problem."

The admiral smiled like the *Mona Lisa*. I should have known.

I exhausted every avenue I could think of: the Base Exchange, the Army supply system in Korea, the Navy supply system in Japan, and department stores in Seoul. No luck.

Late in the afternoon, about an hour before the admiral would show up at his house, I gave up. I stopped off at the officer's club, sat down at the empty bar, and ordered a scotch and water.

A cockroach appeared on the bar and I trapped it under an empty glass. When I offered it to the bartender, a moonlighting soldier, he started a conversation. "You look frustrated, Lieutenant. What's the problem?"

"My admiral has ordered me to get him a blue-and-white checked bedspread for his damn bed, and I can't find one."

"Yeah, I don't think that either the Army or the Koreans have much use for blue-and-white checked bedspreads." He poured me another drink and said, "Nurse this one for half an hour and I'll see if I can help. What size bedspread?"

I shrugged. "Queen, I guess. But don't bust a gut, I've tried everyplace."

He winked and went into the back room.

Twenty-five minutes later he reappeared carrying something under one arm. It was about the size of a pillow and was wrapped in brown paper. He laid it on the bar in front of me. "Will this do, Lieutenant?"

Hesitantly, I unfolded the wrapping. There it was: the prettiest blue-and-white checked bedspread I'd ever seen. "My God," I said. "How—"

"Take it, Lieutenant, compliments of the U.S. Army. But let me give you a tip. When somebody gets you something like this, don't ever ask where it came from. Okay?"

"Okay. And thank you."

An hour later the admiral showed up at his house. I had a fire going in the fireplace and was waiting. He went into the bedroom and came right back out.

"Brian, where in hell did you find that bedspread?"

"Is it okay?"

"It's great. God, it's exactly what I wanted. Where did you find it? I checked every place in WESTPAC and nobody had one."

"Admiral," I said, "I'll bust my buns to get you whatever you want. But don't ever ask where it came from. Okay?"

"You're on," he said. "Jesus, you might make a decent aide yet."

Thus was born the great game we played, from a bottle of rare Kirshwasser to an old bathtub with feet.

Admiral Blackburn was what is called in the Navy a "sailor's sailor," which meant he was a hard charger on liberty. He could knock back a few with the best of them, and he went out of his way to be colorful. This did not always endear him to the local Army brass, who tended to be pretty straight-laced and up tight. (As well they should have been, given their mission in Korea.)

This was epitomized the night that CINC UNC (Commander in Chief, United Nations Command), four-star General Howze, threw a cocktail party at the Yongsan Compound Officer's Club. Mess dress formal uniforms were required, so we all looked pretty snazzy. My admiral looked snazzier than most since he wore his scarlet-lined official Navy boat cloak over his uniform. (Well, it *was* chilly out.) He looked sort of like a caped crusader.

As the evening wore on, the admiral tossed down a few and became the center of a small group of possible admirers. One member of the rapt gaggle was a middle-aged Army nurse who was pushing fifty and her alcohol tolerance level.

When she became a pest, the admiral caught my eye and gave me the get-rid-of-her signal.

I managed to split her away from the clutch around the admiral much like a cutting horse works a cow away from the herd, and I moved her across the room.

At this point, she took exception to being separated from her lustful target. She pushed me aside, spun towards the admiral, and bellowed something unintelligible. Then she charged across the open space between herself and Admiral Blackburn.

Bystanders leaped to safety, the admiral stepped to one side, and she missed him.

She ended her run about twenty feet past my boss, but then she turned for another shot.

A hundred people froze in an open-mouthed tableau . . . all except the admiral. He stepped to a clear spot on the floor, undid his boat cloak, flipped it scarlet side out, and draped it over one arm.

There was absolute silence in the large room.

My admiral looked at the nurse and said, "Hah, Toro."

Scorned and angry, the nurse charged again.

Stepping to one side, the admiral flipped the scarlet-lined cape over her head as she passed by, and then yelled, "Olay."

The nurse crashed into the far wall, where two male officers caught her on the rebound and saved her from falling.

An Army colonel moved to my side and whispered, "Get your boss out of here. *Now.*"

My admiral went quietly.

As we pulled away from the club in the admiral's staff car, he leaned over to me and said, "Perhaps I went a bit too far in there." Perhaps.

We adjourned to the admiral's hooch, where I built a fire in the fireplace while the boss got comfortable and mixed us a couple of night caps.

As he entered the room, he was in a mellow mood, singing, "Throw another aide on the fire, boys, its chilly out tonight."

Taking advantage of his mood, I asked, "Admiral, now that you've gotten to know me, how far do you think I can go in this man's Navy?"

He took his time, sipped his drink, and then said, "You'll make captain, Brian . . . but not early." Alas, no fast track to admiral for me.

I was back on proficiency flying status with my old friend, the SNB, now called a C-45 again. Most of my infrequent flights involved ferrying people or stuff to Japan and back.

All was routine except for the day I had to fly another admiral, not mine, from Seoul to Iwakuni, Japan. It was a beautifully crisp winter day, and I whistled softly to myself as we cruised across the sparkling sea.

The admiral came forward out of the passenger compartment and ripped me a new one. He apparently was not a music buff. Fifteen minutes later, here he came again. Without realizing it, I had cranked up my whistler for an encore.

Lyndon Johnson had beat Barry Goldwater in the November 1964 presidential election, and he was sworn in on January 20, 1965. I didn't care. (I should have.)

Four months into the assignment, I came into the outer office and heard Admiral Blackburn whistling. He had been notified that he'd been selected for a third star and would be reassigned as Commander, U.S. Seventh Fleet. He announced that he was taking me with him as his aide.

In February, the time came to relocate to the U.S. Naval Base at Yokosuka, Japan. The admiral had to fly to Washington to get briefed at the Pentagon before he took command. Pat and the kids were in Tucson, so the admiral arranged for me to fly there instead of Washington; I could accompany my family on the long trek to Japan.

It was in Tucson that I had my first real taste of the power of a three-star's aide. Pat had applied for a passport for herself and the two kids as soon as I told her of the new assignment, but now, several weeks later, the passport still had not arrived. All our travel arrangements were locked in at this point, and we needed her passport within two days. I picked up the phone and called the aide detailer at BUPERS.

The next day, a man came to our door, identified himself as an FBI agent, and handed us the missing passport. We were on our way to Japan.

U.S. Army Photo

Rear Admiral Paul P. (Brick) Blackburn

This picture was taken in South Korea in 1964 when he served as Senior Member, United Nations Armistice Commission. In that capacity he argued with the communist representative at Panmunjom. Yes, the "peace talks" were still going on in 1964. (They still are.) I was along for the ride as the admiral's aide.

15

Vice Admiral Blackburn assumed command of the Seventh Fleet on March 1, 1965. He wasted no time; we went aboard his flagship, the cruiser *Oklahoma City*, and sailed for the South China Sea. There was a war on.

I had to leave Pat and the two kids in temporary quarters: bunk space in an old barracks. Pat took it like a trooper but was concerned that she wouldn't be able to handle the social requirements of an aide's wife.

When I returned to Yokosuka a month later, Pat was famous. Seems the base had put on an amateur production of *South Pacific*, and Pat became the understudy for the Bloody Mary role. On opening night, the primary was ill, so Pat went on stage and belted out "Bali Hai." She was an instant hit.

That did it. I was introduced around the naval base as "Pat's husband."

On March 8th 3,500 U.S. Marines deployed to South Vietnam. They were the first combat force to join the 25,000 U.S. military advisers there.

The Vietnam War grew ever hotter, and my boss was in the thick of the military planning. I was the third person in the room (to pour the coffee) when Commander Seventh Air Force and Commander Seventh Fleet divvied up the air war over North Vietnam.

Since the Air Force strikes would come from land bases in South Vietnam and Thailand, and the Navy strikes would come from aircraft carriers at sea, it made sense to give the Air Force the western part of the country and the Navy the eastern part.

Over and above that, it appeared to me that the driving force behind the *Route Package* structure that evolved that day was the concept of equal publicity. Both commanders knew that headlines in the Washington papers would translate into budget dollars sooner or later, and both commanders intended to take full advantage of it.

Back in the states, Black America's historic march from Selma to Montgomery occurred on March 21-25, 1965.

* * *

Vice Admiral Blackburn scheduled a triumphal visit back to South Korea shortly after he ascended to the Seventh Fleet throne. He was no longer a mere two-star, junior to all those U.S. Army generals in Korea who had been a trifle condescending towards him. Now he had three stars and was king of the hot-damn western Pacific Ocean.

He took his wife and elderly father along . . . and me, of course.

The admiral was a luncheon guest at South Korea's Blue House, their White House, the first day. There was a passel of guests and four of us aides.

We "dog-robbers" were not invited inside, so we went down the road a piece for Korean food. We returned to Blue House an hour later to find that everyone was gone. After a frantic ten minutes we found out the situation: Vice Admiral Blackburn had collapsed at lunch and been rushed to the Army hospital. I begged a ride from one of the other aides and followed in hot pursuit.

I found the admiral's wife and father in the hospital waiting room, distraught as hell. I bullied my way into the admiral's sick room. He was under an oxygen tent, seemingly unconscious.

A doctor in attendance gave me the diagnosis: double pneumonia. And the prognosis was not good.

Suddenly, the admiral stuck a trembling hand out from under the tent and pulled me towards him. "Get them out of here," he whispered.

"Yes, sir." I turned to the doctor and nurse still in the room and said, "Please leave. The admiral wants to speak to me in private."

"No way," said the doc. "We're staying."

"Look," I snapped. "This is the goddamn Commander of the United States Seventh Fleet, and he wants you out of here for a few minutes. Now get the hell out."

They went.

The admiral motioned me to come closer and fumbled with the plastic tent.

Raising the flap, I leaned in close.

"Brian," he whispered, "I know I'm going to be out of it for a while, but I'm going to make it. Don't let anyone, and I mean anyone, know that I'm sick. If word gets out, I'll lose my command." He closed his eyes and went to sleep.

I opened the door and invited the medical staff back in. Then I took care of the admiral's family, went to my old hooch, and had a couple of stiff drinks.

The next morning the admiral was still unconscious, but down at the Army communications center there was an urgent message to him from his chief of staff on the flagship.

> To: COMSEVENTHFLT
> From: ADMINO COMSEVENTFLT
> Subject: Marine Deployment
> CINCPACFLT wants your recommendation re. forthcoming Marine deployment: Chu Lai, Phu Bai, or Danang.

ADMINO COMSEVENTFLT was the admiral's chief of staff back aboard the flagship, a Navy captain. I was in a jam. The admiral couldn't answer it, and I couldn't tell the chief of staff that the admiral was ill. I ignored the message and hoped for the best.

That afternoon the message came again, higher priority. The admiral was still unconscious.

And the same thing occurred the next morning (day two).

That afternoon, the chief of staff, who must have been stressed out, sent a *Flash* message that said CINCPACFLT wanted an answer immediately. The captain went on to say that if he didn't hear from the admiral within an hour he would fly to Seoul to obtain a response.

Time had run out for me. I went down to the message center and sent the demanded response.

> From: COMSEVENTHFLT
> To: CINCPACFLT
> *Info: ADMINO COMSEVENTHFLT*
> Subject: Marine Deployment
> Recommend *Danang.*

The next morning (day three) the admiral woke up and called for his aide. "My God," he said when I entered the room, "the doctors say I've been out for over two days. CINCPACFLT wanted my recommendation about those Marines. Oh shit."

"He got your recommendation yesterday, sir."

The admiral stared at me. "What do you mean? I couldn't send it to him, for Christ's sake. I was unconscious."

"I sent one for you, sir."

"Holy shit."

"Here." I handed him a copy. He stared at it for a long time.

"Why Danang, Brian?"

"You told me some time ago that if the staff can't pick the best option, it probably doesn't make any difference which one you pick."

"Yeah . . . but why Danang?"

"Well, sir, if we win this war it probably won't make any difference where you put those Marines. But if we lose the war, Danang is the only one of the three where it will be easy for them to get out."

Admiral Blackburn looked stunned. "You damn fool," he said, "we aren't going to lose this war."

Twenty minutes later I was summoned to the office of four-star General Howze, commander of all United Nations forces in South Korea.

The secretary ushered me into the general's huge office and closed the door. General Howze and I were alone.

"Good morning, Lieutenant. I hear that Admiral Blackburn is awake now. How does he look?"

"He looks pretty fair, sir, all things considered."

"Good. Now I'm aware that CINCPACFLT has been trying to get a response out of your admiral, so I asked the message center to bring me up to speed on the situation. Imagine my surprise when I saw that the admiral had responded yesterday. While he was unconscious. Who sent that message?"

"I did, sir."

"Did the admiral tell you to send that message before he passed out?"

"No, sir."

"Shit." The general stared at me. "Do you understand that you could go to Leavenworth Prison for this?"

"Yes, sir."

"Then why in God's name did you do it?"

"Because the admiral's last instructions to me before he passed out was not to let anyone know that he was sick."

"Holy Shit." He stared at me again . . . for a very long time. "Okay, Lieutenant, get out of here. And give my regards to your boss."

Many years later I picked up a newspaper and the headline read, "Marines evacuated from Danang without any losses."

On July 24, 1965, Russian-made SAMs attacked a flight of four U.S. F-4Cs. One plane was shot down and three were damaged. It was the first use of SAMs in the war.

Pat settled right into life in Japan. After a few weeks in the abandoned WW-II barracks, we were assigned to base housing. It was a tiny two-bedroom, wood-frame house, and the wind blew through the cracks in the walls, but it was home. (It was sort of on a par with our first home in Sinton, Texas, but safer.)

Japan was probably the safest place in the world for kids; the Japanese doted on them. Six-year-old Kelly would take three-year-old Stuart down to the park several blocks away to play, or they would catch the base bus to the movie theater, and we never had to worry about them. I wonder if it's still that way.

We also had a Mama-san, an elderly woman who came in to clean and iron three days a week. She loved little Stuart and begged us to take her along when we rotated back to the states so she could continue to take care of him. (We should have worked that out.)

And did we have stereo. The Navy Exchange had a vast selection of Japanese stereo equipment that was, next to some German equipment, the best in the world. I added to what I'd purchased in Korea. I designed a vertical stero cabinet and hired a Japanese cabinetmaker to build it. Then I hired the Japanese technician from the Navy Exchange stereo shop to come in every Friday that I was home and "tweak" my system so that we could have perfect music for the weekend. That cost me five bucks a visit.

Pat liked to go into Yokosuka and wander through the commercial district. She had to dodge drunken sailors as they pursued their various vices, but she loved the shopping and the raw seafood.

She also liked to record music; we wound up with over a hundred reels of tape. (All of them obsolete now.)

The U.S. Supreme Court ruled on June 13, 1965, in Miranda vs. Arizona that police must inform suspects of their rights before they can be questioned. On June 29th the U.S. Air Force bombed Hanoi for the first time.

I had one memorable flight as pilot during my year as flag lieutenant. It was August, and we were in port in Yokosuka when the admiral called me into his office.

"Brian, I need you to fly a dog to Iwakuni."

"A dog, sir?"

"Yeah. The admiral stationed over there has his pet poodle here in Yokosuka for some veterinary work. The dog is over whatever ailed it and is ready to go home. Can you handle that?"

"No problem, sir. I'll set it up for tomorrow."

It was easy to schedule a C-45; then I hunted around for a co-pilot. I found a Marine aviator, a major, who was recovering from a bullet wound in his foot. He had been a FAC (Forward Air Controller) with a Marine battalion in South Vietnam. (When I asked him how he managed to get shot in the foot, his answer was vague enough that I suspected he'd done it himself to get out of "Nam.")

The Major had acquired a girlfriend, Betty, who was a nurse at the Yokosuka Naval Hospital. He asked if she could go along for the ride. He pointed out that she could mind the dog. This sounded like a good idea; I have no fondness for poodles.

Now, the Marine's girlfriend had a girlfriend: Linda, the female lieutenant j.g. who had recently become the Seventh Fleet Protocol Officer. (She was stationed in Yokosuka, not on the flagship.) She wanted to go too. No problem; now we had two dog handlers.

We drove out to NAS Atsugi the following morning. The admiral's driver met us there with a white, male poodle on a leash. The dog was as high-strung as I'd expected, but the two women seemed adequate to the task.

I pre-flighted the C-45, got us all strapped in (except for the dog, of course), and launched for MCAS Iwakuni on the western end of Japan. It was a crystal-clear morning, and we had a great view of

Mount Fuji as we cruised past at eight thousand feet.

About an hour into the trip, the major came up on the intercom. "Say, Brian, why don't you give Linda a quick flying lesson. I bet she'd like that. I'll go back and keep Betty and the dog company."

"Well, okay."

The major took off his headset, unstrapped, and crawled out of the cockpit.

Two minutes later, Linda appeared. It took about five minutes to get her strapped into the co-pilot's seat and the headset where it belonged. It took another fifteen minutes to get her to the point where she could hold the bird in level flight.

Then pandemonium broke out back in the passenger compartment. The dog was barking its little head off. *Yap! Yap! Yap!*

"Keep it steady," I told Linda. I loosened my shoulder harness and twisted around so I could see what the hell was going on back there.

Amazingly, the Marine and his girlfriend were joining the "mile high club" right there in the airplane's narrow center passageway. The Marine's bare butt rose and fell in a steady rhythm, and this act had driven the dog bonkers. It raced back and forth over the top of the copulating couple, and each time that it did so, its claws dug into the Marines buttocks. But the man never faltered, never missed a stroke. That was one tough Marine.

1965 was the year that air strikes against North Vietnam began in earnest; 25,000 sorties were flown against NVN in that year. (The sortie count would grow to 79,000 in 1966 and to 108,000 in 1967.)

My greatest contribution to the war effort, either then or later when I flew in it, probably came on a beautiful evening as *Oklahoma City* cruised the calm waters of the South China Sea.

I had friends flying combat missions into Vietnam, so I had asked the communications guys to give me copies of any naval messages that concerned our air strikes.

They obliged. Every day there was a fresh stack of messages in my in-basket, and I scanned them for information. (The Navy had learned to delete all those pesky RUBADWAs from the printed copies.)

We were taking heavy losses. The strategy employed by most of the air wings was to send in large, coordinated strikes (twenty or more aircraft) at low altitude in an effort to degrade the effectiveness of the enemy's surface-to-air missiles. But the SAMs still got kills, and so did enemy small arms fire.

The penetration altitude mentioned most often in the message traffic was three thousand feet. Then it clicked. Back at the University of Washington I'd written a paper that concerned air combat in WW-II. In the course of that research I had encountered the executive summary of a massive strategic bombing study that was completed after the war.

One of its conclusions was that three thousand feet was the worst possible altitude to be at when over enemy territory: the high-altitude weapons could still get you, and small-arms fire from the ground could also reach you. It was the altitude that got you overlapping threats.

I went out onto the deck. The sun had just set, and the sea was so calm that it looked like a huge mirror; the cruiser left tiny ripples in its wake.

The admiral stood by the rail, a lit cigarette in his hand. His eyes were fixed on the far horizon.

"Admiral, excuse me for interrupting your thoughts, but have you ever heard of the *World War Two Strategic Bombing Study*?"

"No." He was irked. "Why?"

"Well, it was the largest single study of American bombing campaign effectiveness in that war. One of its conclusions was that three thousand feet is the worst possible altitude to use over enemy territory."

"Oh yeah? Why?"

"It's the altitude where both the high-altitude and low-altitude weapons can reach you."

"Like the SAMs and the coolie rifles?"

"Yes, sir."

"Okay, why did you feel that this is important today?"

"Because the message traffic I've looked at indicates that our air wings have picked three thousand feet as the preferred altitude going in to the targets."

"Hmmm. I see. I'll think about that."

I'm pretty sure the admiral had that bit of info checked out before he acted. But two days later he sent a message that directed our air wings to avoid three thousand feet; it said to either stay above thirty-five hundred feet and fight the SAMs or go in right down on the deck.

Our losses decreased. I like to think that my conversation with the admiral repaid the Navy's expenses for my Five-Term Program.

About this time, VADM Blackburn pinned bronze leaves onto my collar. I was now a lieutenant commander.

My admiral took one trip without me, and it was the beginning of the end of his career. He had visited an aircraft carrier off the coast of Vietnam and was to fly ashore to rendezvous with his flagship. He was the sole passenger on a COD, a twin-engine support plane derived from the S-2 anti-sub aircraft. His seat tore loose on the cat shot and sent him head first through the after bulkhead. He survived, but he had 120 stitches in his scalp.

While Admiral Blackburn recuperated, Rear Admiral Joseph W. Williams, who was in the area to oversee salvage of a naval vessel that had run aground, was appointed Acting Commander, Seventh Fleet. It was expected that this would be a temporary arrangement, and Vice Admiral Blackburn would resume his command in about eight weeks.

A few days before resuming command, however, the admiral had a seizure while he was at a Japanese resort. The doctors decided it was the result of his head injury; it might have been a one-time event, or it might recur.

The CNO (Chief of Naval Operations) decided to replace him and appointed Vice Admiral Johnny Hyland.

This led to an aide's worst nightmare. On the day of the change of command, December 13, 1965, I had three admirals present in Yokosuka, all claiming to be Commander, Seventh Fleet. And I was in charge of protocol.

Much against my will, VADM Blackburn turned me over to VADM Hyland instead of releasing me from my assignment. I was tired of watching from the sidelines while my colleagues fought the war, and this soured me. I didn't do a very good job for Admiral Hyland in the few months I stayed with him, but he was good about it. When I finally was released, Admiral Hyland told me to contact him if I ever needed help with my career. Admiral Blackburn had given me a similar invitation, so I felt that I had two potential sponsors, the prime benefit of an aide tour.

Because of his health problems, Vice Admiral Blackburn was demoted to Rear Admiral and assigned a staff job in Florida. He retired as soon as he reached thirty years service. (He died of lymph cancer in 1992 at age 83.)

Vice Admiral Hyland was promoted to Commander Pacific Fleet a couple years later, but he lost that job when North Korea captured the USS Pueblo in January 1968. He too retired—the highest-ranking casualty of the *Pueblo Incident.*

So, while both of my admirals had promised future help, when and if I needed it, both were long gone by the time I could have used it.

My biggest problem as I prepared to return to flight duty in the spring of 1966 was that I could no longer pass the vision test. The Navy required its pilots to have 20/20 vision *uncorrected.* I hadn't had that for two years. I'd cheated my way through the last two annual physicals by sneaking in early and memorizing the appropriate lines on the eye chart. Rumor had it that the Navy might soon allow experienced pilots to wear glasses, but that was not yet policy.

Now I was headed back to the cockpit, where vision was important and cheating was a little tougher. BUPERS sent me orders to an F-4 fighter squadron, but I figured I needed another set of eyes up front. The F-4 carried a RIO (Radar Intercept Officer) in the back seat, but he couldn't see forward. The A-6, on the other hand, had a large cockpit with a B/N (Bombardier/Navigator) in a side-by-side seating arrangement. Maybe a B/N could help me get aboard the carrier until the Navy allowed corrective lenses. I used what little clout I had left as an aide to get my orders changed.

The new orders were to VA-196, which was slated to become the first West Coast A-6 squadron. But there were two intermediate stops listed in the orders.

First, I was to spend four months at the University of Southern California (USC). There I would attend USC's *Aviation Safety Course* to learn how to investigate aircraft accidents (and also prevent them).

After that, I was to report to VA-42, the A-6 training RAG in Virginia Beach, Virginia. I was about to be a student again. Twice.

Back on August 11, 1965, a routine traffic stop in South Central Los Angeles sparked the infamous Watts riot. It lasted for six days and left thirty-four dead, over a thousand people injured, nearly four thousand arrested, and hundreds of buildings destroyed.

Fortunately, it was peaceful by the time we arrived in Los Angeles in March 1966. We stayed with Pat's parents in Garden Grove, and my commute to school took me right through the middle of Watts.

The USC Aviation Safety Course was fascinating. We studied things like metal fatigue, stress fractures, witness interrogation, and other things to do with aviation accident prevention and investigation. But by June, Pat and I were ready to leave the Los Angeles basin and head east.

That's Pat (in the middle) dining with VIPs at an embassy bash in Tokyo in 1965. I was off working somewhere and didn't get to eat. The man on Pat's left was head of the Hearst newspaper chain in Asia. Pat enjoyed the conversation.

Dinner on a floating restaurant in Hong Kong

The year was 1965. The flagship, USS *Oklahoma City*, was on a port visit in Hong Kong, and the wives flew down to keep us guys out of trouble.

That's Captain and Mrs. Tarleton from the Seventh Fleet Staff with us. The hotel's sailing yacht carried just the four of us around Hong Kong Island to the south-side restaurant. It was quite a trip.

16

The A-6 was one of the greatest combat aircraft ever. Period. End of discussion. And that's not just my viewpoint; it's the opinion of almost everyone who ever flew one into hostile fire.

A-6A

After Korea, the Navy needed a jet replacement for the mighty Spad. The new plane didn't need to be particularly fast, but it needed to haul a lot of ordnance over great distances. In 1957, the Navy asked for proposals. Eight aircraft companies submitted eleven designs, and the Grumman plan was selected.

A prototype, the A2F-1 (a large, swept-wing, carrier aircraft) first flew on April 19, 1960. In September 1962, as part of the change to DOD's uniform aircraft designation system, it became the A-6A.

The first A-6As sent to the fleet went to VA-42 in February 1963. VA-42's job was to train pilots, B/Ns, and maintenance personnel for the fleet carrier squadrons.

An A-6A was not pretty; it resembled a big tadpole (or a drumstick). It had a large, bulbous nose that housed radar antennae and permitted side-by-side seating for the crew of two. (Actually, the pilot's seat was nine inches forward of the B/N's seat, which was fair.)

It was powered by two Pratt & Whitney J52-P6 turbojet engines, each with 8,500 pounds of thrust. The plane was equipped with powered slats down the entire leading edge of its wings, and it had flaps that stretched along almost all of the wing's trailing edges. Instead of standard ailerons, it used large spoilers (called *flaperons*) on the upper wing surfaces, just ahead of the flaps, to control roll. The wingtips split open to become V-shaped speed brakes.

There was a huge, fixed, air-to-air refueling probe mounted on the centerline of the aircraft forward of the cockpit. It looked sort of like a bent index finger pointed up and forward. It had a ball valve on its tip about the size of a grapefruit. (I stood by the plane at an air show once when a young woman asked me what that thing on the nose was for. I told her it was a ballpoint pen for skywriting. I think she believed it.)

The interior of the cockpit was roomy, especially in comparison to the A-4. There were about six inches between my outboard shoulder and the canopy, which was bowed out so that I could look almost straight down, and a center console gave about ten inches of separation between the two crewmember's shoulders. It was quite comfy.

It also had instrumentation up the kazoo. Between the B/N's knees was a control panel for a computer that had both navigation and attack capabilities. In front of his face was a hood-covered, vertical display for the search/attack radar presentations.

A large armament panel that controlled the airplane's five weapons stations was situated in the middle of the front panel. Both pilot and B/N could reach the armament switches, but they were part of the B/N's function. The pilot could do a manual weapons release in the usual way, with the pickle or trigger on his control stick, or the B/N could set it up for the computer to make the drop.

An A-6 pilot had the world's largest attitude indicator centered on the instrument panel right in front of his face. It was similar in size and appearance to the early TV screens and was called a VDI (Vertical Display Indicator). It had a pale orange glow and showed an artificial horizon across the middle of its screen with puffy white clouds above it. Below the horizon, circles we called "cow plops" were displayed for ground texture. When it got real black outside, you turned up the rosy glow on the VDI, and it looked like you were over Kansas on a sunny day, white clouds above and cow plops below.

When you went into a turn, the VDI told you almost subliminally that you were in a bank; you didn't have to squint at some little VGI (Vertical Gyro Indicator) with its tiny airplane superimposed in front of a tilted black-and-white ball. Of course, we had one of those standard VGIs for back up. And, if worse came to disaster, we still had the old needle-and-ball turn indicator.

Below the VDI was a circular radar screen that showed the horizontal situation. This HSI (Horizontal Situation Indicator) was similar to the surface radar displays on the bridges of ships. I rarely used it.

Dual throttles were mounted in a quadrant on the port side near the pilot's left hand. The tail hook control and flap handle were forward of the throttles.

Strategically placed around the VDI were all the other instruments that would be familiar to almost any pilot: engine instruments, fuel gauges, light controls, etc. (including a radar altimeter). The radio controls were situated on the center panel between the crewmember seats. The human factors people had done a good job.

The A-6A was a "Grumman Ironworks" product. This meant that it was built like a tank. But oh, how it could perform. It could out turn, out climb, and out run every tactical aircraft then in the Navy inventory unless they were in afterburner. I know, because we used to hassle with the other planes whenever we had the chance. The F-4 and the F-14 almost always had to go into *burner* to escape from us in a mock dogfight.

Pat and I rented a nifty little apartment in Virginia Beach,

Virginia, and I got ready to fly jets again, but *that* would have to wait a bit.

In July 1966, we students slated for VA-196 started our curriculum with SERE (Survival, Evasion, Resistance, and Escape) training in northern Maine. It was a lot different from the old survival course in San Diego; after all, there was now a war on. The course was open-ended, so none of us knew when it would be over. (It turned out to last a week.)

The survival phase was short enough that nobody got too hungry. Again, there were no volunteers to kill the bunny. I found some bird's eggs, but I wasn't hungry enough to eat them. There was plenty of cold water in the creeks, so thirst was not an issue.

Our evasion part was exhausting. Two of us climbed to the top of a mountain ridge in order to avoid what we considered to be the prime capture area. We almost stumbled over one of the bad guys who lay in wait for people like us. He woke from his nap and grabbed us.

Most of our time in Maine was spent in a mock POW (Prisoner of War) camp that I thought was damn realistic. I remember being cold, tired, and pissed off. One night I was stripped naked and pushed into a nearby stream of icy-cold water. More water was poured over my head by guards with buckets. This continued until I was convinced that I would get sick and die.

Then there were the *boxes* that we were crammed into for the guard's amusement. Rumor had it that one of us would have snakes poured in on top of them while in the horizontal box. I made it a point to get my turn in the box when I was sure there were no snakes around.

The POW drill used a lot of psychology, and it worked. On the fourth day in the camp, the guards "beat" one of the prisoners right there in the compound, and the rest of us attacked the guards.

By this time, it had all become pretty real to me. It took two men to pry my fingers from the throat of one of the guards; I wanted to kill him. I had crossed a line.

After we returned to Virginia Beach, I went through a refresher instrument course in the TF-9J (a two-place F-9 with a hood in back), then started my A-6 training in August. After a lot of ground school, I flew my new favorite bird for the first time on August 15,

1966.

Our training consisted of the usual stuff: A-6 familiarization, aerobatics, formation flying, tactics, weapons, and navigation. We spent a lot of time on low-level flights through the mountains of Virginia and West Virginia, much of it at night.

The heart of the A-6 was its ability to navigate. The B/N used the computer and radar to guide the pilot to the next checkpoint. Once there, he updated the computer's coordinates, if necessary. The computer reciprocated and slewed the radar crosshairs over to the next checkpoint. Then it was up to the B/N to identify, verify, and track that point while the pilot followed the steering guidance shown on the VDI and the HSI.

The computer generated a curved path on the VDI, so all the pilot had to do was follow the yellow brick road across "Kansas." If you didn't like the simulated road, you could use the steering bugs situated on the periphery of both the VDI and the HSI. (That was usually my preference.)

In theory, the A-6A computer could also guide you through mountains at very low altitudes and keep you at a set distance above the ground. But the terrain clearance mode was still too unreliable to use except in an advisory capacity, so it was up to the pilot to keep the aircraft low, but not too low. The mountains of Virginia are very hard.

We did our live-ordnance training at MCAS Yuma, Arizona. While there, we had (only) one opportunity to carry a full A-6 load of bombs so we could get the feel of it.

On the particular day that springs to mind, I launched with twenty-two MK-82 GP (General Purpose) bombs. They weighed five hundred pounds apiece, so my ordnance load was 11,000 pounds. We headed for the Chocolate Mountain Bombing Range northwest of Yuma.

Part of the drill was to experience twenty-two bombs coming off in a dive and feel the aircraft's reaction. The weapon system's *intervelometer* rippled them off at tiny fractions of a second; this minimized the probability of a bomb-to-bomb collision and also spaced out the impact points on the ground. (An *ejector foot* powered by a small explosive charge pushed each bomb away from the rack to prevent any bomb-to-aircraft collisions.)

My flight that day went according to plan up to a point. I spotted the target, called in hot, and dove at the target. When airspeed, altitude, and pipper placement all came together, I pickled. I felt one bomb kick off. Just one. *Oh shit.*

I started my pullout—a gentle one to keep from overstressing those wings that still held 10,500 pounds of ordnance—and another bomb came off. *What the hell?*

Then another bomb popped off.

"Turn 'em off," I yelled at the B/N.

"I can't," he called back. "I turned off all the switches, but the weapons keep coming off."

Another ejector foot fired as we leveled off about a thousand feet above the sand and headed north, still inside the bombing range (fortunately). The bombs continued to come off, one every five seconds. The last one departed just before we left the range.

"Hey, I figured it out," my B/N said. "I accidentally set the intervelometer for five seconds instead of five hundredths of a second."

Jeeesh.

We found out later that a survey crew was on the ground right in our path. They stood there, mouths open, and watched the bomb blasts march towards them until they dove for cover. As luck would have it, the last bomb hit a few hundred feet short of them.

(The same intervelometer problem bugged me again a year later, in combat this time. I dove on a target a bit northeast of Hanoi and a single bomb came off; the rest then slowly popped off at ten second intervals. I pulled out low and ran up the main highway between Hanoi and Haiphong at a thousand feet, hoping to take out the highway with some of those tardy bombs. Unfortunately, the wind carried every bomb off to the side, and one of them blew up a little farmhouse. I still feel badly about that farmhouse; I had no desire to kill farmers.)

A couple of days later in our Yuma training excursion, I went on a low altitude DR navigation flight around western Arizona. This was like the old days in A-4s where the pilot did the navigating himself. A pilot instructor, not a B/N, occupied the right-hand seat.

My instructor that flight was a senior pilot named Deke—a real hard-ass. When he briefed the flight, he repeatedly stressed that we were to abide by the current regulations and not go any lower than five hundred feet above the terrain. He said this three different times.

We launched and headed north across the desert. I used the radar altimeter to keep the plane five hundred feet above the deck.

Deke spoke up from the right hand seat. "What's the matter, you afraid of the ground?"

Well, I thought, maybe he thinks this is more than five hundred feet. I went down to about two hundred feet.

"You a pussy?" Deke asked.

That did it. I drove that plane right down into the weeds. There was a sharp ridge coming up and I held it right on the deck until I saw Deke's leg muscles tense, then I popped up and over the rocks.

Deke's debrief after the flight was short. "Good hop, once you decided to fly low." (I imagine all that emphasis in the briefing on staying above five hundred feet was just to cover his butt if we hit anything.)

VA-196 had been an A-1 squadron until their old planes were taken away, and everyone was sent to VA-42 for A-6 training back on May 1, 1966. With the subsequent addition of newcomers like me, there was a full complement of aircrew and enlisted men, so we were formed back into a squadron in October. As expected, due to my USC education, I became the squadron's safety officer.

We still had more training to accomplish. When November rolled around, we went into a flurry of FCLP, especially night FCLP, and on November 29 we headed out to sea. I made two touch-and-go landings on the ship followed by six traps. I was then day qualified. On the 30th I did two daytime traps to warm up and then six night traps to become fully carrier qualified in the A-6A.

I cannot begin to describe how night carrier ops with the A-6 in 1966 differed from what they'd been in the A-4 five years before. But I'll try.

For starters, you could see the ship. Someone had decided to turn on the lights. When you were in the groove, you could see the flight deck. The centerline was lit better than before, and the edges of the landing area were also lit. A string of lights that fell from the start of the centerline down the stern to the waterline gave you a three-dimensional feel for the deck. There were even red floodlights to help you when you taxied after a trap. Wonderful.

And now my B/N could call the ball for me. Ken and I had teamed up as we prepared for carrier qualification, so I had a permanent B/N that I could share my secret with. I don't know how he felt about flying aboard with a pilot who had to cheat to pass the vision test, but he took it like a man.

The jet instrument approach to the carrier was now used at night as well as in instrument conditions. You held at 250 knots in a left-hand racetrack pattern at an *initial approach fix* until it was time to descend. (A typical fix might be thirty miles aft of the ship at twenty thousand feet. Each flight was assigned a different altitude, and the distance was a function of altitude.)

Of course you were still obliged to hit your fix and start your penetration exactly on time; airborne aircraft were scheduled to trap aboard at one-minute intervals under night or all-weather conditions. At the fix (and on time), you let CCA know that you were starting down. "Milestone Four-Zero-Seven, commencing." (If you were under radio silence rules, you skipped all the radio calls.)

Popping your speed brakes, you set the throttles for 250 knots, and held a descent rate of four thousand feet per minute until you passed five thousand feet and called your distance. "Milestone Four-Zero-Seven, *platform*, fifteen miles."

You slowed your rate of descent to two thousand feet per minute and then leveled off twelve hundred feet above the water. The speed brakes came in, and you held 250 knots.

At ten miles you called and gave your fuel state. "Milestone Four-Zero-Seven, *gate*, twenty-two hundred."

Somewhere between ten and six miles you dirtied up and slowed to 150 knots.

Between six and three miles you slowed to *donut* speed on the AOA (angle-of-attack) gauge. AOA was used to get the right approach speed because, while the correct airspeed for an approach varies with aircraft weight, AOA is the same regardless of weight.

Passing three miles you reduced power and started down on final approach under CCA control.

At two miles you were at 820 feet, and at one mile you passed through 440 feet.

When you approached a quarter mile astern, CCA turned you

loose. "Milestone Four-Zero-Seven, call the ball."

Now my arrangement with Ken went into play. He would peer over the instrument panel at the ship and give me an advisory over the ICS such as, "You're a little high." Then he'd make the UHF call. "Four-Zero-Seven, Intruder ball, nineteen hundred."

A few seconds later things would come into focus, and I'd tell Ken, "Okay, I have the ball." It worked.

You could tell there was a war on. *Billboard* magazine declared Sergeant Barry Sadler's "The Ballad of the Green Berets" the top song of 1966. At the movies, we watched *Batman* with Adam West, and *The Good, the Bad and the Ugly* with Clint Eastwood.

U.S. Navy Photo

An A-6 launched on the angled deck by one of the two "waist" catapults.

That's a *buddy store* tanker package on the centerline. It, and the two drop tanks, indicate that this bird is off on a tanker mission to refuel other aircraft. Its normal load was twenty-two 500-pound bombs.

17

VA-196 moved to NAS Whidbey Island, Washington, in November 1966. The air station had been home to anti-submarine patrol aircraft like the P-2V and the P-3A, but now it became the West Coast A-6 base.

Whidbey Island is a long, skinny strip of land that runs north and south in the Straits of Juan de Fuca, northwest of Seattle. To get to Seattle from the base, you could take a ferry from the south end of the island; or you could drive to the north end of the island, cross a bridge to the mainland, and then drive south.

Pat and I rented a small house tucked under pine trees in the town of Oak Harbor. (Back when I was finishing up at the University of Washington, real estate agents tried to get us to buy property on Whidbey Island. I declined, confident that the base there would soon close and property values would plummet. Now, I was stationed there, it was booming, and we had to rent.)

At any rate, Pat put the kids in school and took a part- time job at a children's shop in town. I prepared for war.

Our favorite way to prepare for war was to bomb the hell out of Oregon. Of course, we only dropped twenty-five pound Mk-76 practice bombs on a designated target area.

We launched out of Whidbey Island, flew over the civilized coastal belt, and then let down into the Cascade Mountains. After a low-level run through the mountains, we wound up at the Boardman Target Range in eastern Oregon.

A river ran east and west through the range, and our run-in to the target was eastward on the south side of the river. A butte stuck up on the north side of the river, so you had to make sure you were on the right side of the water.

It was winter in Washington, so we got a lot of actual instrument time. Then we got a lot of nighttime. Soon, we flew at night into crummy weather. It was ideal preparation for the A-6 mission: night and all-weather attack.

Our runs at the target were all low-level, at about two hundred feet. Our speed varied, depending on the pilot's mood swings, from

300 knots up to the plane's max of 560 knots (about 640 miles an hour).

The B/N put the radar and computer in search mode and set the plane up on the run-in line. He made sure the radar cursor was on the target; then he stepped both radar and computer into attack mode. From then on, the computer did a weapons release calculation every few feet, and it released the bomb the first time the projected impact was worse than the previous one.

When we ran the target at night in a snowstorm, it all seemed like magic; we pilots never saw the target. (We stayed busy avoiding the ground, which we couldn't see either.)

In early April, we flew aboard USS *Constellation* (CVA 64) for a two-week pre-deployment *work up*. The "Connie," as we all called the ship, was home-ported in San Diego. She was only seven years old, and quite modern, but she was not nuclear powered. Steam from eight boilers drove her four gigantic screws and powered four steam catapults. She drew almost thirty-six feet of water and could make thirty-four knots. Her hull length was 1048 feet, her beam width 129 feet, and her flight deck measured 1063 feet by 252 feet. She was a big one.

A new twist was the catapult tow bar and holdback fitting on the newer aircraft like the A-6. Both were part of the nose wheel strut. A T-bar swung down from the front of the strut, and its crossbar locked into the catapult shuttle. Another bar came down aft of the nose gear and connected to the deck via the ceramic holdback fitting. When the cat fired, the holdback broke. At the end of the catapult run, the tow bar released and folded back up into the nose gear.

In effect, the catapult launched the nose strut, and the rest of the airplane had no choice but to follow.

We were now part of Air Wing Fourteen (CVW-14), and the old rule that squadron numbers tracked to the air wing's number had been pretty well scrapped. VA-55 and VA-146 were aboard with A-4Cs, VF-142 and VF-143 flew F-4Bs, RVAH-12 had RA-5C "recce" birds, and VAH-8 provided KA-3D tanker aircraft. VAW-113 provided our eyes in the sky; they flew the E-2A airborne radar planes. We had nine A-6As. If you counted the helicopters, the air wing had almost seventy aircraft.

Our fighter squadrons had colorful names like Ghost Riders and The Pukin' Dogs. And the light attack guys weren't too square; they were the War Horses and Blue Diamonds. We, however, had acquired the unfortunate name Main Battery (after the main guns on a battleship, of all things) back when the squadron had been a Spad outfit.

Worse, our squadron call sign was Milestone, which the other pilots in the air wing liked to mispronounce as Millstone. (That stopped when the shooting started.)

On April 29, we kissed our wives and kids goodbye and sailed for Southeast Asia and the Vietnam War. It was a sad and solemn farewell.

Unlike my earlier cruises, when Pat had waited for me in Tucson, she stayed in Oak Harbor this time. It was just as well; the wives helped each other when the going got rough.

Yankee Station was a point in the Gulf of Tonkin between North Vietnam and China's Hainan Island. There was a *Dixie Station* down south off the coast of South Vietnam, but our home was Yankee Station.

About a hundred miles northwest, a cruiser or destroyer with the call sign Red Crown used radar and the NTDS (Naval Tactical Data System) to watch and control a large piece of the air war over North Vietnam and the Tonkin Gulf.

A pair of fighter planes called a BARCAP (Barrier Combat Air Patrol) patrolled just off the beach to stop any MIGs that might attempt a strike against Red Crown or the carriers on Yankee Station.

Three aircraft carriers and their escorts usually maneuvered around Point Yankee. Two would take the day watch and one the night shift.

The carriers conducted flight ops on 12-hour shifts broken down into eight 1.5-hour cycles. The first launch of the day might be at 0700, when up to twenty or more aircraft were fired off the four cats at roughly one-minute intervals on each cat. (You could get twenty-four planes airborne in about six minutes if all went well, but it often took a little longer that that.)

They would fly their missions, come back over the ship, and wait for the next cycle to begin at 0830, when the second launch started. When the last bird of the second strike was shot off the cat, or at least moved forward of the landing area, the first plane back from the initial strike appeared in the groove for landing.

After the recovery, there was about one hour to *re-spot* the deck for the third launch. And so it went throughout the day (or night).

When two aircraft carriers conducted flight ops at the same time, their schedules could be staggered, so there were almost always strike birds over North Vietnam to look for moving targets. When only one carrier operated (a normal situation at night) the wily North Vietnamese knew to the minute when the planes were either all on the way in or all on the way out, and none were overhead. For that half-hour, the North Vietnamese came out of their holes and ran their trucks and trains south as fast as they could go.

Constellation arrived at Yankee Station in late May, and on the 28th, Air Wing Fourteen went to war. We started slow; the brass sent us after lesser targets near the DMZ (Demilitarized Zone) that separated the two Vietnams. The targets there were not as well defended as the ones farther north.

I'm pretty sure most of us that went into combat for the first time that day felt like I did: a little scared of the action, but terrified of screwing up or (worse) chickening out. The event itself was almost anti-climactic.

Our target was the Chau Lam highway bridge a short distance inland. It was a beautiful day with little white puffy clouds here and there. The ground was covered with small farms, and it looked so darn peaceful I felt guilty about creating a disturbance. But I did it.

When my turn came, I rolled in and put my load of 500-pound bombs somewhere in the vicinity of the bridge. There was barely any flak, but I jinked like crazy as I exited the target area.

Then it was all over; I was a combat veteran.

Israel's "six-day war" started on June 5th. The Israeli Air Force performed a preemptive strike that wiped out Egypt's airplanes on the ground. Israel then fought Egypt, Jordan, and Syria, and whipped them all. Israel occupied the West Bank, the Gaza Strip, the Sinai Peninsula, and the Golan Heights. We aviators on

Constellation were impressed. Six days. Now that was the way to fight a war.

Target assignments moved farther north, and the ground fire got hotter. We visited places like the Son Cau and Thinh Lac railroad bridges. One strike was unusual in that it was coordinated with another air wing. We approached the beach at about thirteen thousand feet, and another gaggle of airplanes appeared a little off to starboard at a lower altitude. We proceeded on parallel courses towards related targets.

Then an A-4 in the other flight ate a SAM. Everything had been quiet, but suddenly there was a streak of flame up from the ground, and the A-4 exploded. There was no chute, and the two flights trundled on the targets.

That evening there was a knock on my stateroom door, and Ken came in. "I quit," he said. "Turned in my wings."

A quick glance at the empty space above the left pocket of his khaki shirt confirmed that.

I managed to ask, "Why?"

"Well," Ken said, "I started to think about things. At any rate, I'm sorry. Now you'll have to break in a new B/N."

"Yeah, sure looks that way. Any possibility you'll change your mind?"

"Not a chance. This is final."

"Okay, Ken. Good luck."

He turned and left. I sat there and considered how this would affect me. I soon found out.

Perhaps our B/Ns had a higher regard for the crew concept than I did. I wasn't disturbed at the thought of flying with different B/Ns while I waited for Ken's replacement, but the B/Ns had some reservations. They were willing to go up with me on day missions, but they wanted to fly with their own pilot at night. They cited crew coordination issues on system attacks. (Or maybe Ken told them about my little vision problem.)

Our skipper ruled that, until I had a permanent replacement B/N, I would fly day strikes only. This turned out to be a good deal; I was about to specialize in *alpha strikes*.

The alpha strike was a major, coordinated effort by all the squadrons aboard. A typical strike composition included four A-6s, eight F-4s, and eight A-4s supported by an RA-5C photo bird and a KA-3D tanker—twenty-two aircraft on a single strike. (I've led as many as thirty-two aircraft, all headed towards a single target complex.)

My first experience with a real alpha strike was on June 11, 1967. The target was Kep Airfield. A road and railroad came out of Hanoi and ran northeast to China. About thirty miles outside Hanoi, just west of the road and railroad, was a North Vietnamese fighter base called Kep. It was destined to become famous in the minds of the aviators who repeatedly struck it (and the paper-mache' airplane decoy there).

There were multiple SAM sites arrayed about the place, but the main threat in close came from their anti-aircraft guns. There was a veritable forest of 20-mm, 37-mm, and 85-mm gun emplacements situated in a crescent across the north side of the field.

Black puffs of flak from the 85s could reach you before you rolled in, tracers and white puffs from the 37s would stab at you on the way down, and the rapid-fire 20s would try to skin you alive as you bottomed out.

Hanoi sits in the Red River delta about sixty miles inland. Haiphong, another delta city, is a seaport almost due east of Hanoi. Between this delta and the Chinese border lies a mountain chain that runs northwest and parallels the border. The safest way to reach Kep was to coast in over those mountains north of Haiphong and ride them all the way up to Kep, which sits a few miles southward in the delta.

Our flight leader that day was the CO of one of the A-4 squadron's. He planned the strike, ran it, and had a special assignment for me. When the rest of the strike force rolled in heading west, down the runway, I was to turn left, arc around the field for about thirty degrees, and then roll in heading northwest across the runway (and towards the flak sites).

This was not good; it looked to me like I was about to be flak bait.

The strike went as planned, with little opposition until we reached the roll-in point. The fighters went after the flak sites to suppress them, and the attack aircraft dove at the runway. Following orders, I turned left and chugged around the arc while the gunners who hadn't ducked shot at the diving airplanes.

When I rolled in, heading northwest, the F-4s were already off target and had hooked left, away from the flak sites.

The last of the A-4s pulled off target and turned left as my bombs came off.

Looking up from the target, I grimaced. If I pulled off to the left, as planned, and chased my colleagues, I'd be low and belly up to every one of those guns. And I'd be the only plane still in range . . . dead meat. *No way.*

I stayed in the dive, pushed the stick forward for a bit of zero-g to help the acceleration, and headed right for the flak sites.

My B/N screamed, then ripped off his kneepad and hit me over the head with it. He must have thought I was insane.

At the last second, I pulled out in a hard right turn and wound up about fifty feet above the gunner's heads.

I got an up-close and personal look at the Vietnamese gunners as we flew up that long string of AA sites. They sat on metal tractor seats on top of their gun platforms and spun two wheels: one turned the gun platform and the other elevated the gun barrel. But they couldn't spin their little wheels fast enough to track us as we barreled past them at over 500 knots. The few rounds they flung after us while we climbed out didn't catch us.

On June 22, my thirtieth birthday, I killed a train. I've always hated trains. The Southern Pacific tracks run through the middle of Tucson, and they delay automobile traffic at every opportunity. I hate trains.

This morning I had the lead of a small strike headed for a routine target when I spotted a real live train. It must have had about fifty cars and was highballing it for the next safe place to hide.

I called the target, rolled in, and sent twenty-two 500-pound presents to the train. I had the good fortune to catch the train as it went through an S-turn, and my *stick* of bombs cut that sucker into three pieces and disabled the engine.

The rest of the planes in my strike dumped all over the stalled cars. *Constellation* sent planes against the remnants throughout the rest of the day.

The next day, our little squadron "newspaper" headline read, *Gramps kills a train.* Gramps?

* * *

Two days later we hit the Phu Ly railroad yards about thirty miles south of Hanoi. CAG's briefing introduced me to the "big sky" concept.

Other air wings had taken what our CAG viewed as excessive losses while they tried to coordinate and sequence aircraft diving at the target. Their objective had been to avoid mid-air collisions with other strike aircraft and their bombs.

But that allowed the gunners on the ground to concentrate their fire against a handful of airplanes at a time.

CAG's policy was this: stay in formation as long as you can, proceed to the target independently if you have to, and roll in when you get there. There would be many airplanes diving at once from different angles, but it was a "big sky," and chances were that you wouldn't hit another plane or bomb on the way down.

I led the A-6 element and was *pathfinder* for the strike force. We launched and went into what was to be our standard alpha strike rendezvous pattern.

Each squadron was assigned an altitude above the ship in which their flight would rendezvous; separation between flights was normally a thousand feet. The lead flight was given the highest altitude, typically thirteen thousand feet.

After each of the flights joined up at their own altitude, they maneuvered inside the lead-flight's turn and climbed up the bearing angle into their assigned position.

Our launch and rendezvous process took about twenty minutes. When the last flight joined up, I continued my left turn around the carrier until we came up on the westerly heading to our coast-in point. I rolled out of the turn, advanced the power a bit, and started a slow climb.

My B/N got busy on the radar and soon provided a small heading correction. We were on our way.

To my left rode two A-6s, four F-4s, and four A-4s. To my right were my wingman, four F-4s, and four A-4s. It was a glorious sight.

By the time we crossed the coast we'd managed to crawl up to eighteen thousand feet.

CAG called "Feet dry" to let the ship know of our progress. Then he called "Buster," the signal for max speed.

I added full power, lowered the nose, and took us all into a shallow descent that would help us accelerate as we went back down to our planned roll-in altitude of thirteen thousand feet.

All the F-4's went to a hundred percent power plus afterburner and pulled away from us on either flank. Their job was to get ahead of the main body and attack the flak sites to make the gunners keep their heads down while we bombers attacked the target.

We jinked gently to make sure some random 85-mm gun didn't track and nail one of us out of the blue. It took a while for the 85-mm rounds to get to our altitude, so the gunners had to lead us. When we jinked, it made life more difficult for them.

Soon the radios warned of SAM radar activity. Then the first black puffs of 85-mm flak appeared around us, and the jinking became more violent. Someone called a SAM, and all the other planes in our strike disappeared.

Someone else called another SAM, but I didn't see any; I was fixated on the target.

Then we were there: thirteen thousand feet and the roll-in point. I rolled my A-6 over and pulled the plane into its dive.

My B/N flipped the master arm switch and looked for SAMs.

My peripheral vision picked up white puffs, black puffs, and orange tracers. I stared into the gunsight as the pipper tracked towards the target and then—there they were, our aircraft—diving from all sides.

The F-4s had pulled off target; little clouds of smoke from their bombs marked the anti-aircraft AA gun sites. I blinked as I passed between an A-4 and the bombs it had just released.

Somebody cried "Big sky" over the UHF.

Our bombs came off, and I pulled like crazy to come out of the dive above 3500 feet.

We doubled back towards the coast and ran like hell. The flak chased us. Our exit route was the reverse of our inbound course, and our planes streamed together like rivulets that merge into a mountain brook.

There was no attempt to rejoin the original formation; you just tried to find your wingman. If you were to eject, your wingman was the guy who would tell the SAR (Search and Rescue) guys whether or not you had a good chute and, if so, where you were. It was important to have a wingman.

Once we were all over the water, CAG called "Feet wet." We

were safe now. All we had to do was land on an aircraft carrier.

U.S. Navy Photo

USS *Constellation*, CVA 64

She was always just the "Connie" to us.

18

For the next month, most of my flights involved two-plane sorties into the delta area around Nam Dinh and Than Hua, well south of Hanoi. There seemed to be a lot of bridges that needed to be dropped, and we all had our shots at them.

Bridges are hard to kill with dumb bombs. At one point in my life I did the math, and I seem to recall that you had to drop about a hundred dumb bombs on a steel truss bridge in order to have a fifty percent or better chance that you would take out a main segment and close the bridge. We shut down a lot of bridges for a few hours, but they were almost always repaired and back in business by the next day.

We in the A-6 business could put a lot of bombs on target. The empty weight of an A-6A was 28,000 pounds. Max catapult weight was about 58,600 pounds. After accounting for the weight of bomb racks and drop tanks, this left room for eighteen thousand pounds of fuel and eleven thousand pounds of bombs. So, we normally carried twenty-two MK-82 500-pound GP bombs, eleven under each wing. (A flight of four A-6s carried more bombs than a B-52.)

Each bomb was equipped with an M904 nose fuse and (sometimes) also an M905 tail fuse. The fuses were mechanical devices. The nose fuse consisted of a metal propeller held in place by a piece of heavy-gauge wire that ran through a hole in the prop, back through the sway braces that held the bomb in place, and up to a bale in the aircraft's wing station. The ordnance crew put three clips on the short piece of wire that protruded ahead of the propeller. This prevented the wire from coming free ahead of time.

When the bomb was released, the wire stayed with the plane and, despite the three clips, was pulled through the hole in the fuse's prop. When free, the prop spun. After a hundred or so revolutions, the weapon became armed and dangerous.

We didn't find it out until later, of course, but on July 7, 1967, the North Vietnamese Politburo decided to launch a widespread offensive against South Vietnam. The stakes were raised.

* * *

On July 10, we hit the My Xa POL (Petroleum, Oil, and Lubricants) facility with an alpha strike. It was a large storage and transshipment complex that included riverside piers where fuel barges were offloaded.

One of the A-4 skippers was in charge of the mission. He had eight A-4s and two A-6s in the strike (piloted by me and LT Skip Suereth). The skipper's plan was awful. The A-6s were to lead the strike northward until we were all due west of the target. At that point, the two A-4 elements would peel off, dive at the target on an easterly heading, and then run away to the south. In the meantime, Skip and I were to wheel around the target until we were in its northeast quadrant before we rolled in. That would put our bombs last on the target. (It also gave the gunners a long time to shoot at us instead of the A-4s.)

Neither Skip nor I thought much of this scheme, but we did it. The flak became heavy as we reached the A-4 roll-in point, and it seemed to follow Skip and me while we made our partial circle around the POL facility. Skip's bombsight had failed, so when I rolled in, he stayed on my wing.

We stabilized in our dive as the last A-4 pulled off target and fled south. There was not a single fire on the ground, and there had been no secondary explosions.

Skip pickled when I did.

As we bottomed out at 3500 feet, a huge fireball raced skyward behind us and topped out at five thousand feet.

I keyed the UHF and sang out, "Burn baby, burn."

My new B/N arrived, and he was a winner. LTJG Phil Waters was a tall, lanky guy who stayed calm under pressure. Within a couple of weeks I started to refer to him as "Ol' Steely-eye." What upset him was the fact that he had wanted to be a pilot, but his eyesight wasn't good enough. So, here he was, calling the ball for a pilot with worse vision than his.

Now, with a regular B/N again, I was back on the night schedule.

Our night work was of two types: we either ran what were supposed to be (but rarely were) radar-significant targets, or we hunted trucks.

Except for the flak, the system runs against fixed targets were low-level, high-speed runs like we'd practiced at the Boardman, Oregon, target range. Our night targets at that point were outside the Hanoi and Haiphong SAM belts, but the flak could still get real interesting.

The gunners usually went after us with 37-mm, and the tracers would seem to float past the plane like a stream of fiery softballs. Phil kept his head in the radar hood and refused to look out.

One night I said, "Phil, get your head out of the bag and look at this."

"No."

"Come on, they're hosing us down pretty good. Take a look."

"Uh uh."

So I reached over, grabbed him by the back of his collar and pulled him up. He took one quick glance at the tracers floating past and ducked back into the hood like a ground hog who'd seen his shadow.

Hunting for trucks was more fun than the system runs. We'd cruise around in the dark at about two hundred feet and look for movers. Sometimes we could see headlights, and once in a while Phil would get a radar return off a convoy. In either case, we'd roar in fast, so the sound of our engines wouldn't give them too much advance notice. If we were after headlights, I'd rely on my MK-1 MOD-0 eyeballs to make the drop. If it was a system run, Phil cranked in the computer, and let it do its thing, or he'd run the radar cursor onto the target and give me steering followed by, "Ready, ready, hack."

Most of the time we dropped MK-82s when we hunted trucks, but once in a while we'd be loaded with CBUs (Cluster Bomb Units). The CBU was a clamshell canister that fell like a bomb and then opened up at the appropriate time to release dozens of little bomblets similar to hand grenades. One CBU would cover an area the size of a football field with little lethal flashes. They were hell on trucks. We loved them.

This was exciting work, but it was merely a warm up for what was soon to follow.

Our day work went on. On July 23, we flew an alpha strike against the notorious Than Hua railroad bridge. As expected, we didn't drop it.

Thousands of dumb bombs of various sizes were dropped on that bridge over the years without success. (One of the experimental smart weapons took it out later in the war.)

The Vietnamese recognized that they had a good thing there, and they brought in lots of guns to shoot down us "Yankee Air Pirates." I don't know the final score, but I know that the bridge won.

On the next strike something blew up pretty close to me over the Ben Thui thermal power plant. Shrapnel dusted my plane, but there was no significant damage. They missed again.

Once the little A-4 was loaded down with ordnance, it couldn't handle the high speeds that the F-4 and A-6 crews liked. So, the air wing's alpha strike plans against heavily defended, inland targets changed: we dropped off the A-4s soon after we crossed the beach. The A-4s would hit other targets while the F-4s and A-6s raced onward to the main objective. I suspect that the A-4 pilots viewed this humiliation with mixed emotions.

On July 29, fire broke out on the deck of USS *Forestall* while it operated in the South China Sea. A Zuni rocket mounted on an aircraft being readied for flight fired accidentally. The rocket struck another aircraft and set that plane on fire.

As the firefighters closed in, a bomb cooked off and killed or injured most of the firefighters. The explosion blew a hole in the flight deck, and burning fuel fell onto the hangar deck below. The fire ignited more bombs, warheads, and rocket motors as it spread.

Before it was brought under control, the fire killed 134 crewmen, wounded another 161, and destroyed twenty-one aircraft. (Eight months before, a similar fire on the aircraft carrier *Oriskany* had killed 44 sailors and injured 156.)

August opened with a variety pack of odd targets: rafts on a river brought four secondary explosions, good hits on a cave complex yielded a lot of dust, and we blew up a batch of shrimp boats. (I have no idea why we were sent after shrimp boats.) We then proceeded to bomb some truck storage sites (dirt parking lots).

* * *

On August 11, USAF F-105 Thunderchiefs cut Hanoi's Paul Doumer Bridge. They had to drop a hundred tons of bombs to do it.

About this time we started to plant *seeds*. These were MK-82 SNAKEYE bombs with special fuses and retarding fins. When we dropped a seed, the tail fins popped open to form four speed brakes that decelerated the weapon before impact.

Seeds were always dropped into shallow water or marshland where they burrowed into the soft bottom. Then they lay doggo until something, man or machine, came past and tried to leave. That's when they detonated. A man could approach a seed; he just couldn't leave.

The wily U.S. war planners liked to have us fly through flak to lay seeds down in ferry crossings to stop traffic. The wily Vietnamese then floated empty oil drums down the stream to set off all the seeds. It took them about half an hour to reopen a ferry crossing after we seeded it. Once in a while, our planners would have seeds laid down in a ferry crossing at night and then hit it with regular bombs the next morning. (To set off our own seeds? Revenge against the guys throwing the oil drums into the water? Who knew?)

The middle of August saw us up north again; we were finally allowed to attack the key highway bridges around Haiphong. We'd been frustrated with Haiphong for some time. From a distance, we could see Soviet freighters offloading SAMs and AA ammunition onto the Haiphong piers, and we knew that trucks carried the stuff over the seven bridges to the mainland, but we weren't allowed near the freighters, the piers, or the bridges. We were now directed to hit the bridges. We still couldn't go near the freighters or the piers, but at least we could attack the bridges.

It took three days to drop all the bridges. The North Vietnamese threw everything they had at our strikes for the first two days, and then they ran out of missiles and ammunition. On the third day, with only light opposition, our strikes finally took out the bridges. The Navy lost a batch of airplanes and pilots doing it.

Incredibly, we were then ordered to stay at least ten miles away from Haiphong and its bridges. We could see the missiles and ammo that came off the ships. We watched the bridges as they were repaired, and then we saw the trucks move across them once more. Then, after the North Vietnamese SAM and AA sites were once more re-armed and ready for us, we were sent in to drop the bridges again.

After we lost more planes and crews doing it, the area was once more put on the restricted list. This was sheer madness, a trademark of the entire war.

On the 20th I had a near encounter with a MIG. Phil and I were cruising around the coastline south of Haiphong while we looked for the proverbial target of opportunity. The area was dotted with thunderstorms, and I couldn't see much, so Phil worked the radar.

I was bored. Soon the fingers of my left hand started to tap a rhythm on the throttle heads to accompany the musical beat that I heard in my headset. Rat-tata. Rat-tata. Rat-tata-tat. Then it struck me: that was the sound a MIG's track radar made in our warning system. I let out a whoop and broke into a thunderstorm cell.

That afternoon, trailed by a couple of F-4s eager for a kill, we went back up there and trolled for MIGs. Of course, none came out to play.

August 21, 1967, was a black day for VA-196: we lost three aircraft and six comrades in a five-minute period. CDR Leo Profilet, the skipper, led an alpha strike against the Duc Noi rail yards four miles north of Hanoi.

Everyone knew this would be a tough one. Some of us who were not on the raid went into the CIC (Combat Information Center) to listen to the radio calls.

One of the B/Ns on the raid had been a professional trumpet player before he entered the Navy and, right after the skipper called "Feet dry," the sounds of a trumpet playing the cavalry charge came over the UHF. It sent goose bumps down my spine. Writing about it sends them again.

Being August, the whole area was dotted with huge thunderstorms, and the strike had to wander around some to get to the target. The radio was alive with SAM calls as the strike force began its attack.

CDR Profilet called "Rolling in" and then ate a SAM half way through his dive.

His wingman's B/N watched the lead crew eject and called out, "Two good chutes. Two good chutes."

The three surviving A-6s joined up as they dodged thunderstorms and fled northeast. The weather forced them farther north than they intended—across the Chinese border.

Back on the ship we heard the radio crackle with static, and then someone called, "MIGs . . . MIGs . . . MIGs at six o'clock." That was all.

LT Phil Bloomer, pilot of the one crew that survived, told us he broke hard right into the center of a massive thunderstorm cell when he spotted the fighters.

The Chinese MIGs shot down the other two A-6s. Of the four men downed at the Chinese border, only the trumpet player, LT Bob Flynn, survived the ordeal. The Chinese kept him a prisoner until March 15, 1973.

In a naval aviation squadron, the executive officer is the second-in-command and is slated to become that unit's next commanding officer. Therefore, succession is almost always smooth. It was in this case. The XO, CDR Ed Bauer, replaced our lost CO and became the new skipper. The next senior officer became the acting executive officer.

August 24 was better. I put bombs onto a bridge and got a huge secondary explosion. I must have caught something interesting on the bridge.

August 28, 1968, became a footnote to history when ten thousand anti-war demonstrators took to the streets at the Democratic Party's Convention in Chicago. Twenty-six thousand police and National Guard soldiers subdued them.

On August 31 I had a serious encounter with multiple SAMs targeted at little old me. I was leading a small strike against a bridge south of Hanoi.

It was close enough to the big city that our SAM warning system went to *singer-low* when we were still several miles south of the target. This indicated that SAM radars were searching for us. Then the warning system went to *singer-high*, an indication that at least one SAM radar was tracking us.

Someone called "SAMs" over the radio, and I went into a hard turn. (The basic maneuver to fight a SAM was a hard turn towards the missile to make it overshoot.) I had no idea where the SAM was, but I wasn't about to sit there and let it track me.

For the next few minutes I kept my A-6 at full power and in one hard turn after another as the warning system and radio calls indicated there were multiple SAMs in our vicinity, and some were tracking us. I didn't see the missiles that came up behind me; I was fixated on the target again. Now that I'd spotted it, I wasn't about to lose track of it in the melee.

As we approached the bridge, I found myself in a ridiculous situation: I'd lost so much altitude in the course of all those hard turns that I was down to three thousand feet. I was not only too low to roll-in; I was below minimum pullout altitude.

I leveled the wings and began a slow climb over the bridge. When the target disappeared under the A-6's big nose, I counted to four, pickled off the bombs, and started a right turn towards the sea.

Steely-eye had a good look at our target from his right-hand seat. He whooped when he saw our bombs cover the bridge.

I jinked left and back to the right. "Is it down?"

"It's down," he said. "The center span is down. How did you do that?"

"Pure skill, sonny. Pure skill."

After we trapped back aboard *Constellation*, my wingman came up to me in the debriefing room. "Man," he said, "you did a great job avoiding those SAMs. I counted nine of them, six coming right up your butt, and every time I was about to call, 'Break left' or 'Break right,' you did it before I made the call."

"Must be instinct," I said. "I never saw them."

Skill, instinct, or dumb luck, the Navy awarded me a DFC (Distinguished Flying Cross) for leading that raid and dropping the bridge.

By that time I'd also earned three Air Medals and two Navy Commendation Medals. With one notable exception, that DFC was my last individual combat award.

Soon after that raid, the new CO stood up at an AOM in our ready room and made an announcement: "I'm tired of writing up award recommendations. From now on, if any of you think you deserve a medal, you'll have to write up the award nomination yourself."

"Wait a minute," I objected. "You mean we're supposed to write up *ourselves* for medals?"

"That's exactly what I mean."

"I don't think that's right," I said. "I'm not going to do it."

"Well then, Brian, you're not going to get any more medals."

And that was that.

Nevertheless, I came close a few days later. I led a large strike against a target well north of Hanoi . . . and I couldn't find it. The weather was terrible: there were thunderstorms all over the place. I wasn't about to hang us all out to dry up there, so when I couldn't find the target, I led the strike back towards the beach and better weather. I figured we could split up there and attack whatever we could find.

Suddenly, I saw a mass of railroad tracks through a small break in the clouds. *Hot damn—some kind of railroad marshalling yard—a good target.* I keyed the UHF and called "Follow me."

I rolled into a steep dive, and black puffs of 85-mm gunfire erupted all around. I swept the gunsight pipper up to the middle of the maze of tracks and pickled.

We were in and out of clouds as I recovered from the dive and climbed out. When we topped out above the clouds, I brought the power back and turned towards the beach.

The other strike birds came up and joined on us one at a time. I looked them over; they'd all dropped their ordnance. Up to then, I wasn't sure my flight had actually followed me down the chute.

John (Toy) Mattell led the second section of A-6s on that strike. He came up to me in the debriefing room after we trapped aboard and said, "Brian, I'll follow you anywhere, but don't you *ever* take me there again."

The next day the air wing's intelligence officer came to see me. "When you rolled in on that railroad yard yesterday, did you know it was the big one by Kep?"

"Nope. It was just the only good target around."

"That's too bad. If you'd said that you knew, we were told to write you up for a Navy Cross." (The Navy Cross is second to the

Medal of Honor. Those are the only two medals the Navy can award that will change your career and your life.)

Me (with sun glasses) and my B/N, Phil Waters in 1967.

I usually referred to Phil as "Ol' Steely-Eye."

After a night raid into North Vietnam, 1967

Yeah, that's an illegal beer in my hand.

19

We spent most of September off the line for R&R (Rest and Recreation) in Japan and Hong Kong. We partied like it was our last chance. Then came October.

That month started in a routine manner with day strikes against an assortment of bridges, military facilities, and an unsuspecting boat yard.

One of those missions was noteworthy: the target was a railroad bridge complex about three miles south of the Chinese border. Because of the nearness to China, our strike leader was under the direct supervision of the President of the United States. Yes, President Johnson was on the radio. He asked questions, ordered us to make individual attacks out of a racetrack pattern (as if it were a stateside bombing range), dictated dive angles and headings. He was a huge pain in the ass. The strike leader's tact and diplomacy were exemplary.

On the twelfth, Phil and I got down to some serious night work. We struck the Cat Bi Airfield at Haiphong and got hosed down with 37-mm and 20-mm fire while we made our low-level system run in from seaward.

The next two nights we went after trucks in the Hanoi-Haiphong-Nam Dinh triangle (commonly called the *Iron Triangle*).

All three of these sorties are asterisked in my flight logbook to indicate exciting times.

To hunt trucks with the A-6 system, we relied on a new technology called AMTI (Airborne Moving Target Indicator). On one sweep of the radar antenna the significant items generated a radar return. On the next sweep the polarity was reversed, and all the returns were erased except for those that had moved. Everything you saw on radar was moving. Sweet.

We ran our night hunts at 360 knots and two hundred feet, the minimum altitude to release CBUs. (The clamshell needed time to open and disperse the bomblets.) Once again, I can't think of another aircraft that would let you feel comfortable while you did such stuff.

One thing better than a good AMTI run was to spot headlights. One night we coasted in east of Nam Dinh and turned northwest. To my great delight, a line of about twenty sets of headlights came towards us. I told Steely-eye to forget the system and come up for air. We ran right down the convoy while I sang "Yankee Doodle went to town" and pickled off CBUs in time to the music. We left a string of fires along the road.

On October 26, 1967, Lieutenant Commander (now Arizona Senator) John McCain, flew his A-4 on a strike into Hanoi and ate a SAM. He ejected and landed in Western Lake in central Hanoi. Since he was the son of Admiral McCain, Commander-in-Chief of the Pacific Fleet, this garnered considerable attention in the press.

The next night, October 27, Phil and I ran Hanoi. It was the wildest ride of my life. The planners wanted three strings of seeds placed in the marshy waterway on Hanoi's eastern flank. The skipper selected three crews: his own, one of the hotshot junior officer crews, and us.

The skipper came up to me prior to the brief. "Brian, we'll be going in at ten-minute intervals. Which slot do you want?"

"I'll go first," I said.

The skipper looked puzzled. "I figured you'd want to be last. Why first?"

"Not Tail-End Charlie. No thanks. I figure the first man in might catch them by surprise."

"Okay. You got it," he said.

Boy, was I wrong about catching them by surprise.

The desired location of the three strings of seeds pretty well dictated our approach to the target. Phil and I needed to come in from the south, cross the southeast part of Hanoi, and then drop our weapons between town and the Gia Lam Airport.

Phil and I laid out our route with a lot of consideration for the terrain. We would stay low through the karst mountains south of Hanoi in an attempt to keep out of the SAM envelope for as long as possible. Phil was sure he could keep us out of the karst using the radar, but I marked minimum altitudes on my strip chart just to be sure.

Our plan looked reasonable. We'd coast-in at the "armpit" (a curve in the coastline south of Nam Dinh), fly northwest through the rough terrain until we were south of Hanoi, then break out of the karst and make a high-speed, low-altitude run the last thirty miles to the target. It would take us about four minutes to get from the mountains to the target.

It was a clear, moonless night when we launched. Everything went as planned until we emerged from a pass between two 1500-foot karst mountains and turned towards Hanoi. Terrain was no longer a problem: it was flat and low all the way to the target, and I eased the A-6 down to two hundred feet.

We immediately got singer-low, and the bright red SAM warning light started to blink on and off; they knew we were out there, but they couldn't lock on yet. I pushed the twin throttles full forward and steadied up on our course to the target. The heavy plane responded and accelerated towards five hundred knots.

With twenty miles still to go, the SAM warning light came on steady, and singer-high sounded in our headsets; they had a lock on us.

I went down. When the radar altimeter read a hundred feet, the SAM light started blinking again; we were back to singer-low. The waters of the meandering Red River rushed by, first on one side and then the other. The flak came, sporadic at first and then more intense. Steely-eye had his head in the scope. I had no inclination to invite him to look.

At about ten miles (eighty seconds) to go, all hell broke loose. I couldn't even estimate how many guns were shooting at us. Off to our left, the muzzle flashes formed a solid band that stretched for several miles along the west side of the city. The string of guns to our right was shorter and less dense, but they were closer.

Flak lit up the area around us to the point where I could see the buildings and streets that rushed towards us. A broad street appeared ahead, and it was right on our course. I descended, and we roared down the street at rooftop level. I had a brief thought about the Grand Canyon and the cable that hung between the two rims; the cable I'd always missed somehow. I didn't want to hit a wire right then.

The tracers formed a dense canopy close over our head. They

were high because the buildings on either side shielded us: we were a little too low for the anti-aircraft rounds to find us. But all those rounds had to hit something. The gunners on our left were blowing the hell out of whatever was to our immediate right, and the gunners over there were reciprocating. Whatever damage we were about to do, it was modest compared to what these folks were doing to their own city.

Then, in the space of about five seconds, the flak stopped, we were out of the street and over the river again, and then we were at the target. I climbed to two hundred feet, and the seeds came off. The plane ballooned up when the eleven thousand pounds of weapons were released, and the first SAM came right up our tail.

Phil shouted a warning into the ICS. "SAM, SAM, SAM at six o'clock!"

I could see a rosy glow in the rear view mirrors that I assumed was the approaching missile, and I broke hard right and down. We were almost upside down in a 120-degree-bank turn descending through two hundred feet when the SAM went off a little behind us and outside our turn radius. I snapped the wings level on a southeasterly heading.

"Another SAM at six," Phil said.

We were below a hundred feet now, and I was reluctant to go any lower right there.

"It's tracking . . . it's tracking," Phil said, his voice growing ever louder. Then, "Pull!"

I pulled for all I was worth. We soared skyward, and the SAM detonated below us.

Phil called another one: "SAM closing!"

We were now climbing through four thousand feet. Then Phil screamed, "It's got us! It's got us!"

Rolling inverted, I pulled until I felt the plane shudder near a stall. The missile went off above us as the plane's nose came down into a steep dive. I rolled upright, and again pulled until I felt the plane nibble at a high-speed stall. The fireball from the last SAM had illuminated the Red River almost under us, and I dropped the starboard wing a little so that we'd pull out over the water. We might need the extra few feet.

"SAM at six," Phil called.

There was nothing more I could do. Right then I was more

worried about slamming into the river than about the damn missile. The SAM went off a little above us right as we bottomed out. The flash lit up tiny ripples on the water a few feet below.

We came up out of that maneuver like a scalded cat and clawed our way up the wall headed for higher altitudes. I picked what I figured was the shortest route to the sea and ran for it.

"There's another SAM," Phil said. But his voice was much softer now.

Now headed for twenty thousand feet, I asked, "Where is it?"

"Way back. I don't think it can catch us." He paused a few seconds, then said, "It blew. It was a couple of miles back."

Our course would take us near Haiphong. I didn't care. They couldn't get us now; fate was on our side. Then we were over water. I keyed the UHF button and said, "Milestone One is feet wet."

One of the BARCAP fighter pilots stationed just off the coast came up in response. "Say, Milestone, that was real pretty. Would you mind doing that again?"

The debriefings by our three crews and the BARCAP were consistent: Phil and I had drawn almost all of the enemy's fire. The second crew across the target had faced one SAM and moderate flak. The third crew drew nothing but light flak.

Constellation's commanding officer brought medicinal whiskey from the infirmary down to our ready room so we could celebrate our success. He and our squadron skipper decided that awards were in order. Phil and I were to be nominated for the Navy Cross, and the other two crews were to be nominated for Silver Stars. The skipper even backed away from his edict this one time and ordered the squadron intelligence officers to write up the recommendations; they would have to be routed all the way up the chain of command to the Secretary of the Navy for approval.

Next morning one of the mechanics brought me the throttle quadrant from the plane I'd flown the night before. With a grin he showed me that the steel throttle arms were bent forward eighteen degrees. Nobody could straighten them out.

The intelligence officers from the carrier division staff, the ship, and the air wing got together, studied the debrief reports, and declared me to be, "the most shot-at man in the history of the world."

On November 2, my buddy, LCDR Jim Cameron, the squadron operations officer, came into my stateroom with a glum expression. "The planners have decided that one more string of seeds is needed in that marsh area next to Hanoi. The skipper wants to know if you'll go back in."

"You tell the skipper," I said, "that I'll go back in there as soon as everyone else in the squadron has taken their turn in the barrel."

So, my roommate, LCDR Dick Morrow, was assigned the mission. Dick wrote a letter to his wife, handed me his wedding ring for safekeeping, and then he and his B/N, LT Jim Wright, flew into Hanoi and their deaths.

The BARCAP fighter pilots who witnessed their run saw a fireball roll along the ground about three miles short of the target.

I've come to regret very much my decision not to go that night. I should have gone. I think I had a much better chance of surviving that trip than Dick did. I'd already done it once.

Months later the Secretary of the Navy responded to the award recommendations: all three crews from the first raid would receive Silver Stars. Every admiral up the chain of command had approved the Navy Cross recommendations for Phil and me, but SECNAV had downgraded our awards to Silver Stars. No explanation was given.

We had three more weeks of combat that turned out to be routine compared to what had gone before. Then it was time to sail for home.

Surprise. The Navy had come up with a great idea: a contract Boeing-707 would pick up a planeload of *Constellation*'s combat aviators in Japan and fly them home. These deserving ones would beat the ship home by ten days.

Then *Constellation*'s skipper modified that concept a bit: the flyable A-3s and A-6s would TRANSPAC (fly across the Pacific). That would free up some seats on the 707 for his ship's-company officers.

The Navy had replaced our lost A-6s on a one-for-one basis, so we still had nine planes, but one was not flyable. So, there would be eight A-6s and three A-3s. Those of us selected to fly ourselves home instead of riding in comfort and splendor were pissed. Thus began one of the stranger adventures of my flying career.

On November 19, we flew the TRANSPAC birds from the ship into NAS Atsugi, Japan. The spare parts that remained on *Constellation* were to be transferred over to the replacement carrier, so our planes were in sad shape. And if we downed a plane on deck, we had to ride the ship home with it. (Once on our way, if we downed a plane, the crew had to stay with it until it was repaired and flyable. We could envision an extended stay at NAS Atsugi or on Wake Island.) We gritted our teeth and launched for Japan.

NAS Atsugi's radar was down, and there was a low overcast. No problem: we could use our radar and computer to shoot our own approach. Oh yeah? When we broke out of the overcast, I could see that our computer had brought us down about a mile to the right of the runway. I did a hairy S-turn to the left and landed. It was a bad omen.

Now we had to wait around until the ship left for the states, so it was November 26 when we launched on the four-hour flight to our first refueling stop: Wake Island. There were still three A-3s and eight A-6s in the gaggle. We figured that we'd be low on fuel when we reached Hawaii, so we wanted to get there in daylight. The plan was to launch from Atsugi two hours before dawn, so we could refuel at Wake and then get to Hawaii before sunset. The A-3s were to lead all the way across because they had celestial navigation capabilities we did not.

We had to climb out through a thick overcast, so we made individual IFR departures. When we broke out on top, I couldn't see any of the other plane's lights, so we took up the course to Wake and hoped for the best. I tried to rendezvous on a white light until I realized it was a star. At dawn we found the rest of the flight.

The refueling at Wake took longer than anticipated; it would be dark when we got to Hawaii. The flight to Oahu took 5.2 hours. We were low on fuel, it was night, and there were huge thunderstorms all around NAS Barbers Point when we arrived. The flight leader broke us up into two-plane elements for the instrument penetrations into Barbers Point.

I tried to pass the lead to my wingman. "Skip, you'll have to take us down. My VDI is blank, and the back-up VGI is cocked off at a thirty-degree angle."

"Negative," Skip said. "I don't have any attitude indicator."

"You what?"

"Yeah." he said. "My VDI is blank too, and the VGI spins like a top."

Giving up, I called Barbers Point Approach Control. We shot an instrument penetration right through the middle of a thunderstorm. It took a lot of concentration to keep the plane level; I had to hold thirty degrees of bank indicated on the VGI.

Skip clung to my wing like a leach.

A few minutes later we broke out under the storm at five hundred feet, and the runway lights lay before us. I called for landing. "Barbers Approach, this is Milestone Four-Zero-Four. I have the field in sight, request section landing."

"Section landing?"

"Roger. There are two of us up here." I dirtied up the plane and Skip followed suite.

"Disapproved Milestone. Barbers Point doesn't allow section landings."

"Very well, Barbers. Which of us do you want to eject?"

"Eject?"

"Yeah. Neither of us has the fuel to go around. If you don't allow section landings, one of us will land, and the other will eject over the field. Which one of us do you want to eject?" We were now about ten seconds from touchdown.

"You're cleared for a section landing, Milestone."

"Thank you."

By the time we got unstrapped and wrote up all the gripes on our planes (most of which would not get fixed until we got home) it was after 9:00 p.m., and every food source on the base was closed. Some decided to forego chow, but several of us walked out to the main road and stuck out our thumbs. A derelict truck with a load of pineapples picked us up and took us to some little ramshackle late-night hamburger stand at a road intersection. We ate, hitchhiked back to the base, and fell into our BOQ beds, exhausted.

We slept late and lounged around the BOQ the next day. That night we prepared to fly to NAS Alameda outside San Francisco.

We would refuel there and then fly home to NAS Whidbey Island. The admiral in charge of Whidbey Island wanted us to arrive right after lunch, so he could host a welcome-home event at the airfield. That meant another pre-dawn launch.

There were a bunch of other Navy jets at NAS Barbers Point that needed to get to California, so they were sent with us to take advantage of the A-3's celestial navigation capability. There would be twenty of us. Twenty airplanes.

The weather was lousy, but *meteorology* guaranteed that the top of all clouds was at twenty thousand feet. *Guaranteed.* We'd launch one at a time, fly out on instruments until we were on top, and then rendezvous on the Barbers Point zero-nine-zero radial at forty miles. A night rendezvous of twenty airplanes promised to be fun. Then it got worse.

The cloud layer went up past forty thousand feet, higher than we could get with our full fuel loads. Twenty of us were out there in the soup together.

Then somebody called, "There's a hole on the zero-eight-zero radial, eighty miles."

Our flight leader came up. "How big is it?"

"Oh, it's about four miles across and runs from twenty thousand to twenty-four thousand."

"Okay," our leader said, "everyone rendezvous there."

Twenty jet airplanes flew into that little black, round ball of air and attempted to join up. There were flashing lights everywhere. I had to take wild evasive action twice to prevent mid-air collisions. But we did it. And then a twenty-plane formation headed east and climbed into the soup. The fact that we all lived through this was a miracle.

We broke out of the clouds about two hundred miles east of Oahu at forty-one thousand feet. The first rays of dawn came soon thereafter. The flight to California was the longest of our TRANSPAC trek: 5.3 hours. My legs were cramping by the time we approached the coast at San Francisco and let down for NAS Alameda.

Refueling didn't take long this time, but when we climbed back into our cockpits, a messenger arrived from NAS Alameda Base Operations. The Whidbey Island admiral would be late, so we were ordered to delay our departure for home. We were pissed. But orders are orders, so we sat around under the wings of our airplanes and waited for the signal to go.

After two hours, the message that we could come home arrived. An hour and a half later our A-6s roared over the runway at NAS Whidbey Island in an eight-plane parade formation and broke for landing.

The tower cleared us to land and then added some instructions. "Milestone flight, you are to hold on the taxiway after landing until you're all together. Then you will taxi in at hundred-foot intervals. You will all fold your wings on my signal. The admiral wants you to look pretty as you taxi in."

Fortunately, I was not the flight leader. He came back with a meek, "Wilco, anything else?"

"Yes, sir. The admiral wants you to park, in order, so the planes face the wooden platform in the hangar doorway. Then you are to shut down, climb out, and stand at attention in front of your planes while the admiral gives a speech."

"Which hangar door has the admiral's podium in it?"

"You can't miss it, sir. There are about a hundred women and kids in front of it."

Then, there they were: our wives, our kids, and the squadron's widows with their kids.

We did what we were told. We rolled up to our respective slots, spun to face the hangar, and shut down. We clambered out of our cockpits, tucked our hardhats under our left arms, and stood at attention in front of our weary A-6s.

A yellow police tape held the civilians back. I could see Pat in the front of the crowd, right behind the tape. I spotted little Kelly and tiny Stuart; they clutched Pat's dress.

The admiral strode up to the podium that was mounted on top of the wooden platform and clicked the mike on. "Ladies and gentlemen—"

Lifting the yellow tape, Pat ducked under it and ran towards me, our kids in pursuit. The crowd followed her; they stampeded right through the tape and ran towards our line of airplanes.

The admiral said, "Shit . . . ah, forget it." He threw down his notes.

Pat flew into my arms. I was home.

Mom and Dad in Tucson with
Grandma Swonder on her 82nd birthday.

20

Home. The first home that I remember was the farm in Minnesota. It was 1942, a bad year for most people in the world. In my little world, Mom was diagnosed with tuberculosis and incarcerated in a TB sanitarium in Bemidji, Minnesota; Dad went to Bremerton, Washington, to be a ship fitter foreman in the shipyard there; I went to live with Grandpa and Grandma Swonder (Svonder) on the farm. I was five years old.

I don't recall being sad about this; the farm was an interesting place, and my grandparents took good care of me. Every evening I'd sit on the living room's linoleum floor, by the pot-bellied wood stove, while Grandpa listened to the console radio and moved colored pins around on the big *National Geographic* map of the world he had stapled to one wall. There were blue pins for our troops, red pins for the "Ruskies," white pins for the "Krauts," and yellow pins for the "Japs." Grandpa kept up to date on the fighting positions around the world.

The farm was (still is) situated southwest of Alexandria, Minnesota, and the nearest neighbor was the Rudyall farm about a mile and a half away. There was a pasture, a forest, a lake, and several small fields. I had a dog named Trigger and a Red Ryder BB gun. I could eat strawberries off the vine in summer and build snowmen in winter. I was a happy boy.

When I turned six, I went to school in a little one-room schoolhouse about three miles away. There were about twenty kids in the school, distributed through the twelve grades, one or two per grade. The bigger boys picked on me and made my life at school as miserable as possible. In other words, everything was normal. Walking to school through deep snow has become a "Yah, right," joke. But that's what I did. That's what we all did. If there was a storm, Grandma would walk with me until the school was in sight.

Grandma lived in the kitchen. She got up well before sunrise, added more wood to the big, black stove in the kitchen, and started to cook. She usually finished well after dark. Like Grandpa, she'd been born in Czechoslovakia (she called it Bohemia). The two met and married here in the new country and had twelve children, eight of whom lived to adulthood.

By the time I went to live with them, Grandpa was tall and thin; Grandma was pudgy. They were exactly what you would expect of an elderly, old-world couple. They were wonderful people.

There were two small bedrooms just off the living room. Grandma and Grandpa slept in one; I slept in the other. We kept the doors open, so heat from the wood stove in the living room could sneak in. Later, when some of my aunts were there, I was relegated to a bed in the attic. I used to worry about the "boogieman" and the "pookoes" when I was up there. Fortunately, the pookoes only ate you if you went into the woods alone after dark.

There were "thunder mugs" under the beds if you needed to pee in the night, and there was a chemical toilet under the stairs leading to the attic. But the principal facility was the outhouse about twenty yards downhill. If we were lucky, there was a Sears-Roebuck Catalog to read and use for toilet paper. When that was gone, we used corncobs from which the kernels had been removed for food. Perhaps that explains a few things about my nature.

When the war ended, my six aunts came home to the farm to celebrate. Most of them brought boyfriends along who were soon to become my uncles. The men were fresh from the battlefields of Germany and the ships on the Pacific. They all sat around the kitchen late at night, drank beer, ate terribly smelly cheese, and talked about the war. I snuck as close as I could and listened.

On my tenth birthday, Aunt Jeanette bought me a .22 bolt-action rifle. I immediately became the scourge of the woods; no squirrel was safe. That lasted until I watched one die at my feet: when its little eyes glazed over, I quit shooting squirrels.

Finally, Mom was released from the sanitarium, Dad came home, and we were a regular family again. Dad went back to his pre-war career as a traveling salesman, this time for Westinghouse Electric. We moved around Minnesota a lot, sometimes living in a house trailer (now called a mobile home) and sometimes renting apartments or small houses.

For a while we rented an apartment above a garage on a small farm, and I got my first horse. Dad agreed to help the farmer at harvest time in exchange for boarding the horse. Dad also bought a McClellan cavalry saddle for me. I didn't want a cavalry saddle; I wanted a cowboy saddle like Roy Rogers used. So, Dad took the

McClellan back, and I had to ride bareback. (There's a lesson there somewhere.)

My uncle Eddie had a farm in the northwest corner of North Dakota, and my aunt Fritzi had married one of his neighbors, a cowboy type named Cornwall (called Con). Con had a combination ranch and wheat farm. In most years, hail wiped out his wheat crop, so he ran whiteface cattle to convert the trampled wheat into beef. During a visit to Con and Fritzi, Dad went in with Con to buy a palomino colt, a stallion, and he gave his share to me. Wow. Now I owned part of a palomino stallion, just like Roy Rogers.

I spent the next summer at Con's ranch. Unfortunately, or perhaps for the better, the palomino was still too young to ride, so I wound up on good, old, faithful Jerry, a docile strawberry roan.

That summer was educational. I got to watch ecstasy incarnate when a barn-raised calf got its first look at the great outdoors, I watched a batch of piglets being born, and I witnessed the palomino "servicing" a neighbor's mare. (Apparently stallions can do that at a younger age than they can be ridden.) I also got to drive a team of horses pulling a load of hay, and I learned how to drive a truck.

My uncle Frank had taught me how to swim by throwing me off a rowboat in the middle of a lake. Uncle Frank rowed away, and I learned how to swim.

Now Uncle Con was about to teach me how to drive. He had this old dump truck with some of the floorboards missing from the cab. One day he drove me out into the middle of the hilly horse pasture for my lesson. (Northwestern North Dakota is all rolling hills with few trees.) After Uncle Con showed me how to use the clutch, brake, and gas pedal, he got out. "Drive it home," he said, and he walked away.

After some effort, I got the thing into gear, and it rolled forward. Unfortunately, it headed down into a swale and rolled faster and faster. I gripped the steering wheel, got the truck out of gear and back into neutral, and tried to avoid the large rocks scattered about as the truck accelerated down the slope.

Then, while I stretched for the brake pedal, we hit a rock. The truck lurched, I bounced up in the air and, when I descended, I went right on down through a gaping hole where the floorboards should have been. I managed to hang onto the steering wheel, but I wound up with my feet dragging on the ground behind me.

The truck went through the bottom of the swale and slowed as it rolled up the far side. Then it stopped and started to roll backwards. Now my feet were out in front of me, still dragging on the ground. The truck repeated this back and forth several times until it finally expended all its energy and sat idling at the bottom of the swale. I dragged myself back up into the cab, practiced a few swear words that I had recently heard, and then drove the truck back to the farmhouse.

I ate the five meals a day that the hard-working crew ate, and became extremely fat. When I returned to Minnesota in the fall, Mom took one look at me and put me on a banana diet. That's all the milk and orange juice you can drink, and all the bananas you want. After two days, you don't want any more bananas, and the diet part kicks in.

Mom suffered a relapse and had to go back into the TB sanitarium. The doctors there pronounced her dead on two occasions, but she survived—more through sheer will then anything else. When she was released in May of 1950 she had only half of one lung remaining, and the doctors told Dad to get her to Arizona within thirty days, or she would die for sure.

We hooked up the house trailer and headed for Phoenix; Dad had talked Westinghouse into making him the Sales Manager for Southern Arizona. We arrived in Phoenix on my thirteenth birthday.

A year later Dad relocated us to Tucson. He purchased a nice little house on the east side and bought me a horse and saddle. This time the saddle looked a lot like the one Roy used.

The huge, and quite famous, Conquistador Hotel was also situated on the eastern edge of Tucson (between Broadway and Fifth Street, where the Conquistador Shopping Mall is now). Well behind the hotel was a riding stable that catered to hotel guests and others. It also boarded horses.

We lived about a mile northeast of the stable, so we boarded my horse there. Dad struck a deal with Charley Counts, the stable owner (and a dead ringer for Buddy Ebsen of *Beverly Hillbillies* fame): I would work at the stable for my horse's room and board.

* * *

My horse turned out to be pretty worthless. It was what we called "barn sour." The first day I rode it away from the stables it balked, took control, and galloped full tilt for home. As we approached the complex of wooden corrals at a dead run, it became apparent that the horse was going to cut a corner too tight and slam into the corral railings. A second before we hit, I swung my right leg up onto the horse's rump and saved it from damage when the horse careened into the wooden poles.

After the horse bounced off the corral, I swung my leg back where it belonged, and I was "tall in the saddle" as the stupid beast staggered to a halt.

A fellow teenager in a beat-up cowboy hat witnessed this fiasco. "Wow," he said. "I've never seen anything like that before. Where you from?"

"Minnesota," I said. Thus it was that I became known around the stable as the "Minnesota Cowboy."

We got rid of the horse, but I continued to work at the stable whenever I wasn't at school. You couldn't have kept me away. As "salary" for stable chores, Charley Counts let me use Misty Blue, his prize Quarter Horse, as my own.

I made a tidy little income astride Misty Blue as a trail-ride guide for tourists, but the bonus money was in "breaking" recalcitrant horses. There was a horse dealer nearby who specialized in selling palomino horses to easterners for their little know-nothing kids to ride. (More Roy Rogers fans.) We called him "Sam, the used-palomino man."

Now, you get palominos by inbreeding, with the expected result: most of them are high-strung or plain nuts. The used-palomino man made money by selling them for big bucks and then buying them back for peanuts when Daddy discovered that Junior couldn't handle them. In between, I took my cut.

The first day that Daddy brought Junior out to ride his new palomino, the horse would go about a hundred yards away, then turn and walk back home; Junior couldn't stop the horse.

Despite my initial sorry record in this regard, I had become an expert at handling this behavior. As Daddy pleaded with Junior to take control and ride that expensive horse, I would swagger up: hat on head, chaps on legs, and spurs on boots. Slapping my leg with a four-foot leather quirt, I'd say, "The horse is barn sour, mister. I can cure that for ten bucks."

"Do it," Daddy would say, and Junior would dismount.

Then I'd swing up on the beast and head out. After a hundred yards, the horse would try to swing around and head back home. At this point, I'd slew the horse's head with a rein so that he was pointed away from the stable, and then I'd crack him across the butt with that quirt. (The business end of the quirt was a "beaver tail" filled with buckshot. It made a *crack* when it slapped that scared the hell out of pretty much any horse.)

The palomino would inevitably lurch into a panicked run—away from the stable. When the horse was winded, I'd bring it back and turn it over to Junior. That lad was then able to ride away on a very peaceful palomino, and I'd collect my ten bucks for ten minutes of work from a satisfied Daddy.

Of course the fix wasn't permanent, and eventually Daddy would sell the horse back to Sam for pennies on the dollar. I think I "cured" some horses several times.

Through the course of his Westinghouse sales efforts, Dad got to know Marcellus Rix, foreman of the Eureka Ranch (Bar XL brand). The Eureka ran several thousand head of whiteface Hereford cattle on 120 sections (76,800 acres) about sixty miles northwest of Willcox, Arizona. Mister Rix agreed to take me on for a summer as an unpaid cowhand. I jumped at the chance. It turned out to be an adventure worthy of a fifteen-year-old boy with cowboy dreams in his head.

The rich easterners who owned the ranch seldom visited, so Marcellus and his wife lived in the big main house. A short distance downhill from the main house, nestled in a grove of tall cottonwoods, was the ranch headquarters complex: a large cookhouse with an apartment for the Hispanic woman who did the cooking, a bunkhouse, and the home corrals. The bunkhouse was occupied by two Hispanic cowboys, an Anglo farm hand who tended the alfalfa fields and maintained the heavy equipment, and me.

My first big lesson in the real world happened the evening the farm hand came back from town drunk. He was stumbling around, and I teased him about it. He suddenly snarled something and staggered towards the bunkhouse about twenty yards away.

"Run," whispered Manuel, one of the cowboys. "He is *borracho* and goes for his rifle. Run."

I hesitated a moment . . . and then I ran. As I ducked into a dense cove of trees about a hundred yards from the bunkhouse, a rifle cracked. The bullet buzzed past my ear and struck a nearby tree. I'd been shot at for the first time. I hid in the woods until I was sure that the farm hand was asleep, and then I snuck back to my bed.

I was very proud when Marcellus sent me off alone to the high country of the Galiuro Mountains to check the water in the ranch's stock tanks. It took me all morning to make the rounds up there, and I didn't hurry. It was beautiful country, and I enjoyed watching the antelope. Then, when it was time to head back down to the ranch, I did a stupid thing: I pointed my horse in a wide detour to the west in order to see new territory.

In late afternoon, I found myself on a long ridge leading down to the valley all right, but it was going to make me late getting home. To my right was a steep shale slide that appeared to lead down to a dry streambed that turned off in the direction I wanted to go. I decided to risk the descent and turned the cow pony downhill. We slid down the shale slope, creating small avalanches, until the horse pulled up short. We were on the lip of a sheer drop of about twenty feet to the streambed. I figured there was no way the horse was going to survive that jump; we had to turn around and, somehow, make it back up to the top of the ridge.

Then I realized how far we were from where the ranch hands would expect to find us if they had to search. If the horse and I wound up crippled in a fall, it would be days before we'd be found . . . if ever. With that in mind, I slid off the horse, grabbed his tail, and swung his head around.

He knew exactly what to do: heaving and humping, he struggled up the shale slope. I hung on to his tail and tried not to throw the poor animal off balance. We finally made it and stood, panting and sweaty, back on firm ground. I swear that the horse gave me an exasperated look.

It was sundown, and Marcellus Rix had the cowboys saddling up to go look for me, when I rode into the home corral. Marcellus also gave me an exasperated look.

My closest call, however, came when the three of us cowhands were pushing a small herd of cattle up a dirt road with a fence on the right and a dense patch of mesquite off to the left. Being the junior member of this crew, I was riding "drag" back in the dust behind the cattle.

Suddenly, a yearling steer broke out of the herd and ran off into the brush on the left. I yelled "I'll get him" and put spurs to my horse.

The yearling disappeared into a thick line of fifteen-foot mesquite trees, and I followed at a dead run. I crossed my arms in front of my face to ward off the thorny branches as we exploded through the line of trees . . . into space. We were airborne, about twenty feet above a boulder-strewn dry riverbed.

In slow motion I will remember forever, the horse, with me still in the saddle, did a casual summersault and fell upside down. I realized that I'd be crushed to death if I were still under the horse when we landed, so I grabbed the saddle's pommel and pushed sideways hard as I could. Then *slam*, we hit.

The horse and I landed on our backs, side by side in the soft sand. Miraculously, we'd missed all the boulders. Both of us lay still for a moment and looked at each other with very big eyes. For those few seconds, that horse and I communicated on a higher plane. Then we struggled to our feet, and I rode back to the herd in time to see Manuel return the stray yearling to the herd.

September came, and I returned to Tucson and school. My most notable memory of that senior year was my first kiss. I'd been entirely too busy with horses to mess around with girls. At any rate, one night at a back-yard party, dancing under the spell of moonlight and soft music, I kissed Jeannine Bartoe. She promptly stuck her tongue in my mouth. (What could you expect from a girl with a French name?) That got my attention.

Marcellus Rix had invited me back for the following summer and, after graduation from Tucson High in the spring, I high-tailed it out to the Eureka Ranch. I didn't last long. Along with my high-school diploma, I'd acquired an attitude that got me fired after two weeks, and I slunk back to Tucson in disgrace.

I arrived in time to sign up to be an extra in the movie *Oklahoma* that was about to start filming in southern Arizona. I was instructed to let my hair grow and return to the Santa Rita Hotel in two weeks to catch a bus to the shoot.

On the appointed day, I arrived at the hotel and saw a long list of names posted on the door. There had been a budget cut, and everyone whose name was below the red line was off the project. My name was the first one *under* the red line. Strike two.

Charley Counts, the stable owner, somehow managed to get the contract to provide horses for Gene Autry's Flying-A Productions while they filmed thirty-minute TV westerns out at the Old Tucson movie set. (They starred Richard Arlen, an old-time, character actor.)

Since I was the oldest of the three teens working at the stable, and I was the one with a driver's license, Charley put me in charge of the effort. I had a truck, a horse trailer, a dozen horses, and an assistant: my buddy Gene Davis. (Gene was the kid who dubbed me the Minnesota Cowboy.)

The two of us had a grand time out at Old Tucson. Charley paid us to take care of the horses, and the production company paid us whenever we acted as extras. If we stood around in street scenes we got a few bucks. If we galloped a horse into town shouting "prunes, prunes" (the correct words would be dubbed later) then we got twenty bucks. All told, we made pretty good money for a couple of teenagers on horseback.

Gene and I almost made it into acting. The director wanted a thirty-minute program about a white boy lost in the desert and the Indian boy who rescues him. I was to be the white boy, and Gene was to play the Indian. We were to do several stunts on horseback that Gene and I practiced. Then, the day we were to start filming, the production company folded: the producer had absconded to Mexico with all the funds. (Years later he was arrested as he crossed back into Arizona at Nogales.) Strike three.

On my first day as a freshman at the University of Arizona School of Agriculture, I had to take an IQ test. I must have done well; I was immediately offered a two-year, full-ride scholarship. Dad was especially happy when I gave back the tuition check he'd written that morning.

My major problem in college that year was getting a date. I had just turned seventeen and was considered way too juvenile by the freshman girls; they wanted to date older upperclassmen.

Then, my buddy Gene came to my assistance by getting me a blind date with a high-school girl: Pat Richards. It didn't go well, but she agreed to a second date. When I went to pick her up, her mother ruefully informed me that Pat had decided to go to the football game with the girls instead. I stormed down there, found her, and gave her a piece of my mind. This apparently impressed her; we started to date.

Pat's last name was not Richards: it was Estudillo. But I didn't learn that until she signed the wedding license, much later. Pat's mother, Charlotte Rubi, claimed to be a direct descendent of the Marquis de Rubi, the Spanish nobleman sent to the new world in 1767 to inspect the network of padres and conquistadores. The Marquis, no fool he, wound up with Spanish land grants to much of what became the American Southwest. As a descendent, Charlotte joked (or maybe it wasn't a joke) that she was the rightful owner of New Mexico and Arizona.

A man who owned trading posts in northern Arizona befriended Charlotte's father and installed him as manager of one of them. So, Charlotte grew up on the Navajo reservation. Photographs indicate that she grew up pretty much as the Navajos did.

At sixteen, Charlotte wound up married to a slick talker from the Estudillo clan and soon gave birth to Margaret Patricia. Pat's early years were spent in Winslow, Arizona, before Charlotte left Señor Estudillo behind and moved to Tucson.

When I met Pat, she was sixteen, and her mother was a very attractive thirty-two. In fact, when I went to pick up Pat for our first date, and her mother answered the door, I thought Gene had set me up with an older woman. Talk about panic.

Pat and I weathered a sometimes-rocky relationship before I went into the Navy. She had a temper, and I had an attitude. Once, when I was angry about something and about to break up with her, a horse I was working with kicked her in the head. I figured if we broke up right then, her mother would sue me for damages. Besides, I saw that she handled adversity (not to mention a kick in the head) pretty well.

So, I continued dating her right up until I went into flight school. Then, being without female companionship throughout flight training made me susceptible. I wound up proposing to her while flying back to Texas after a brief Christmas leave in Tucson. I wrote my proposal on the back of a barf bag conveniently stashed in the back of the seat ahead. Amazingly, she accepted.

And now I was home, with Pat, Kelly, and Stuart. The twins, Marquita and Matthew, would be born nine months later.

Me on Misty Blue (1954)

21

Training for the next deployment started January 2, 1968; we were due back on Yankee Station in June. *Constellation* had lost sixteen aircraft and twenty-six crewmen during the 1967 cruise, and we were serious about our preparation for going back on the line. We practiced as before; we bombed the hell out of the Boardman, Oregon, target range.

Running Boardman low altitude at night seemed rather tame after our experience at Hanoi, but it wasn't without its thrills.

One dark night we came out of the mountains and settled into our first bomb run at 360 knots, two hundred feet above the sagebrush.

"That's strange," Phil said. "The radar's screwed up. It's showing a mirror image."

"What do you mean, mirror image?"

"It shows us on the left side of the river instead of the right side."

"Oh, shit." I pulled up hard. I don't know how close we came to that butte on the north side of the river, but it had to be a near miss. There was nothing wrong with the radar. We were on the wrong side of the river. Someone had parked a truck or a van over there that Phil had mistaken for the radar-reflective target.

On March 31, 1968, President Lyndon B. Johnson announced that the United States would stop bombing raids in the heart of North Vietnam (the Iron Triangle). He also stated that he would not seek re-election.

We had overstressed the wings of our original A-6As, so they had to be converted into KA-6D tankers that wouldn't be faced with high-g turns any more. As a result, we received a batch of brand new replacement A-6As.

In April, we added three A-6B aircraft to our stable. The A-6B was a stripped-down A-6 with special equipment to handle the General Dynamics AGM-78 Standard ARM, a new anti-radiation missile built to replace the older AGM-45 Shrike.

The equipment on board the A-6B was supposed to detect and locate SAM radars. We would then fire the Standard ARM missile. In theory, the missile would home in on the radar and kill it. It was a big weapon: fifteen feet long and 1,370 pounds. Its advantages over the Shrike were a longer range (fifty-six miles), a larger warhead (215 pounds), and a better seeker. We hadn't been in the anti-radar business before, so we had some learning to do.

Phil and I were one of three crews selected to train on the Standard ARM. For that, we flew the A-6Bs to the Point Mugu Naval Air Weapons Station on the coast south of Oxnard, California. There wasn't much for the pilot to do; the B/N and the missile did all the work. The pilot's contribution was to get the plane airborne.

This was not quite as simple as it sounds. At this point there were no instruments in the A-6Bs except those associated with the missile system, and there was a low overcast over the base every morning. So, to get in an early flight, we had to figure out a way to do instrument departures without any instruments. (This was worse than the old days in the A-4.)

We solved the problem in typical naval aviation fashion. The bottoms of the morning cloud deck were generally a couple of hundred feet of so above the ground, and the tops were always around four or five thousand feet, so we punted. We'd get airborne and hold the plane right down on the deck until we picked up about four hundred knots. Then we'd level the wings, pull the bird into a steep climb, and hope we broke out on top before we ran out of airspeed. We always did. By the time we came back from our morning run, the clouds had burned off, and we could land.

Most of our work over the ten days we spent at Point Mugu involved practice against their radar test sites. On two occasions, Phil and I flew down to southern Arizona and ran the Army's Fort Huachuca Electronic Test Range. It was boring work and meant time away from home. I doubted that the system would be very effective, and I think our later experience with it in combat bore that out. (The system improved later.)

We had a B/N in the squadron who attracted bad luck on liberty like a magnet draws iron. Of course the fact that he drank way too much didn't help. I'll call him "Moe" to protect the guilty. I had my first glimpse of his curse while at Point Mugu.

One night we were in town celebrating something or other, and Moe had to pee. He went down the hallway to the men's room but found it crowded. Since he couldn't wait, he looked for an alternative and spotted a back door. He raced out the door, found himself in a dark alley, and commenced peeing against the wall. While he stood there, he looked up and found himself staring into an open bedroom window. There was a semi-clad woman on the bed, and a man coming at him with a drawn revolver.

The police came and hauled Moe away to jail. We managed to get him released the next day. (There will be more about Moe later.)

That spring, I had the opportunity to land an A-6 with one wheel up. Phil and I finished a post-maintenance check flight on one of our birds, came back over the airfield, and broke in the usual manner. When the airspeed dropped below 250 knots, I lowered the landing gear. I looked at the landing gear position indicator and got a rude shock: the starboard main mount showed a *barber pole* instead of *down.*

I recycled the landing gear to no effect. The port main mount and the nose gear registered down and locked, but the starboard main showed "barber pole" again.

After waving off, I flew close aboard past the tower, and the crew there confirmed that we had a problem: the starboard landing gear was stuck inside the plane.

The crash trucks rolled while I orbited the field to burn down to minimum fuel. We decided to forego foam on the runway; I'd catch the emergency arresting gear cable near the start of the runway. This cable was not attached to hydraulic engines like aboard ship; it was attached to heavy chains that would be dragged through the grass on either side of the runway.

We landed in the center of the runway, with our tail hook down, and caught the cable. I used back stick to keep the nose up as long as possible, then planted the nose wheel and used left stick and rudder to hold the starboard wing off the runway.

After about a thousand feet of roll, the chains had slowed us way down, and the lower half of the starboard wingtip speed brake settled onto the runway. The plane slewed to the right and stopped.

I shut down the engines and opened the canopy while we still had hydraulic pressure. Then we safed our ejection seats and scrambled out of the airplane.

There was no fire. The only apparent damage to the airplane was that one corner of the lower starboard speed brake had been ground off. Phil and I trotted off into the grass and sat down to watch.

A crane arrived soon after the crash trucks, and so did our squadron maintenance chief. Cables were attached to the plane's built-in lift points, and the crane hoisted the A-6 up to a wings-level position.

At that point, two things happened in quick succession: the fire marshal picked up an axe and swung it at the starboard main mount door, and our maintenance chief attacked the fire marshal.

Calmer heads and hands intervened. It turned out that the fire marshal just wanted to gain access to the release mechanism to make the door open and the gear come down. The actions of our maintenance chief were clear: he just wanted to defend his airplane.

Total damage to the plane turned out to be that wing tip speed brake and the axe hole in the landing gear door. It was, therefore, declared an *incident* instead of an *accident*. (This kept my aviation accident record clean.)

In late May we left the kids with Pat's folks in Los Angeles and drove down to San Diego. I moved my gear onto the ship, and we spent the night in Coronado with good friends from my aide days.

Next day we drove to Tucson for a one-night visit with my parents and then drove back to San Diego. The plan was for us to spend the last night before the ship sailed with our friends again. But we pulled up to a wake in progress.

The widow came out to the car and broke the news to us: her husband had been killed while we were in Tucson. He had fired a practice rocket from an S-2 anti-submarine aircraft, and that rocket ignited the other rockets in the pod. They all exploded and ripped the starboard wing off his plane. The S-2 didn't have ejection seats, so he had to sit there while his aircraft spiraled into the Pacific.

Two evenings before I'd asked him to help Pat if I got killed, and now it was he who was gone. (Fate.) On that very sad note, I kissed Pat goodbye the next morning and went off to war, again.

Constellation sailed for WESTPAC on May 29, 1968. On June

5th, Robert F. Kennedy was shot and killed in Los Angeles. One could sense that momentous currents flowed across the United States and our war in Vietnam.

Air Wing Fourteen's composition had changed: two A-7 squadrons (VA-27 and VA-97) had replaced our two A-4 squadrons. The LTV (Ling-Temco-Vought) A-7 was a sawed-off version of the F-8 Crusader fighter plane. The F-8 had been a long-bodied aircraft with shoulder-mounted wings that rotated up during slow flight to increase angle of attack while the fuselage stayed down so that the pilot could see to land.

To make an A-7, LTV cut two feet out of the F-8's fuselage and fixed the wing so it didn't rotate. A lot of avionics were then crammed into the single-place plane in an attempt to allow the pilot to do what the two-man crew of the A-6 did. Its detractors knew the A-7 as the "SLUF" (Short Little Ugly . . . Fellow).

Air Wing 14 went back into combat on June 28. The war was different now. It appeared that our government was trying to play head games with the North Vietnamese. I don't know if this confused the enemy, but it sure confused us. There were more restrictions than targets.

We started out with small day strikes against trivial targets: bridges, ferry crossings, and piers. I managed to blow up some railroad boxcars on July 2. That cheered me up for a day.

The following week we began night work. Now we could run trivial targets around the clock. Almost all of our work was south of the Iron Triangle, down around Nam Dinh, Thanh Hoa, and Vinh.

Those of us who had received the Standard ARM training also flew some A-6B sorties in a vain attempt to kill SAM radars. During the entire 1968 cruise I flew the A-6B a dozen times and fired one missile with no apparent results.

When the North Vietnamese sensed a Standard ARM in the air, they'd shut down the radars in the area for a minute or two, and the missile would get lost. Of course this was of some value to the strike birds in the air, but not a heck of a lot.

One morning I read in the *Stars and Stripes* that Secretary of Defense Robert McNamara had denied that there was a shortage of bombs. Then I went up and launched with ten MK-82 bombs instead of my normal load of twenty-two. This went on for a couple of weeks, then our bomb load went back up to twenty-two. (It was a "distribution problem," not a "shortage.")

On August 20 we lost an A-6B operationally (not due to combat), but the crew was recovered. LTJG Dan Brandenstein took the flight surgeon up for a hop. They lost power right after launch and pancaked into the water. Both crewmembers were recovered, and Dan went on to eventually become an astronaut.

The next day Phil and I fired an AGM-45 Shrike anti-radar missile with unknown results.

A week later we caught some trucks on the road and left eight fires behind us. Ho hum. Most of our work had now become nighttime searches for trucks headed south, and it was pretty dull. Every now and then, however, we'd stumble into a flak trap and get hosed down pretty good. That always got the adrenaline moving again.

The intelligence types reported that a large convoy of ammunition was thought to be secluded in a village south of Nam Dinh, and four of us were sent to blow it up. Our instructions were to strike any suspicious sites but to avoid the big church in the middle of the village.

We set up a racetrack pattern over the place and took turns flinging two bombs at a time into likely places. After half an hour of this, we had zero results. Then one of the guys called "Screw this" over the radio, and a few seconds later the church and everything within two hundred yards of it disappeared in a huge explosion. Must have been a lucky miss.

One day, four of us were up in the area between Nam Dinh and Thanh Hua when a flak sight opened up on the other section.

Without giving it a lot of thought, I rolled in on the flak sight and wound up inside a funnel of 37-mm tracer rounds. The orange balls zipped by close aboard on all sides. It occurred to me that the head-on cross-section of the plane was so small that the odds of a hit right then were pretty low, but when I pulled out, and they got a shot at the plane's silhouette, the odds would go way up.

So, we were in a game of "chicken." I didn't pickle; I stayed in the dive.

Steely-eye got real nervous. I did too.

Then the tracers stopped, and the gunners ran for their bunkers.

Teeth clenched, I pickled and pulled. We bottomed out below a thousand feet, but we beat the fireball that came out of the complex when our bombs touched off their ammunition supply.

About that time our cost-conscious United States Congress figured that once an aviator reached the rank of lieutenant commander (major), which I was, he wouldn't be sent on any more risky flights, and he should, therefore, have his flight pay reduced. I led an alpha strike into North Vietnam the day my flight pay was reduced by a hundred dollars a month.

One of the A-7 pilots was a friend of mine from earlier times. He sometimes bragged to me how the A-7 could do anything we could do in an A-6, and he could do it without a B/N.

I was sitting in my stateroom writing a letter one night, when the door flew open with a bang. There stood my friend, caked in sweat, red lines from his oxygen mask embedded in his face.

His voice cracking, he said, "You remember how I've told you that we could do anything you could do?"

"Yeah," I said, "I remember."

"Well, we can't." He turned, slammed the door, and stomped away.

I never learned what had caused this confession. He was shot down by AA fire the next day.

On the night of September 18, Phil and I had to divert to the Marine airstrip at Chu Lai; the bombs had failed to come off one of our racks, and the ship didn't want us back aboard that way.

The Marines there welcomed us with open arms. While their ordnance people removed the bombs, the Marine captain in charge of their A-6 line took us into the line shack, got us some hot coffee, and regaled us with stories about how difficult it was for them to get spare parts for their A-6 systems. Once the bombs were removed, the Marines helped us to get our plane started and out of there.

As we crossed the beach and turned toward the ship, Phil tried to pick up *Constellation* on radar. "Strange," he reported, "the radar is down."

We found the ship the old fashioned way, with TACAN, and trapped aboard.

Twenty minutes later, we found out why the radar didn't work: while we enjoyed their hospitality, the Marines had opened up the plane's nose and stolen the radar antennae.

September 30, 1968, marked the day the nine-hundredth U.S. aircraft was shot down over North Vietnam. It was one of our A-6s. The two crewmen, LTJG Larry Van Rensalaar and LT Dominic Spinelli, were declared MIA (Missing in Action).

October saw almost all night AMTI runs. Since we didn't operate in the Iron Triangle any more, the trucks enjoyed a head start on their trip south. We tried to get as many of them as we could when they came out of their safe zone.

We were on a routine night AMTI run when Phil picked up a bunch of trucks in a line at a ferry crossing. We came in low and fast, and hit the head of the line. When we turned to leave, Phil leaned forward, looked past me and declared that we had hit the ferry and one or more of the lead trucks. Out of bombs, we used the tactical frequency to report the location of the ferry crossing and its line of trucks, then we headed home.

As we went "feet wet," Skip Suereth came up on the air. He explained that he had a full load of bombs, but his radar had failed. He suggested we lead him back to the ferry site so he could "buddy bomb" off us.

No problem. We rendezvoused, and Phil set up the computer for another run at the ferry crossing. Normal night formation practice was for the leader to have his formation lights on dim and steady while the wingman had all his lights on bright and flashing. This was not, of course, the rule in combat, but I set my formation lights to dim and steady for Skip's benefit.

I set up the run at about two thousand feet so that any gunners on the ground wouldn't see my dim formation lights. Skip tucked in under my starboard wing.

Approaching the target, I could see there were still a couple of small fires burning. At about three miles, a couple of 37-mm sites opened up on us and hosed us down pretty well.

Phil gave a "Ready . . . ready . . . hack" over the UHF, and Skip pickled.

As we broke away from the target I saw several secondary explosions on the line of trucks—and saw bright lights showing on Skip's plane. He'd neglected to turn off all his lights when we went feet dry. No wonder we got hosed down.

By the time Phil and I reported in to *Constellation*, we were *low state*. One hunt, two attacks, and a rendezvous had eaten up most of our fuel. I called the ship for a tanker and permission to land. The recovery was already in progress, so getting an okay to land was not a problem. Fuel was another matter, however.

We got radar vectors to a KA-3D tanker that came out to meet us. I slid in behind him, and he let out his drogue. I did one more check of our fuel gauge and puckered a little. If we couldn't get more fuel in the next few minutes, Phil and I would have to eject and go for a swim.

Nervous, I blew the first two attempts at the basket, and sweat poured off my palms as I slid in for my third try. I connected.

Afraid to take my eyes off the tanker and the basket, I keyed what I thought was the ICS button and shouted to Phil, "Are we taking on fuel? Are we taking on fuel?"

The unconcerned voice of the KA-3D pilot came back at me. "Yeah, you're taking on fuel. Don't sweat it."

Oh oh. I'd lost my cool on UHF, for all to hear. *Damn.*

The tanker took us right down to the ships one-eighty position and cast me loose.

I dirtied up and came around to land while the tanker turned upwind and positioned himself to give us another shot of fuel if we boltered. We trapped.

On October 13, Phil and I flew bureau number 154154 up to NAS Atsugi, Japan, for repairs to some combat damage. When we crawled out of the plane, a grizzled old American strolled up and introduced himself as the man in charge of repairs to our aircraft.

Smiling, he asked, "When do you want her back?"

"Soon as she's ready."

"You don't understand," he said. "When do you want her back?"

I got the message. "Well," I said, "we could use a couple of nights in Tokyo." "Can you have her ready day after tomorrow?"

"Funny," he said, "that's when I figured she'd be ready for you."

Phil and I caught a cab into Tokyo and had a great time, especially at a cabaret called Mama Zimbashi's Night and Day. Mama, it turned out, was the inspiration for Milton Caniff's "Dragon Lady" in his popular comic strip *Terry and the Pirates*. Mama and I hit it off. She must have been seventy, but she could still dance the mazurka. And, I discovered, so could I.

On the 31st of October, President Johnson declared an end to the bombing of North Vietnam. We would now concentrate on South Vietnam and Laos.

1968 was becoming a big year for the music industry. James Taylor, Joni Mitchell, and The Carpenters all started their musical careers, and Led Zeppelin was formed. *The Graduate* was on the screen, and "Mrs. Robinson" by Simon and Garfunkel was all over radio.

A-6As

Note the refueling probes perched above the white radar domes on the noses. Those are drop tanks slung under the wings.

22

I was the squadron maintenance officer during the 1968 cruise. The A-6 was a complicated airplane, and it was difficult to keep the birds in a full-system status. I was, of course, eager to break all known maintenance records. About this time in the cruise, I began to see the results of my early decisions, and they were generally good.

Spare parts shortages were always a problem. Yankee Station was at the end of a very long supply chain, and combat priorities were often not enough to offset the multiple opportunities for screw-ups. Even when the parts made it on board, it was easy to lose them in the maze of spaces used for storage throughout the ship.

So I figured I needed a wheeler-dealer for my materials officer. I picked LTJG John Casterline. He would deny it, but I remember that our initial conversation went something like this:

"Cas, I'm about to make you my materials officer."

"Oh shit."

"Yeah, Cas, I know what you're thinking. It's a dull job with no glory."

"It's a pain in the ass."

"That too. But it won't be like that for you."

"Oh? Why so?"

"Because you're going to steal. I know that down in your heart of hearts you'd rather swipe something than get it honestly."

"Sir, I am an officer and a gentleman."

"Good. That'll make it easier to fool everyone. How are you at seduction?"

"Seduction?"

"If need be, I want you to seduce the supply officer's wife. Whatever it takes to get us parts. Understand?"

"What does she look like?"

"Beats me. Get lucky. And one other thing, I want you to learn the bowels of this ship. Stuff gets lost down there all the time. I bet within a few days you can find stuff down there that we needed last week and couldn't get."

"All right. I'll give it a shot. This might be fun."

It was. Within twenty-four hours Cas found all sorts of stuff we needed.

Then I turned the entire maintenance operation over to the warrant officers. I gathered together the junior officers who had been appointed to be the various division officers within the maintenance department and briefed them.

"Gents, you have a job and a half to do in the air. You don't have enough time to plan and fly one or two missions a day and still run your shop. Let the warrant officers and the chiefs run it."

"You mean you don't want us to do our jobs?"

"Not exactly. I want you to do the administrative bullshit that you always handle, but leave the hour-by-hour details to the warrants. If they want to change work assignments, let them. If they want to repair 403 before they start on 407, let them. Let them pick the priorities."

"That seems like you want us to turn the warrant officers and the chiefs loose and get out of their way."

"Damn good idea," I said. "Wish I'd thought of it."

"Sounds like we're about to place a hell of a load on our warrants."

"They'll love it," I said.

And they did. We broke all prior records for full-system A-6 availability on a cruise.

When we were in port, the warrant officers still ran the maintenance department; we aviators were busy on the beach. But I tried to meet with the warrants every day, just to keep an eye on them.

One day when the ship was tied up to the carrier pier at Naval Station Subic Bay in the Philippine Islands, I treated the warrants to lunch at the Subic Bay Officers Club. I'd been to some formal event earlier and was still in my full-dress white uniform, the one with the high, tight collar. My after-lunch conversation with the warrant officers went on a long time; late afternoon arrived, and we were still at our table.

A large gaggle of aviators from the ship came in and rearranged a section of the restaurant to form three long tables that jutted out from one wall like three piers. There were about twenty chairs at each table. Over the next half hour, the three tables filled up. Guys from VA-196 occupied the table in the middle, while the two A-7 squadrons filled up the other two. Smelling trouble, I stayed away.

Sure enough, here it came. The A-6 table had the waiters deliver saucers of milk to each of the A-7 drivers. The message was clear: they were "pussy cats."

In retaliation, the A-7 pilots sent "flaming hookers" to everyone at the A-6 table. (To make one, you put an ounce of drambui in a wine glass and light it. To drink it properly, you have to toss down most of the liquid and leave the flame still alive in the glass. If you do it correctly, you won't burn yourself. It's an art.)

The warrant officers wisely decided it was time to return to the ship. I should have gone with them. Instead, I joined my comrades at the center table. A flaming hooker soon appeared in front of me.

Now, this was not my first flaming hooker. I took the wine glass between thumb and fingers, put my thumb to my lower lip as I tipped the glass, and tossed some liquid into my mouth. It was all done in one smooth motion. Then I held the glass out in front of me and, sure enough, the flame still flickered in it. And I hadn't burned myself.

However, a thin trickle of flame from a wayward drip lay on my right sleeve. The man next to me, in a helpful mood, patted it out with his hand. This action spilled the remains of the drink, still aflame, down the front of my white uniform. In one second, I was on fire from my waist to my face.

Everyone at the table threw a liquid at me. I was pelted with water, milk, coffee, and many alcoholic beverages. The net effect, however, was to put out the fire. My hands and face were fine; my white uniform was a singed mess.

The Subic Bay Officer's Club was not a place to get rowdy. That club was meant for the staid "black shoe" officers of the surface Navy. The only reason that aviators of the "brown shoe" Navy went there was to get away from the mayhem at the NAS Cubi Point Officer's Club.

Subic was such a huge naval base that NAS Cubi Point was just a small part of it. And the most important part of NAS Cubi Point, besides the runway, was its storied officer's club. In the 1950s the club had been a bamboo and palm thatch building with tons of atmosphere and not much light, sort of like a Tiki Torch Restaurant.

It sat on a bluff and faced west across Subic Bay. Sunset views could be spectacular.

By 1967 that wonderful old refuge had been demolished to make way for a brick and steel, modernistic, split-level, oblong box. The door was on the east side. When you entered, you were on the upper level. If you walked forward about fifteen feet you came to a railing and could look down on the dining area that occupied a lower level about six feet below. If you looked westward across the sunken dining area, your gaze went over the full-length bar and out the plate-glass windows to the bay and the sunset. Offices, a closet, and the two *heads* (rest rooms) were on the upper level to the left of the entrance; the stairway down to the lower level was to the right.

One of the light attack squadrons had a four-foot statue of a knight that was their totem. When the squadron went to the club, the knight went with them. A junior officer was assigned to stand guard over the statue at all times.

Of course the other squadrons routinely plotted to steal the statue.

On a Saturday night, three of the junior officers from a sister squadron (not us) put their plan into action. Culprit A was to be sequestered in the closet on the upper level next to the railing. When Culprit B knocked on the closet door, Culprit A was to jump out of the closet, vault over the railing to the dining area floor six feet below and grab the man guarding the statue. Culprit C was to step away from his nearby table on the lower level, grab the statue, and toss it up to Culprit B who waited on the upper level. Culprit B would then run out the door and escape in a base taxi that he'd rented.

About nine o'clock that evening. they put the plan into action. Culprit A went into the closet and Culprit B ordered a base taxi. Culprit C hung out at his table near the statue. But the seeds of disaster had been sown: Culprit A took a bottle in with him, and the base taxi took a long time to get there.

When the taxi pulled up, Culprit B banged on the closet door with his fist and ran several feet down the railing into his catcher's position.

Culprit A failed to appear, but the statue's guard turned to look at the source of the noise on the upper level.

A man of action, Culprit C seized the moment, grabbed the

statue, and tossed it skyward.

As planned, Culprit B caught it, ran out the door, and took off in the taxi.

Several members of the aggrieved squadron ran after the taxi. Unfortunately for Culprit B, the taxi driver refused to exceed the parking lot speed limit of ten miles an hour. The cab was overtaken, its rightful owners retrieved the statue, and Culprit B was pummeled a little. Then victors and culprits adjourned to the bar together.

About ten o'clock Sunday morning, someone bumped into the closet door and woke up Culprit A. The sound registered with the groggy pilot: it was the assault signal. He jumped out of the closet and vaulted over the railing. He landed with a large splat on the Sunday buffet table just as the admiral, dressed in his go-to-church Navy dress white uniform, was about to ladle gravy onto his biscuits.

On one visit to Subic Bay, a typhoon roared through the Tonkin Gulf, and the other carriers had to get out of there. Back at the Pentagon, the Air Force launched a budget-battle strike against the Navy with the claim that they could hit North Vietnam in bad weather such as this, while the Navy couldn't. Within hours, I had a weird mission.

My task was to fly an A-6 armed with *one* MK-82 bomb from NAS Cubi Point in the Philippines to the coast of North Vietnam, and then loft the bomb onto enemy territory. We were not to go over land because there were no SAR assets available should we have to eject.

So, that's what Steely-eye and I did.

Back at the Pentagon, the Navy could then retort to the Air Force, "Liar, liar, pants on fire."

Obviously, we pilots and B/Ns spent a lot of time at the Cubi Point Officer's Club whenever the ship was in Subic Bay. Some of us drank too much, especially Moe.

One afternoon, about sunset, Moe, another squadron mate, and I left the club early to return to the ship. For some unremembered reason, we left by the club's back door, the one on the view side overlooking the steep slopes that cascaded down to the flat terrain that skirted the bay. I led the way out the door and, deep in conversation with my mates, turned left down the narrow dirt road that ran between the cliff and the club. After walking about twenty feet, I noticed that Moe was no longer with us.

We looked around, but Moe had disappeared. We surmised that he had gone back into the club. We missed Moe the next day, but missing squadron mates was not an unusual occurrence when in port.

The next afternoon, again about sundown, I was back in the Cubi Point Officer's Club, enjoying the view as the sun sank behind the mountains across the bay. Suddenly, a motion outside, across the dirt road, at the edge of the cliff, caught my eye. A hand reached up over the edge of the cliff and grabbed one of the guardrail posts. A scraggly, dirty, bruised body followed the hand up to the guardrail. It was Moe.

He had *not* gone back into the club the previous evening; he'd fallen over the guardrail and down the slope. He woke up the next morning and spent the entire day clawing his way back up to the club. Naturally, we brought him in and bought him a drink.

I shouldn't leave the impression that I was merely a clean-living observer of bad behavior. I had my share of regrettable moments. One evening several of us, well under the influence, took over the bandstand in the Cubi Club. I played the piano and sang; three colleagues did their own imitations of musicians.

One of my squadron mates sidled up to me and whispered, "There are two captains at the bar who recognize you from your aide days. They're talking about how disgusting your behavior is. You better cool it."

Forget it. I was not in a cooling frame of mind.

A few weeks later I received a short letter from my old boss, Admiral Blackburn. It read, " I know I told you to be colorful, Brian, but not THAT colorful."

Buddy stores for aerial refueling were always in short supply. They broke easily, and most repairs had to be done at NAS Cubi Point or back stateside.

I first realized that our maintenance record would be just fine when I walked about the hangar deck one night after we pulled out of Subic Bay, looked up, and saw a dozen buddy stores stowed in the overhead. We were allotted *three*.

The next day a naval message came to *Constellation* that wanted to know if we could spare a buddy store for another carrier; seems the entire supply at Cubi Point had disappeared. My three warrant officers looked innocent as angels.

Somewhere in this time frame, the Navy relented and allowed experienced pilots to stay on flight status with vision less than 20/20 if corrective lenses got them up to that standard. I broke out my civilian glasses and was grateful to be able to see targets and to call the ball on my very own again.

My glasses didn't make everything perfect, however. One muggy South China Sea night I was about to catapult off the ship. I ran up the power, checked the gauges, flicked on my lights to signal my readiness to go, and jammed my head back against the headrest.

The air conditioner went to high blower and pumped lots of cold air into the cockpit; it felt good. Then my glasses fogged over, and the catapult fired. I couldn't see a damn thing. I yelled and tried to rip my glasses off, but they were stuck to my head under the hard hat.

I rotated off the end of the cat shot and cleaned up the aircraft by feel. We'd climbed through two hundred feet by the time I managed to pull the glasses down on my nose so I could see the instrument panel.

Pat was pregnant when I left, and late September was the appointed time for her to deliver. The end of September came and went, and then the first week of October

In the second week of October I finally received a letter from Pat. She said she hoped the Red Cross telegram had reached me. Then she went on to say how glad she was that *they* were here, and *they* were healthy. (*What telegram? They?*)

Reading fast, I was on page three of the letter before I found out there were only two of them. Pat had given birth to twins on September 21, a girl we named Marquita, and a boy we decided to call Matthew. The doctor who delivered them had been as surprised as Pat to learn there was more than one.

Now and then we were sent into Laos in support of U.S. ground forces that were in trouble. My wingman and I were diverted there late one afternoon to help out a company of Army rangers that was about to be overrun by the North Vietnamese. It took us a good half hour to get there. We were passed from one controller to the next until we arrived on scene, and the airborne FAC turned us over to a grunt with a UHF radio. We circled the area at thirteen thousand feet.

The ranger's camp was on a knoll at the south end of a large clearing surrounded by forest. The Army FAC in the camp gave us directions. "Milestone, we're marking our position with smoke."

"Roger that. I see yellow smoke."

"That's us," the FAC said. "Now look about two hundred clicks north, the center of the clearing."

"I see the clearing. Don't see anybody moving down there."

"Trust me, the gooks are there all right, about a thousand of them. Put a couple of bombs into the middle of the clearing."

"Will do. Break, Milestone Two, two bombs each."

Two clicks from my wingman told me that he understood. I rolled in east to west, with the second A-6 following a short distance behind." As we pulled off target, four white clouds of smoke erupted in the middle of the clearing.

"Wowee," the FAC screamed into the radio. "Right on! Can you do that again?"

"We can do that ten more times."

"Holy shit. Do it."

"Roger that."

For the next ten minutes we dive-bombed the hell out of that clearing. Each run was followed by a whoop from our FAC and a request to move the next bombs here or there.

When our fuel state began to make me nervous, we still had four bombs each. I called our FAC. "We have to go, amigo. We'll give you one last pass with a double shot. Where do you want it?"

"North end of the clearing," he said. "Everything else is pretty well wasted."

We gave him our last salvo and climbed out to the northeast.

"Thank you, Milestones. You saved our bacon. Request you stay on this frequency for a few minutes."

"Wilco."

Three minutes later the now-faint voice of our FAC cut through the static. "Milestones, we have an estimated body count of 340 so far. The rest have hightailed it. Thanks again. Cleared to switch."

"Adios, Ranger. Good luck." That was sobering. We didn't really deal in dead bodies, just bridges and trucks and stuff like that.

Moe's luck in Subic continued to be bad. One evening he stood outside the plate glass windows of the Cubi Point Officer's Club and decided to do a "pressed ham." He dropped his trousers and shorts, bent over, and shoved his bare buttocks against the glass. Unfortunately for Moe, he pressed too hard; the glass shattered and sent him sprawling into the dining area amid a hail of broken glass. Only a few stitches were required.

In March when Johnson had ruled out bombing in the populated areas around Hanoi and Haiphong, the Vietnamese had moved their guns and missiles south to where we were still active. In October when the President ordered an end to the bombing in all of North Vietnam, the guns and missiles seemed to trek on down to South Vietnam and Laos.

On December 18 we lost an A-6 crew over South Vietnam, shot down by AA fire. Pilot LTJG John Babcock and B/N LT Gary Mayer were listed as MIA, but their status was later changed to KIA (Killed in Action).

The very next day we lost another A-6 and crew, this time over Laos. The rescue folks managed to pull out our B/N, LT Bob Colyar, but the pilot, LT Mike Bouchard, was presumed to be KIA. Bob reported that he heard the pilot's revolver followed by many rifle shots, a pause, another revolver shot, and then a final rifle shot.

My last combat sortie was on December 20th. We sailed for Subic Bay on the 21st and spent Christmas in port.

The day before *Constellation* was to sail back to Yankee Station for one last at-sea period, I received the best present I could expect, orders to report to the U.S. Naval Postgraduate School in Monterey, California. I was headed back to school.

The squadron could have held me until the cruise was scheduled to end in January, but the CO let me go.

And Skip, who had been my roommate for this cruise, and my

wingman on so many occasions, also went home early. This time we didn't have to fly ourselves home; we caught a MAC (Military Air Charter) flight out of Clark Air Force Base. Skip and I separated in Hawaii.

When I got off the plane at the San Francisco International Airport, I was dressed in my service dress blue uniform.

An ill-dressed hippie came towards me on the other side of the velvet-rope traffic divider. He tried to spit on me when we passed, but I saw it coming and jinked left. If the SAMs and the AA fire hadn't hit me, why the hell should that turd?

Constellation lost nine planes in combat and seven more to operational accidents during the 1968 cruise. Eleven aircrew were killed or missing, and five of them were ours.

My flight log for 1967 and 1968 recorded 183 combat missions with VA-196. One third of the air crews scheduled to make both the 1967 cruise and the 1968 cruise with me came home on time; the rest were either dead or POWs who had many long years of prison and torture to go. One third.

The *Intruder Association* web site states that VA-196 flew more combat sorties and sustained a higher loss rate than any other carrier-based squadron involved in the Vietnam War. I am proud to have been a part of that squadron.

Together again – 1969

This was taken in the beachfront home we rented in Monterey, California, while I went to graduate school.

23

In January 1969, Pat and I rented a five-bedroom, two-story house a block from the water on Monterey Bay. It was a mile from the Naval Postgraduate School and about two miles around the bay from Monterey's Fisherman's Wharf. The owners begged me to buy the house from them for $ 32,000. I thought it was overpriced and declined. (Yeah, I do know what that house is worth today.)

In my defense, I borrowed all I could against my insurance policies and bought four acres northwest of Tucson. That land eventually became the family homestead.

My major was to be Operations Research and Systems Analysis, an interdisciplinary field started by physicists in London during World War Two who had to figure out how best to employ Britain's new invention: radar. The team was successful and went on to solve many other operational problems to assist the war effort. O.R. as it soon was called, used research techniques, probability, statistics, physics, economics, and several of the other black arts to analyze military operations and recommend improvements.

The school's Monterey campus had once been the famed Del Monte Resort, so it was beautiful. Peacocks roamed around the place to add a touch of color, as if that was needed. Our classes included officers from all branches of service and many countries so, on the rare occasions when we wore our uniforms, we were pretty colorful also. It was a great refuge from the war.

The month I started school, Richard Nixon took over as President. I thought the war had wound down. Nixon must have thought otherwise.

When I went down to the NALF (Navy Auxiliary Landing Field) that was tucked away in a canyon behind Monterey, I expected to find my old friend, the Bug Smasher. But there wasn't a C-45 around. Instead, lined up for our flying enjoyment, were several US-2s, the utility version of the S-2 Tracker, a twin-engine bird that had been around since 1952 in an anti-submarine role and as a COD aircraft.

The US-2 was a high-wing plane with two 1,525-hp prop engines. It had good range—840 nautical miles in six hours at 140 knots—and a top speed of 230 knots (downhill). It carried a pilot, co-pilot, and several passengers.

What I found new and strange was that the throttle quadrant was on the cockpit ceiling. When you landed, you flew with one hand on the yoke and the other on the throttles above your inboard shoulder. I felt as if I were a straphanger on a streetcar.

U.S. Navy Photo

S-2 Tracker

School was enjoyable, but I wasn't the brightest kid in the class, and I had to work at it. I studied six hours a day, seven days a week, and managed a respectable B average.

Pat took some college courses, volunteered at the military dental office, and joined little theatre.

I sometimes took care of the four kids while I studied. The two older ones fought; the two babies crawled around on the floor and giggled every time they bumped into each other.

Our course curriculum included six weeks away from the school on an "experience tour" prior to the last academic quarter. Students were assigned to various military analysis shops around the country to give us a taste of the real thing, and to help us with our principle remaining task: the master's thesis.

I was assigned to CNA (the Center for Naval Analysis) in

Arlington, Virginia. There, I was put to work cataloging the bomb impact data that had been collected since we started blowing up Vietnam back in March 1965. I was stunned at how much data we had; it seemed that every single bomb impact had been plotted and saved. And much of it was on post-strike BDA (Bomb Damage Assessment) photos.

About the third day I was there, I received a phone call from one of my Monterey professors. "Brian," he said, "you might not know this, but I do analysis for the Secretary of Defense, and I'm here at the Pentagon while you guys are on your experience tour."

"So you're like one of those famous 'Whiz Kids' that McNamara had around?"

"Yeah, sort of. Anyway, we have a problem that I figure you're a natural to help us with."

"What's that?"

"The Secretary is about to cancel the Navy A-6 program because he thinks its radar bombing isn't accurate. I told him that I knew an analyst who might be able to prove him wrong."

"You mean me?"

"I mean you. You've flown the A-6 in combat, you've been through almost two years of training at Monterey, and you have all that bomb impact data right there at CNA. Want the job?"

"Well, what happens when I go back to school?"

"Not a problem. The Secretary wants your completed study in four weeks. You'll be done before you have to go back to Monterey. Brian, if you don't do this, the A-6 program is dead. The Secretary is serious."

"Okay. You got me. How do I start?"

"Beats me, Brian. It's your baby now."

It took me two days to figure out what to do, and then I got busy. I took the results of all the A-6 radar bomb runs in North Vietnam and plotted the center of each string of bomb craters. A stick of twenty-two bombs can leave a pattern of impacts that ranges from several hundred feet to over a thousand feet long, depending upon the interval the B/N set and other factors. Since B/Ns tried to put the center of the bomb stick on the target, I used the distance from the center of the target to the center of the stick as the miss distance. In most cases, I could also deduce the run-in heading from the impact string and knowledge of how a crew would attack each target.

Then I divided this "massaged" data into three sets: the first set included those cases where the misses were distributed all around the target. The second was where the misses were either short or long (at six o'clock or twelve o'clock). The third set contained the cast-offs where I couldn't tell what was what.

When you make a level system bomb run against a radar-significant target, the main source of errors is altitude and airspeed. System errors on those two factors will put you long or short, not left or right.

I reasoned that the data set with misses all around the target represented targets that were not radar-significant; the B/N had been forced to target a set of coordinates (from outdated charts).

Conversely, I figured that the set of data with the misses in the six o'clock and twelve o'clock positions were the result of runs against targets that actually were radar significant.

One way to measure bombing accuracy is the CEP (Circular Error Probable). It is the circle around a target's bulls-eye such that half the bombs you drop can be expected to land inside that circle.

I don't remember the exact figures, but if one used both sets of data, the A-6 radar-bombing capability didn't look very good: the CEP was about a thousand feet. But when you considered just the target set that appeared to represent actual radar-significant targets, the CEP came in at under two hundred feet. That was a major difference, and better than the CEPs for visual dive-bomb runs in combat.

The conclusion was clear: the A-6 could hit a target using radar, but only when the target showed up on radar. *Duh!* I wrote it up and gave it to my mentor over at the Pentagon.

A week later, I was about to leave CNA and go home, when the professor called. "The Secretary loved your analysis," he said. "He's decided not to cancel the A-6 program."

"Wow," I said, "that's great."

"And you've written your master's thesis."

"What?"

"Yeah. When we get back to Monterey, I'll have myself designated your thesis advisor. You'll have to put a few ribbons and bows on your paper, but you're almost done. That okay with you?"

"You bet, sir. That's fine with me."

"There's one other thing, Brian. If you want it, there's a job for you on the Secretary's staff when you graduate."

I was silent for several seconds. "Well—"

"But I have to tell you, if you take the job, you'll probably never fly again. They'll keep you there. Are you interested?"

Strangely, I agonize over little decisions while big ones seem to pop out of me. "No, sir," I said. "I've got a flying career, I'll stick with it. But thank you. Thanks for everything." (I have often wondered . . .)

My A-6 study circulated around the Navy's analytic community. Shortly before I graduated, I received an incendiary letter from a Ph.D. working for the Navy in Hawaii. He lambasted my data, my analysis, my conclusions, and my gall. I showed the letter to my mentor. He scanned it and threw it in the trash.

In April 1971, I was promoted to Navy commander and received my degree: Master of Science in Operations Research and Systems Analysis. I also received orders to my next post, an office in the Pentagon called OP-511F. I was stunned; I'd expected another squadron assignment.

I called my detailer at BUPERS. This elicited zero sympathy. He chuckled and said, "It's called a 'Payback Tour,' Commander. The Pentagon has a critical need for people with a degree in systems analysis. The Navy gave you an education, and now the Navy wants you to use it."

Pat and I bought a little house out in Fairfax, Virginia, right outside the "beltway." Pat parlayed her experience as a volunteer in the Monterey dental office to garner a chair-side dental assistant job. I began what is a way of life at one time or another for most American military men: I commuted to the Pentagon.

It turned out that OP-511 collected all the aircraft and flight data for naval aviation and published over a hundred different periodic reports each year. By data I mean number of flights, landings, hours in the air, fuel used, oil used, maintenance done, etc. This was for every single airplane in the Navy and Marine Corps.

OP-511F, the subordinate shop to which I was assigned, wrote computer programs in COBOL (Computer Business Oriented Language) to collect the data, massage it, and print the reports. I was destined to replace the commander who ran the shop when he rotated out.

I'd been there two weeks when a question was raised about my lack of speed when I programmed in COBOL. I was slower than my boss had expected. I defended myself. "Hey, I'm not a computer type, you know."

Captain Pete Swanson, head of OP-511, and the others in the room were astounded. "You're not?"

"No. My degree is in Operations Research and Systems Analysis, not Computer Systems Analysis."

"Oh oh," the captain said. "What computer experience do you have?"

"Well, I took a course at the University of Washington back in 1962. We poked a wire into eight holes in the back of this black box to write simple programs."

"A black box?"

"Yes, sir. Then at Monterey we had one class in FORTRAN. That's it."

"Damn."

Captain Swanson took me upstairs to see the admiral. The captain explained the situation and said the shop would like to keep me, but my background was not what had been requested.

The admiral grunted and looked at me. "Sorry about the screw up, Commander. If you want to leave, I'll find you a more appropriate slot someplace else here in the Pentagon. If you want to stay, we'll be glad to have you."

"I'll stay, sir." (Better the devil you know.)

So, my detailer had sent me to the Pentagon because they were desperate for computer systems analysts—but I was an operations research systems analyst—and the dumbass detailer didn't know the difference.

But I soon discovered that I enjoyed computer programming; it was sort of like doing crossword puzzles. It took a while, but I got pretty good at it.

In those days, we designed each program by use of a flow chart, and then we translated the flow chart into code on paper. Next, we sat down at a keypunch machine and converted our written code into holes on IBM cards, one card per line of code. Then we boxed up the cards (my programs all ran to around three thousand cards apiece) and sent them down to the computer room where they were stacked into hoppers and run through the giant machines with blinking lights.

The computers were IBM-360s when I first got there, but they were swapped out for Univac-1108s after a few months.

Debugging was a laborious process. You would make a fix, type a new card, submit the entire box, and then wait a day to see if it worked. And woe unto you if a card got out of sequence; it took forever to find it.

I developed a program to track the Navy's aircraft inventory, which consisted of several thousand planes. When I started to test it, the program ran fine with a hundred planes, and it ran fine with a thousand planes. Then, on Friday morning, the shop that had asked for the program called. They wanted to run it for real. They needed the information it could provide, and they needed it on Monday.

"No sweat," I said. "The program works great." I plugged in all the aircraft, one card per airplane/unit combination, sent the box down to the computer room, and went home for the weekend. That night the program blew up.

Saturday morning I went back to my office and tried to identify the problem. I returned to the card set where the program had run with a thousand planes and added the rest in a few hundred at a time. Since it was the weekend, I got one-hour turnaround instead of overnight. The program ran every time until I was down to the last batch of cats, and dogs . . . and then it quit on me.

By Sunday evening I'd solved the problem. There was one ancient C-45 that had been parked on a Saudi Arabian airstrip for a decade or more. If I left that one plane out of the inventory, my program ran to perfection. But if I included it, the program self-destructed.

So, I did the rational thing: I took that maverick C-45's card and threw it in the burn bag. That tired, old bird is probably still there—sand in the cockpit and hairy scorpions in the wheel wells—cause it ain't in the inventory any more.

Those of us with wings flew out of Andrews Air Force Base. In my case, I got to fly the US-2 some more. Oh joy. So, I had two more years of dull flying. There's an old aviation saying that goes, "Flying is hours and hours of sheer boredom interspersed with moments of stark terror." I guess I'd had enough stark terror, so now

I got the hours and hours of boredom.

We did lose an engine on one flight, but I was merely the copilot, and the pilot was an old prop hand who handled it well. Besides, it was a sunny afternoon, and Andrews AFB was only ten miles away when it happened.

Back at the shop, I replaced my first boss and became OP-511F, then I replaced Captain Swanson when he left. I became OP-511 and more or less ran the whole show. I even had a pretty secretary.

My new office connected to the main one by a door and a little pass-through window next to my desk. My secretary sat right outside the little window; it had been designed so that she and I could pass papers back and forth. If I needed privacy, I could slide a recessed panel to close it off.

One day I bent over and ripped the stitches out of my trouser crotch. I shared this tidbit with my secretary, and she suggested that I let her sew them up. Great. I closed the door and window, stripped off my trousers, sat down, opened the window, and passed my pants out to the secretary. (I wonder what the troops in the outer office thought when they saw this operation.) Then I closed the window and went on about my work.

The door suddenly flew open and there stood the senior captain for whom I worked. I hadn't seen him face to face in two months, and here he was, right in front of my desk.

"Well," I said as I stood up, "it seems you've caught me with my pants down."

On February 3, 1972, I screened for command of a squadron, but my name was way down the schedule: XO in 1974, CO in 1975.

I called my detailer. "Look," I said. "I'll be almost up for captain by the time I get to be a squadron skipper. I won't be able to compete for air wing commander; there won't be enough time. You have to change this."

"Sorry," he said. "Admiral Zumwalt, the new Chief of Naval Operations, wants to experiment with some lieutenant commanders as squadron COs, so we picked a dozen to go into open command slots early. To do that, we had to delay a bunch of commanders. You're one of the unlucky ones."

If either Vice Admiral Blackburn or Vice Admiral Hyland had

still been in the Navy, I could have called them. Here was the opportunity for the help that each man had promised. Unfortunately, they were both history by then.

The shop that managed fuel for all of naval aviation got wind of my aircraft inventory program. The captain that ran that office asked me if we could modify the program to estimate fuel requirements for the next ten years, by fiscal year, on an aircraft-by-aircraft basis.

"No sweat," I told him.

We already had flight hours and fuel usage data by type airplane for prior years, so I took my roster of airplanes and applied those factors to get projected flight hours per year and the concomitant fuel requirements for each aircraft in the inventory. I also put in the ability to inflate or deflate the base-line flight hours year-by-year. Then I got tricky; I added in the ability for the captain to vary the cost of fuel year-to-year with inflation factors. I was proud of the program, but the captain soon deflated my ego.

"The cost of aviation gasoline and jet fuel hasn't changed in twenty years," he said. "Why in hell did you put in inflation factors?"

He said that in 1973. Hah!

I labored on in my comfortable position. I was somewhat frustrated, but the job was a good one, and my secretary could mend trousers. Life was good. Then it got better.

In July 1973, I was ordered to report to VA-42, the A-6 RAG (training squadron), in Virginia Beach, Virginia. I was to be that squadron's operations officer while I waited for my XO/CO command tour. I was to fly again.

24

Pat and I sold our home in Fairfax and bought a house down the coast in Virginia Beach, Virginia, home of NAS Oceana. That in itself was an experience. The Navy had recently announced a reshuffle of ships and squadrons that brought a major influx of Navy personnel to Norfolk and Virginia Beach.

By the time I got there, houses were scarce. I found a new development I liked, but only the model home remained for sale. I hesitated, but a charter bus pulled up outside, and a herd of Navy wives charged the building.

"I'll take it," I cried.

When I checked in, VA-42 had a new skipper and an old problem: the squadron was six months behind schedule on student throughput. Commander Tom Shanahan, the new commanding officer, had been one of the second-tour pilots I flew with back in VA-56 when I was a nugget. According to him, his first action as CO had been to call BUPERS and ask them to send me down as his ops boss. I was flattered; I almost believed it.

In a squadron, the commanding officer takes care of the big picture and is the designated "good guy." The executive officer takes care of the unpleasant stuff and is the "bad guy" whenever one is required. Then there are four department heads: the administrative officer handles all the paper work, the maintenance officer gets the planes ready to fly, the safety officer tries to keep the operation safe, and the operations officer does everything else.

Since I was the operations officer, the officers who wrote the flight schedule worked for me. Our instructors and students all reported to the director of training, and he worked for me. If we spent too much on fuel, or bombs, or whatever, it was my fault. In VA-42, ops boss was an interesting job.

It was easy to see why the squadron was behind schedule: it had gone through the motions and not much more.

For example, if Ensign Smith was scheduled for a formation flight that needed good weather, and the weather was lousy, the flight was cancelled. If a two-plane formation flight was scheduled, and only one plane was available, both sorties were cancelled.

And the sailors down on the hangar deck were not about to bust their chops to get airplanes ready when so many flights wound up canceled.

Change was required. I got the CO's approval and then broke out some new policies. Every student had to be prepared for his next flight in the training syllabus, of course, but now he also had to be ready for the next flight that could go in bad weather. If students were scheduled for a two-plane formation flight and just one plane was available, both students had better be prepared: one of them was going to take that up bird and do a syllabus flight that needed only one plane.

We also got a little innovative. If the weather was lousy there in Virginia, and we were behind in syllabus flights that needed good weather, instructors and students flew the planes to someplace with good weather, and then operated out of that airfield for the rest of the day, or longer.

A sudden high-level interest in the use of their product spurred the maintenance troops to get planes turned around quicker. If they could get a plane up, it flew.

But I think the acey-deucey board incident is what turned the corner for us. I walked into the squadron ready room one afternoon and found an instructor and his student playing acey-deucey (a version of backgammon popular in the U.S. Navy).

Suddenly, the squawk box rattled and *maintenance control* informed the duty officer at his desk in the corner that the airplane for the next flight was ready.

Keying the talk lever, the duty officer said, "Roger that. Thanks." Then he turned to the two players and said, "Your plane is ready."

"Yeah, yeah," the instructor said. "We're almost done here."

I put the coffee pot back on the warmer and looked at the flight schedule posted on the large whiteboard that covered most of one wall. The two players waiting for this airplane to come up were already late.

"Get out of those chairs and into that cockpit," I yelled. "Our sailors busted their asses to get that plane ready for you, and here you sit playing a damn dice game."

The two leapt from their chairs, stared at me for a second, and then ran for the door.

Furious, I snatched the acey-deucey board off the table and gave it to the duty officer. "Lock this up," I ordered. "I don't want to see the damn thing out here again until this squadron is back on schedule."

"But, sir."

"You heard me, mister. Lock it up."

One of our enlisted men was pushing a broom over in the corner and heard all this. I didn't think too much about it at the time; I had to brief the CO on what I'd done. There was bound to be a minor rebellion among the ranks of the instructors, and I needed him to back me up.

He did.

Two days later, everyone in the squadron assembled in the base theatre for a scheduled *all hands meeting.*

Commander Shanahan gave a few opening remarks from a podium on the stage, then he asked me to come up and brief everyone on our progress.

When I stepped up on the stage, several hundred sailors burst into applause. It stunned me. It had to have been about my tantrum in the ready room. That sailor in the corner must have passed the word to his buddies that somebody "upstairs" had stood up for them and their hard work.

On October 6, 1973, Egypt and Syria attacked Israel in an attempt to regain some of the land they'd lost in previous wars. This "October War" lasted until October 22 on the Syrian front and until October 26 on the Egyptian front. Syria gained nothing; Egypt got a bit of the Sinai back.

Commander Shanahan came up with his own idea: he did some research, polled the troops, and put us on a "four-tens" schedule. Everyone would work ten-hour days for four days and then, if we had met out goals, we'd take a three-day weekend. Every week.

After some doubts, I became a convert; it worked. By January we had eliminated the backlog and, in a suitable ceremony in the ready room, I unlocked our acey-deucey board.

By the summer of 1974, after one year under new management,

the squadron's student completions were well ahead of schedule instead of six months behind.

I was in a unique position in VA-42: I was a student pilot again, but now the instructors worked for me. In a way, the fact that I had to go through the student syllabus myself gave me some added insight into the process.

We flew the latest version of the A-6, the A-6E. It came out in 1971 and had pretty much the same airframe, but it had a new digital computer, multi-mode radar, and a new weapons release system. It also had higher-thrust engines and increased landing weight. (The A-6E TRAM, the A-6E SWIP, and then the A-6F models would follow later, after my time.) We were still a few years shy of the modern "smart bomb" era, although we did get to play around with some of the prototype laser-guided bombs.

Of course I had to go through instrument refresher training again. I went over to VF-43 and flew twenty hours in the back seat of a TA-4 (a humpback A-4 with tandem seats). I then worked my way through VA-42's A-6 syllabus in 108 hours of pilot time.

One of my favorite days as a naval aviator occurred when we took a batch of students, myself included, to El Centro, California, for weapons training.

On the first morning there, four of us took off for the target range. We were Panther Flight. Each of us carried twelve of those blue MK-76 practice bombs. The target was unmanned, so an instructor, one of my guys, circled the target above our pattern to call our hits.

After making my radio call, I rolled in on the target from thirteen thousand feet. I hadn't done this since 1968, but it felt natural, as if I had put on long-lost slippers.

"I don't believe this," the instructor called out as I pulled off target. "Panther One, you got a bull's-eye."

Grinning, I keyed the mike. "Roger that." I came around and rolled in for my second pass.

"Holy shit," came over the radio. "Another bull's-eye, Panther One."

"Roger that." I felt as if I was in a "zone," like a basketball player that hits shot after shot, almost unconscious. My third pass got a milder response.

"Panther One, your hit is ten feet at three o'clock."

But still on a roll, I knew my fourth drop was in before I got the call, it just felt that way.

"Panther One, you got another bull's-eye. I don't believe this shit."

The rest of the flight went pretty much that way. Seven of my twelve hits were bull's-eyes, and the rest were real close.

I was the last pilot to walk into the hangar after the flight. My instructors and our students stood in an arc and stared at me with awe. God, it felt good. That must be what the rock stars feel when they get out of the limo and face the crowd.

The instructor who'd called the hits said, "Commander, that is the greatest exhibition of bombing I have ever seen. How in hell do you do it?"

"Can't tell you," I said. "Wish I could. I just felt it today. But don't get too enthusiastic; tomorrow I won't be able to hit my ass with either hand."

And I couldn't. By noon the next day, my aura of infallibility had crumbled. Damn!

In June 1974 I started intensive FCLP training, almost all of it at night. For some reason I struggled with the landings, and the LSOs worried about me. (Maybe I should have tried it without my glasses on.) At any rate, on July 15 and 16 I got eight day traps and six night traps; I was carrier qualified once again.

On August 7, 1974, I flew my last flight as a student; it was a final instrument check flight in a VF-43 TA-4C. Then I was on my way across the hangar to join VA-35 as executive officer.

Attack Squadron Thirty Five was one of the oldest squadrons in the Navy. It dated back to 1934 when it started out life as VB-3B flying fabric-covered BG-1 biplanes from wood-decked carriers. The squadron even flew in the search of the Pacific Ocean for Amelia Earhart. Later, as VA-35, the squadron saw action on twenty-eight U.S. aircraft carriers and one British carrier.

When I joined VA-35, it was part of Carrier Air Wing Eight (CVW-8). We had twelve A-6E attack aircraft and four KA-6D tankers. We were the Black Panthers, but our call sign was *Raygun*.

You could now read a new magazine called *People*. *The Sting*, *The Exorcist*, and Mel Brook's *Blazing Saddles* were on the big screens. "Kung Fu Fighting" by Carl Douglas was on the radio. On August 9, two days after I joined VA-35, President Nixon resigned and Gerald Ford took command of the nation.

25

VA-35 had just returned from a seven-month cruise in the Mediterranean Sea aboard USS *America* (CVA 66), but there was no slack. *America*, with CVW-8 back aboard, was due to sail September 6 for the North Atlantic on Exercise Northern Merger.

It was a made-up CVW-8, however: three of its squadrons were on loan from other air wings. For this exercise the air wing had two F-4J squadrons (VF-103 and VF-213), two A-7C squadrons (VA-82 and VA-86), RVAH-1 flying the RA-5C photo bird, VAW-126 with E-2B Hawkeye airborne radar planes, a Marine detachment from VMCJ-2 with EA-6A jammers, a detachment of SH-3G helos from HC-2, and us: VA-35.

For me, it was a quick immersion into carrier life. For those who'd been back only one month after a long cruise, it must have been a huge pain in the behind.

America was similar to *Constellation*: she was new and modern but not nuclear powered. One of the first things I noticed about *America* (CVA 66) was that she had no nickname. And I never heard anyone say anything cute about "Route 66."

We had started operations with *America* back on August 27, and I had eight traps before we left for the North Atlantic. Ah, the North Atlantic— "poopy suit" country.

I believe the suit's name came about because, once in it, you may have to go "poopy" before you get out of it. It is a rubber suit that encloses your entire body except for your hands and head. It's not like a form-fitting wet suit; it's bulky and looks similar to the astronaut's outfit, but it's dark gray. There's a slit in the belly about three feet long. It's the entry to a rubber tunnel that extends about a foot out from the suit.

It takes a major effort to get into it. First you put on waffle-weave long johns and warm socks. You may also put on a regular flight suit, but I never did. Then you sit down in a chair with the suit on the deck in front of you, facing away from you.

You put your feet through the slit and into the rubber booties. Then you stand up, pull the suit up behind you, and cram your head and upper torso through the slit so that you are completely inside the suit. You push your head upwards through the neck hole that stretches to allow your head to pass before it snaps back to form a watertight seal around your neck. Then you jam your hands into the suit's arms and out the wrist holes. They also snap back to form watertight seals.

But you aren't done yet. Now you have to take the rubber tunnel you used to enter the slit in the tummy, roll it up, and tuck it into a zippered pouch. This seals your body, except for your head and hands, inside the suit.

An extra-large torso harness goes on outside the poopy suit. After that, you sit down and sweat.

There's an air hose that sticks out of the suit on your left side. If you're lucky, there's an air hose built into your ready-room seat that you can connect to the suit's hose to give you cool air while you wait to man your airplane. If there is no air, you sit and wait while sweat collects in all the low points. Once you waddle to your plane and crawl into the cockpit, you can connect your suit to an air source in the airplane.

All of this is designed to keep you alive for a few more minutes if you have to eject into the icy waters that make up the North Atlantic. But you better be close to the carrier, with a helicopter overhead, or you're still in deep poopy.

NATO Exercise Northern Merger started September 16th and lasted for ten days. It dealt with joint operations and a simulated amphibious assault on Denmark. The British aircraft carrier HMS Ark Royal, with her superb pilots, joined us for the exercise. (The Brits don't use LSOs; their pilots are on their own. They do, however, keep an open bar in the wardroom.)

The Soviets were also around. Their surface vessels were almost always in sight, and their Bear and Badger bombers attempted numerous overflights. Our fighters, and sometimes we attack types, intercepted them and flew on the bomber's wing while they transited the operations area. I flew eight sorties, three of them tanker flights to refuel the fighter planes that harassed the commies.

Then we had a black day: two of our A-6s collided and we lost all four of the crewmen. Commander Ron Hyde, the squadron skipper, had to write the letters home.

On September 29 we broke off from the other NATO forces and steamed for Portsmouth, England for five days of liberty. Most of us headed for London and turned into tourists during our brief visit.

America returned to the Norfolk Naval Base on October 12, but we flew home to NAS Oceana on the 10th, while the ship was still two days at sea.

After the exercise, we settled down to routine operations in preparation for our next cruise. I didn't have a lot to do. XO is one of those "waiting jobs," sort of like vice president, where your main concern is the health of the boss. Like any good XO, I tried to keep problems off the shoulders of my CO.

Race relations played a role in the squadron's daily life. After the race riots aboard aircraft carriers *Kitty Hawk* and *Constellation* in 1972, the Navy had instituted sensitivity training and other anti-discrimination measures. We never had a serious problem in VA-35 while I was there, but the possibility lurked just below the surface.

As an A-6 pilot, I practiced flying low through the mountains at night and in lousy weather. I learned that B/Ns are braver than pilots. I might get nervous about our fuel state, but the B/Ns would treat it as a trivial problem saying, "We got enough for one more pass."

I might doubt the system's ability to take us through mountain passes I couldn't see, but the B/Ns never lost faith. I think it's easier when you don't sign for the plane.

On May 3, 1975, USS *Nimitz* (CVAN 68), was commissioned. It had taken seven years to build her. She was the prototype for the newest series of nuclear-powered aircraft carriers, the *Nimitz* Class. (*Nimitz* was featured in the movie *The Final Countdown*.)

In June, the Navy altered aircraft carrier designations to reflect that the big ships now had multiple missions, not just attack, and *Nimitz* became CVN 68 instead of CVAN 68. She was to be the new home for CVW-8 and VA-35.

Ten days after *Nimitz* was launched, I trapped aboard her for the first time. We worked with the ship right up until July 16, 1975, when the air wing moved aboard, and we left for Guantanamo Bay, Cuba on the start of the ship's shakedown cruise.

After the Caribbean we swung back to the North Atlantic again.

Oh joy.

In the tail-hook Navy, a pilot's ability to trap aboard the carrier is his primary skill. It is what he is. So, the LSOs grade each and every pass he makes at the deck. There are four grades: OK, Fair, No-grade, and Dangerous. Of course the LSOs can make amplifying remarks in their logbook. For example, "Fair (LHAW) 4" translates as "Fair, a little high all the way, caught the fourth wire." The goal is always "OK 3."

The squadron ready rooms display what is called the "Greenie Board." It's a large sheet of white board marked off into a matrix. The pilot's names are listed, one per row, down the left side. The columns are numbered from one to some number expected to exceed the number of landing attempts to be tried that cruise.

Every time a pilot traps aboard, their score is indicated on the Greenie Board by a different color in the matrix square for that pass: green for an OK, yellow for a Fair, white (no color) for a No-grade, and red for Dangerous. Red colored squares are very rare. The pilots almost always take a wave off, or the LSO waves them off, before they qualify for a red box on the matrix. I earned one in the North Atlantic.

My B/N and I had been on a long, tedious flight down the Norwegian coast to the Netherlands and back. We arrived at the ship late in the afternoon of a dreary, overcast sky. The entire world looked desolate and cold up there: gray ocean, gray sky, and gray ship. Approach Control warned us that heavy swells were pushing the ship around a bit.

We came in on an instrument approach even though the ship could be seen from a long way out. The approach felt fine until—in close—the ship's stern jumped to starboard about thirty feet.

My reaction should have been to wave off, but I was tired and wanted to get home right damn now. I slammed the throttles forward and pulled in the speed brakes, rolled right and then back to the left, jerked the throttles back and put the brakes out again. And trapped.

This maneuver was accompanied by an anguished scream from my B/N that I heard without benefit of the ICS.

The air wing LSO, the head guy out there on the platform, took me aside and debriefed me quietly. "That was a dangerous, dangerous pass," he said. "It was also the finest piece of flying I've ever seen. But you get a red box on the Greenie Board for everyone to see. We can't let you get by with this."

It was a bitter pill, a humiliation that stared me in the face every time I entered the ready room. But I agreed; it had to be done.

We had brief liberties in Portsmouth, England, and in Wilhelmshaven, Germany. *Nimitz*'s captain achieved some notoriety with us when he kicked the German harbor pilot off the bridge as we entered Wilhelmshaven harbor and took the ship in himself. He apparently lost faith in the harbor pilot's ability to control the big ship. Whatever the reason, our captain handled it well, and we dropped anchor right where we were supposed to drop it.

The Germans were fascinated with the nuclear ship, and we ran a lot of tours for them. One day I escorted a group of old men around the ship, and we finished back on the flight deck. "Well," I asked their leader, "what do you think of her?"

'Ja," he said, "das boot make gut target."

Then I noticed the miniature submarine pin in his lapel.

Nimitz returned to Norfolk on September 24. As usual, we flew our birds back to NAS Oceana a day earlier. On October 1 the ship went back into the yard for what is called a "post-shakedown availability." That's a pre-planned maintenance event to fix whatever wasn't built right.

Soon thereafter I re-learned a couple of lessons: it's easy to get lost, and "get-home-itis" can be dangerous.

I needed to get home to Tucson for some now-forgotten reason, so I grabbed LCDR Mike Currie for my B/N, commandeered an A-6B, and launched for Tucson. To make it interesting, we decided to quit the air traffic route structure over New Mexico and drop down into a low-level sandblower route that ended in southern Arizona. Since we were in an A-6B tanker, we had none of the fancy navigation equipment of the A-6E, but neither of us was worried.

We had a grand time as we zipped up dry riverbeds and skipped over low, scrub-covered ridges. I was thrilled when I thought I recognized terrain I'd once ridden as a teen-age cowboy, so I forgot the chart and pointed with confidence at various land marks dredged from memory.

For some reason Mike didn't seem convinced.

After about ten minutes of this, I said, "Okay, when I pop up over that ridge ahead you'll see Tucson." I popped-up and . . . no Tucson. *Sumbitch.*

The three Cs when you get lost are climb, conserve, and confess. I climbed up to twenty thousand feet, throttled back to max conserve, and tried to orient myself. Tucson should have been in plain sight about fifty miles to the southwest. No such luck.

Staring at the fuel gauge for a few seconds made me decided it was time to confess. I came up on Guard Channel and called, "Mayday, mayday, mayday. This is Alpha Juliet Five-One-Four over eastern Arizona. I am lost and low state. Request assistance."

A few long seconds later, the radio burped. "Five-One-Four, this is Albuquerque Center. Squawk seven-two-zero-zero."

I dialed in the numbers on our IFF system. "Roger Albuquerque, squawking."

"We have you Five-One-Four. Where you headed?"

"Davis-Monthan Air Force Base in Tucson."

"Roger that. Your steer is two-zero-five degrees, one hundred and fifty miles."

"Thank you, Albuquerque."

Much relieved, I turned to that heading. A few minutes later I could see Tucson emerge from the desert background. We did an idle descent to the Air Force base and landed with a little over a thousand pounds of fuel—enough for another ten minutes.

The next day we headed back to NAS Oceana. The weather looked great all the way across, but I filed IFR to get into the high-altitude structure. Right after we leveled off at Flight Level Four-One-Zero (41,000 feet), we had an electrical problem. The radio still worked okay, but the electronic navigation equipment (TACAN and ADF) was out

Right then I should have aborted the flight and landed back in Tucson. But I wanted to get back to Virginia Beach, and the weather was forecast to be good all the way, so we faked it. We picked visible landmarks off an Air Navigation Chart and followed the same track as we would have on instruments. We didn't tell Air Traffic Control about our little problem. We reported as if we were on the TACAN airways.

Then our fuel plan started to erode. The jet stream that was supposed to help us had gone away, and our emergency fuel supply went with it. We would have enough gas to get to NAS Oceana, of course, but no extra. No problem, I figured. The weather forecast was still good.

There was another golden opportunity to abort the flight and land when we were over Kentucky. The weather there was beautiful and we still had lots of gas. I didn't do that.

Right after we started our let down into Virginia Beach, the weather turned sour—real fast. It was like instant fog had rolled in. All of a sudden, the airfields up and down the coast reported that ceiling and visibility had gone down, close to minimums.

We were screwed. We didn't have enough fuel to go anyplace else. Matter of fact, we had barely enough to make it to the runway. Instead of the long, slow descent at idle power that I'd counted on, we had to shoot a GCA (Ground Controlled Approach).

We were in the soup about three miles out on final approach when Oceana threatened to close the airfield; it was right at minimums.

So I lied. I told Approach Control I had the field in sight and was landing. I descended right on down through minimums, spotted the runway, and landed. I checked our fuel gauge while we taxied in. It read zero.

About half an hour later, the plane captain came up to me in the squadron ready room where I was still busy with the "yellow sheet" (maintenance gripes). He held out a smooth stick about four feet long.

"Commander," he said, "we didn't believe the fuel gauge on that bird you brought back, so we stuck this stick down into the main fuel cell. You see any wet on it?"

"Nope. Looks dry as a bone. You telling me I was flat out of gas?"

"Yes, sir. That's exactly what I'm telling you. You are one lucky—"

"Thank you, sailor."

On December 10, 1975, I saluted the outgoing squadron commanding officer and said, "I relieve you, sir."

With those words, I took command of Attack Squadron Thirty-Five. The largest carrier-based squadron in the world, we had twelve

A-6E bombers and four KA-6D tankers to be flown and maintained by fifty officers and five hundred enlisted men. And we would sail aboard the newest and most capable aircraft carrier the world had ever seen.

U.S. Navy Photo

The new Commanding Officer.
He looks serious, doesn't he.

VA-35 A-6s over Sardinia – 1976.

I’m flying the lead A-6.

26

Bryan Compton, captain of the *Nimitz*, was pissed. It was obvious from the tone of *Nimitz*'s last message to me. It read, "Well, where are my A-6s?"

His A-6s were frozen solid to the parking ramp back at NAS Oceana, that's where they were. And he knew it. I had already responded to two prior messages on the subject, but the captain was not known to give slack.

This was no way to begin my command tour. I put on my green cold-weather flight jacket, tugged my aviation green fore-and-aft cap down tight, and went out in the winter storm to check on progress.

Half a dozen airmen knelt on the inch of ice that surrounded the most likely airplane. Two men worked on each wheel; they chipped away with ice picks and any other sharp instrument they could find. Farther up the aircraft line, a similar group worked on a second bird. Tarps had been thrown over the airframes to protect them from the sleet.

The man in charge of the aircraft line, an experienced warrant officer, moved from one plane to another and willed the ice to crumble away. It didn't look promising; sleet still came slanting down and ice formed almost as fast as the men could chip it away.

I called everyone over to the first plane and said, "Okay guys, focus all you've got on one plane. That's all I ask. I just want one plane to show up overhead *Nimitz* and shut them up.

It took another two hours, but the guys gave me that one airplane. When it reported in over *Nimitz* it was sent back home; the carrier was encased in ice.

CVW-8 moved aboard on January 14th, and *Nimitz* shoved off for the Caribbean on February 1 (good timing) for refresher training. We operated around Guantanamo Bay, Cuba, and Roosevelt Roads, Puerto Rico, for the next two months.

Then the ship returned to the Norfolk area, and the air wing shuttled back and forth between NAS Oceana and *Nimitz* for three months. After a bit of this, we were ready to go do the cruise and get it over.

The Navy still had racial problems, and we all had gone through sensitivity training. The warrant officer who ran the squadron's aircraft line had his own technique. He was a big man, an ex-boxer who had sparred with professional heavyweights, and he ran a good line operation. I'll call him "Big John."

Our line division worked out of an old ramshackle hut about a hundred feet from the modern hangar that housed the rest of us. It must have been left over from an earlier era. The line personnel took care of the aircraft; they fueled them, cleaned them, polished them, and stroked them. They did not perform true maintenance; that was the function of the trained men inside the hangar.

About twenty young, low-rated airmen made up the line crew, and they were a cross section of a failed America. Many were high school dropouts, and some were the result of President Johnson's edict that a percentage of the recruits accepted by the armed forces be mentally challenged. (Hell, it worked for Congress.) They were all, however, responsive to good leadership, and Big John gave it to them.

One afternoon a heavy rain hit us, and the crew sought shelter inside the line shack. Big John ordered everyone to go out and make sure all the canopies were closed and engine intakes covered. Men dashed through the rain towards the airplanes.

But one scrawny black kid stayed in the line shack. Big John pointed at the airplanes and said, "Go."

"No, sir," the kid said. "I ain't goin' out in that shit and get wet."

Standing under the shack's downspout was a large rain barrel that was now full of water. Big John bent over, grabbed the kid by his ankles, stepped outside, and stuffed him head first down into the rain barrel.

After a few good shakes, Big John pulled the kid out and dropped him on the pavement. Then he pointed at the airplanes and said, "You're already wet. You goin' now?"

"Yes, sir." And the kid ran all the way out to the aircraft line.

Thank God, Big John was black.

One day as I worked in my office on the second deck of the hangar, the door flew open and banged against the wall. A young, very disheveled sailor stepped up to my desk and said, "Sir, you're prejudiced against us Hispanics."

Leaning back, I put my pen down. "Son," I said, "my wife's maiden name was Estudillo. Any questions?"

He blinked a couple of times, stood up straight, grinned, gave me a reasonable imitation of a salute, and said, "No, sir."

A similar intrusion happened a few days later. It was an Anglo kid this time. He opened with, "Sir, request you put me in the brig, cause if you don't . . . well, I'll get my shotgun and blow your damn head off."

I obliged him. When he got out of the brig a few days later he was mellow again.

Nimitz sailed for the "Med" on July 7, 1976. Two nuclear-powered cruisers, USS *South Carolina* and USS *California*, were on our flanks. This would be the first time in ten years that American nuclear-powered ships entered the Mediterranean Sea.

There was a long-standing cold war game where Soviet ships and long-range aircraft tracked American aircraft carriers across the Atlantic and monitored their entry into the Mediterranean Sea. But this was *Nimitz*, a new breed of cat.

The first night out of port, the captain turned *Nimitz* south and ran at high speed. By dawn we were far over the horizon from the task force.

For the rest of the transit, we flew under stealth conditions. All flights were done NORDO (no radio), and the ship allowed no emissions: no radar, no TACAN, nothing.

All aircraft stayed right on the deck after launch and flew out a specified course for a hundred miles or more before they climbed. The E-2 radar plane did the same and kept the radar off until they were at altitude and far away from the ship. The E-2 would then control the airborne aircraft and give them coded steers to a false carrier position. The planes would penetrate to that fake position, turn, and fly to the real ship at low altitude.

We tracked the Soviet aircraft while they flew over the rest of the task force and searched in vain for our carrier. When we sailed past the Pillars of Hercules and entered the Mediterranean Sea, the commies still hadn't found *Nimitz*.

* * *

We had a pretty routine cruise, but the liberty was lousy; none of the ports along the Riviera would let us near because we were nuclear. The few places that let us in were not great attractions. Tunis was no place to relax, and Taranto, down at the instep of Italy's boot, was worse. The rest of the time we pulled into Naples for liberty. But we had to anchor far out, so the boat ride in took a long time. (The ride back out to the ship seemed to take longer.) Naples was not that bad, but whoever said, "See Naples and die," knew what he was talking about.

As squadron commanding officer, I had to dispense justice for offenses that did not warrant a court martial. This *non-judicial punishment* was done at a proceeding called Captain's Mast.

I stood behind a podium while the executive officer read the charges, and the investigating officer read his report. Then I asked the witnesses and the accused for their input. It took about fifteen minutes to adjudicate each case.

These events were held about once a month and usually had six or seven cases to judge. Punishment was almost always a restriction from liberty, although I could sentence a man to the brig.

The Marines aboard a naval vessel have two primary duties: guard the captain and run the brig. (They hardly ever climb the rigging and shoot at the officers on enemy ships any more.)

At one of these masts, a young sailor with fire in his eyes was brought before me. He was fed up with the Navy and his supervisors. He'd been charged with insolence, and it was a clear-cut case; hell, he was insolent to me during Captain's Mast. I sentenced him to ten days in the brig on bread and water.

On the tenth day the Marines brought the sailor back before me at a Captain's Mast convened especially for him. He came to attention in front of the podium and looked me right in the eye.

I looked back and said, "Do you want another tour in the brig, sailor?"

"Sir—no, sir. Please don't send me back, sir."

"Well, are you ready to show respect where it is due?"

"Sir—yes, sir."

"Very well. You are hereby released. Return to duty."

"Thank you, sir. Thank you."

He did a snappy about face and marched out of the ready room.

God, those Marines do good work.

One afternoon when I returned to the ship, the flaps on my A-6 wouldn't come down. I recycled the flap switch, popped and reset circuit breakers, and called the ship for advice. All attempts failed. Since my landing speed would be about thirty knots faster than in a flaps-down configuration, I expected to be told to Bingo into some Italian airstrip.

Then Captain Compton came up on the radio. "Don't sweat it," he said, "I'll make up the speed for you."

The water boiled around the ship's stern and she leaped forward like a racehorse out of the gate. Within a few minutes the captain had enough wind across the deck that I could bring my plane in with the flaps up. What an incredible ship.

After dinner one evening *Nimitz* took off at high speed for the east end of the Mediterranean; some crisis was afoot in Lebanon. CAG called all of us squadron skippers together.

"Do *not,*" he said, "say that we're at war. We are merely supposed to position the task force in a proactive contingency mode. There is no war. Repeat. There is no war."

Calling my officers together in the squadron ready room, I told them that the haste was merely to get into position in case we were needed. We were *not* at war, and we must not use that term.

Early the next morning I was summoned to CAG's stateroom. He was not a happy man. "Why in hell," he asked, "did you put out the word that we were at war?"

"I never said that, CAG. I told all my officers that we were *not* at war. I'll check this out."

Then it occurred to me: my maintenance officer had not been at the meeting. He'd been on the hangar deck with a sick airplane.

It took mere minutes to discover the answer. The maintenance officer had called a dawn meeting of the maintenance chiefs. When everyone was assembled, he roared out, "Gentlemen, we are at war."

What he meant, I found out, was that we were at war against that constant enemy of naval aircraft: rust.

Command makes you responsible for the lives of other people, and the decisions can be tough ones. The operations officer and the squadron LSO came to my stateroom one evening. The visit was about a pilot I'll call "Johnny."

"Skipper," the ops boss said, "we're here to recommend a *Pilot's Disposition Board* on Johnny. The LSOs all agree; he's not 'hacking' the night traps. They're afraid that Johnny will cream himself. He should be grounded."

The LSO nodded. They both looked at me to make the problem go away.

I thought back to the nights in the A-4, and how scared I'd been when I wasn't sure that I could "hack it." And how, the more I did it, the better I got. It was a matter of confidence.

"Put him out tomorrow night," I said, "and every night until I tell you to stop."

"He might kill—"

"Just do it, Ops. And I want an LSO report on him after every trap he makes."

"Yes, sir."

Johnny flew every night for the next three nights. I imagine he scared himself—and his B/N—because he scared me a couple of times, and I was merely watching him on the TV monitor that covered all the landing approaches.

On the fourth night, I looked at the schedule, and Johnny wasn't on it. I summoned my ops officer. "Why isn't Johnny on the schedule for tonight."

"Weather's supposed to be dog shit, Skipper. I kept him off the schedule."

"Send him out, Ops. Send him out."

"Okay, Skipper. It's your call."

My ops boss was right: the weather *was* dog shit. I was glued to the TV monitor as Johnny came down through the worst of it . . . like he was on rails.

He earned an "OK 3" from the LSO. That was the end of Johnny's problem. Last I saw of him, he was a damn good aviator.

My experiences in the Vietnam War convinced me that we naval aviators went into shooting wars unprepared to plan, brief, and lead strikes against enemy targets. Since my aircrews had a fair amount of spare time, I kicked off a program to address that shortfall.

I selected a theoretical enemy target, picked a crew more or less at random, and had them plan an alpha strike against that target. When they were ready, they briefed the VA-35 crews in our ready room. The other aviators questioned and complained. Then I critiqued. We did several of these during the cruise.

The Soviet Navy was deploying some extremely well armed cruisers and destroyers. Between their defensive missiles and high-rate-of-fire guns, it looked like attacking them would be a real hairy mission. So, I focused on the development of tactics with which to do that.

One of these involved an A-6 (me) with two A-7 wingmen. We'd use our system to find the target ship at long range and then run in at very low altitude to delay radar detection. At a few miles from the "enemy" ship, the A-7s would turn away from us, one to the left and one to the right, and yo-yo high (soar). After a few seconds, we'd pull up and loft our weapons at the ship as the two A-7s rolled in for dive attacks from two different directions. This would give the Soviet sailors three targets in three quadrants all at the same time. It might have worked; we'll likely never know.

Many years later I was told that the Navy had adopted the practice strike mission briefings and some of the airborne attack tactics I worked out. If nothing else, it made me feel good about my contributions.

At this point, I was senior to everyone on *Nimitz* except the ship's captain, and I'd been informed that I was too senior to be considered for a CAG's job. That meant that my flying days were numbered, and my chances of making admiral were slim. Without being a CAG, command of a ship was highly unlikely. The best I could hope for was to be selected for captain and then get command of a major shore base, something like NAS Oceana.

In December, I received my orders. "When relieved as CO of Attack Squadron Thirty-Five in March 1977, you will proceed to the Pentagon and report to the Chief, Studies, Analysis, and Gaming Agency of the Organization of the Joint Chiefs of Staff."

Another damn payback tour. Well, I would be up before the captain selection board in a few months. If I was selected, and then screened for a major shore command, maybe I could escape from the

Pentagon. Maybe.

On January 21, 1997, I made the last carrier landing of my career, and it was a memorable one. We were south of Italy and the weather was terrible. The Mediterranean was rough, and low clouds scudded past the ship. My B/N, Mike Currie, and I launched in late afternoon; it would be a night recovery.

At the end of our flight, we entered the holding pattern behind the ship and waited for our penetration time.

One minute before we were to start our descent, the *Nimitz* CCA came up on the radio. "Raygun Five-Zero-One, your new Charlie time is plus eight." Our recovery had been delayed eight minutes.

"Raygun Five-Zero-One, Wilco." I set up my racetrack pattern to arrive at the penetration fix eight minutes later.

As that time neared, CCA came up for us again. "Raygun Five-Zero-One, continue to hold, we have a crash on deck."

Oh oh. "Raygun Five-Zero-One, Wilco." I started to think about fuel.

Ten minutes later, CCA called us again. "Raygun Five-Zero-One, you are cleared to commence your penetration."

"Roger that. Raygun Five-Zero-One will commence in two minutes."

I turned toward the fix and checked our fuel. On arrival at the fix, I reduced power to eighty percent, popped the speed brakes, and settled into a four thousand foot-per-minute rate of descent. We were in and out of thick cloud layers, and night had come. It was black outside, really black, except when lightning glowed through the murk. Then Saint Elmo's fire danced across the windscreen, and I could see a thin layer of ice on the Plexiglas.

CCA called again. "Raygun Five-Zero-One, Raygun Five-Zero-One, level off and hold. We have another crash on deck."

Mike and I looked at each other. This was about to get very dicey. "Wilco. Raygun Five-Zero-One is level at ten thousand. What's the Bingo field?"

"There is no Bingo field. They're all closed due to weather."

"Understand. How many ahead of us for Charlie?"

"None, Raygun. You're the last one out there. We'll call you down when the crippled bird is out of the way. Stand by."

"Wilco." This was now beyond dicey. The good news was that

some of the ice had flaked off. The fuel gauge continued to haunt me.

"Raygun Five-Zero-One, you are cleared to descend. Your signal is Charlie. The ceiling is a hundred feet, and visibility is a quarter mile in heavy rain."

"Wilco. Raygun Five-Zero-One commencing."

Mike tapped the fuel gauge. It read eleven hundred pounds. We had enough for one pass at the deck, and just one pass. And there was no airborne tanker available. If we were waived off or boltered we had no choice but to eject. The water temperature meant that, even with our poopy suits on, we'd be unconscious in a few minutes and dead in a few more.

We dirtied up, and CCA talked us down the final approach. I whispered my prayer once again. "Come on, God, one more time." Rain pounded against the canopy.

The CCA controller gave us his last call. "Raygun Five-Zero-One, you're at a quarter mile. Call the ball."

Mike called it. "Intruder ball, five hundred."

And we trapped. "OK 3."

Our flyoff to NAS Oceana was on February 5th, two days before *Nimitz* pulled into Norfolk. We planned to rendezvous all our aircraft and have a dramatic sixteen-plane flyover to impress the brass and the dependents that waited for us at Oceana, but the weather intervened. The clouds started at five hundred feet, and someone from another squadron reported that he was at forty thousand and was still in it.

As we came off the cat, I called my guys and told them to proceed independently and switch to Oceana Control for instrument approaches. There were moans of disappointment.

Then one of my guys called. "We're in a hole big enough for us to join up. It's fifty miles on the ship's three-three-zero radial"

I keyed the UHF. "How big?"

"Its about four miles across and runs from twelve thousand up to about fourteen thousand."

Visions of the twenty-plane rendezvous in that hole east of Hawaii in 1967 flashed before my eyes. If we did rendezvous in that hole, we'd still have to fly a sixteen-plane formation down through the soup on an instrument approach.

We were now thirty minutes from home after a cruise where the squadron lost no airplanes, had no deaths, and had no major injuries. I made my decision. "Negative. Get instrument approaches."

So, there was no grand and glorious finish to the cruise, but we were home, and Pat's kiss made the pain go away.

As usual, Pat had borne the brunt of family problems while I had been at sea. Our youngest son Matthew came down with juvenile diabetes while I was on cruise, and that was now a major factor in our lives.

On the humorous side, teen-age Stuart had tried to move Pat's car a few feet in order to open the garage door, and he managed to strike a visitor's car also parked in the driveway.

Six weeks after I returned, our daughter Kelly turned eighteen, married a recently discharged sailor, and followed him to a ranch in Colorado. (We would have preferred she go to college, but Pat and I no longer had a vote.) Events on the home front suddenly were happening faster than at my job.

On March 31, 1977, amid all the pomp and pageantry of a naval change of command ceremony, Commander George O'Brien, my executive officer, saluted me and said, "I relieve you, sir."

With that, George took over the squadron. Over the next few months, VA-35 was presented with top Atlantic Fleet awards for both operational effectiveness and safety that we had earned during our cruise. George, of course, got to hang the awards on *his* wall. (He ultimately went on to nuclear school and command of the newest nuclear aircraft carrier at that time, USS *Eisenhower.* But he didn't make admiral. Strange.)

After twenty-one years, my operational flying days were over. I was three months shy of my fortieth birthday. I had 3,669 hours of pilot flight time and 652 carrier landings, 163 of them at night. I had flown thirteen different types of aircraft. More importantly, I had an equal number of take offs and landings.

U.S. Navy Photo

The officers of Attack Squadron Thirty Five, 1977

I'm in the middle of the first row, fifth from either end. The man to my left is my Executive Officer, George O'Brien. They were a great crew.

U.S. Navy Photo

USS *Nimitz*, CVN-68

VA-35's A-6s are parked along the starboard deck edge with their wings folded.

The last flight home – 5 February 1977

This was taken as the squadron flew back in to Naval Air Station Oceana, Virginia, from USS *Nimitz* at the end of my last cruise. Two more A-6 flights and I'd be gone, off to the Pentagon.

27

Now I was part of the Studies, Analysis, and Gaming Agency of the Organization of the Joint Chiefs of Staff. It was an interesting place. For starters, our office space was in a huge vault in the Pentagon's basement. SAGA, as it was called, had three functions.

One team prepared and then war-gamed the RISOP (Red Integrated Strategic Operations Plan) against the SIOP (Strategic Integrated Operations Plan). In effect, they pretended to be the Soviet strategic planners and tried to figure out how to destroy the United States with their nuclear arsenal. Their theoretical plan was then gamed against our real one.

Another team set up a totally different kind of war-game. They created tension-building scenarios that culminated in crisis-management exercises. Top-level government figures were then invited to participate in the exercises. The purpose of each drill was to educate and prepare the decision makers for possible real-world crises, and for everyone involved to learn from the pseudo experience.

The third team did other analyses of interest to the JCS. They were called the Special Studies Division, and I wound up as Chief, Special Studies Division of the Studies, Analysis, and Gaming Agency of the Organization of the Joint Chiefs of Staff. Try putting *that* on a business card.

We put the house up for sale, and Pat stayed back in Virginia Beach while the kids finished school. I expected to screen for captain, and I was pretty sure I'd also screen for a major shore command. If that happened, I figured I'd be on my way to the new base in a year, maybe less. So, I rented a house in Fairfax, Virginia, a decent commute from the Pentagon, and waited. Pat and the kids moved up a few months later, and I waited some more.

I made captain, and then I screened for a major shore command shortly thereafter. I eagerly dialed the number for the captain detailer at BUPERS.

"Where am I going, and when?" I asked.

"You're on the JCS staff," he said. "You're not going anywhere until your four-year tour is up."

"What?"

"Yeah. New policy. The JCS was bitching about losing officers shortly after they got there, so now everyone who goes there gets a full four-year tour."

"But—"

"There is good news, Captain. If you behave yourself and don't complain, you'll get one of the really good commands when you finally do leave."

"Oh yeah? Like what?"

"One of the big air stations like Oceana, Alameda, or maybe even Rota, Spain."

That did sound pretty good. "Okay. I'll be quiet. When should I call back?"

"About six months before your tour is up. Good luck, Captain."

Should have bought a house.

There were usually about a dozen of us in Special Studies engaged in two or three simultaneous analytic efforts. A major struggle in the JCS at the time was to create a more rigorous basis for the allocation of defense funds, one that was closely tied to actual military capabilities and requirements. It came to be known as TFCA (Total Force Capability Assessment). Our job was to set up an analytic process that functioned something like a black box: pump in scenarios and capabilities, and out would come budget allocations for airplanes, ships, etc.

Naturally, each service was extremely interested in how such analyses would be performed. So, it came to pass that a large part of my job was to referee the planning sessions while representatives of the four armed services fought over the assumptions, scenarios, and methodologies that would be used in the analysis.

As I had observed earlier in my career, "In the great global battle between the United States Air Force and the United States Navy, anything that happens to the enemy is purely coincidental."

One of our studies looked at a Soviet Pact invasion of NATO territories in a drive to the Atlantic, and what NATO forces could do about it. We used computer-based war-gaming, static force comparison methodologies, and analyses of the humdrum supply and sustainability issues. Under the assumptions given, *no nukes*, the results did not look good for our side.

When I briefed the JCS Operations Deputies in the "tank" (the JCS conference room), there was a quiet pause at the end of the briefing. I waited for questions.

The Navy four-star admiral finally asked, "In your study, Captain, what kind of effect did the sealift of supplies from the United States have on the outcome in this non-nuclear scenario?"

"Admiral," I said, "in this scenario, sealift ships get to the European coast line just in time to do another Dunkirk." (Meaning that the ships would wind up rescuing our soldiers from the beaches instead of offloading supplies).

My statement was met with stony silence.

As we filed out of the room, my boss whispered to me, "I hope you know that you just blew your shot at admiral." What? Again?

Out of the blue I was asked to do a one-person study of the impacts of modern-technology weapons on the defense of North Norway. It was one of those "bonding" exercises between our government and the government of Norway. I don't think anyone on either side expected it to turn up anything of value. I fooled them.

To start off, I was flown to Norway and then escorted by the Norwegian Army up to the northern regions, far north of the Arctic Circle. (It was a fascinating tour, especially since I am half Norwegian on my father's side. Dad's mother, Ragna, was born in a little town about half way up the Norwegian coast.)

The military problem was pretty straightforward: in case of war, the Soviets were expected to race across the Finnish flat lands on paved highways they had helped finance, and then charge down one or more of the narrow valleys that run north and south along Norway's spine. The Norwegians would try to stop them in the steep-sided valleys. My job was to explore ways that new technology could help.

I found several. A prime example concerned the defense against air attack. I looked at the situation as a Russian pilot would: how do I attack the ground forces without getting shot down?

Coming down the valley did not look like a good way to survive. I reasoned that the pilot would do a high-speed attack across the narrow valleys at a ninety-degree angle, flying low, just high enough to clear the ridgelines. He would be in sight of the Norwegian ground forces for about twenty seconds or so; long enough to drop area weapons like the CBUs we'd used in Vietnam, but not long enough for anti-aircraft weapons or missiles in the valley to have a good crack at him.

After I concluded the study, the Norwegians were delighted with it. And, therefore, so were the powers in the U.S. government. I was flown to Oslo to brief the Norwegian military brass.

When I got to the part about Soviet pilots running low-level attacks across the valleys, a grizzled general balked. "You tell us," he said, "that the solution is to put men armed with shoulder fired missiles up on the ridgeline. Do you have any idea how difficult it will be to get them up there? That is one hell of a climb."

"Yes, sir. You lift them up there with helicopters."

"Well, the tops of those ridges are heavily forested. How do you propose to get the men out of the helicopters and down on the ground?"

"You do like we did in Vietnam when we needed to clear a landing place; you drop a bomb there to knock down the trees. I recommend you prepare such sites ahead of time."

"Hmmmm," said the general. "That could work."

In 1979 my team was tasked to study what would happen if Iraq and Iran fought a war. We studied the situation and predicted that they would stalemate in ten days. Our report was greeted with a large ho-hum.

I understand that changed shortly after I left SAGA when the two countries actually did go to war. I heard that our study became a top seller in the Pentagon and went to three printings.

By the way, the two countries stalemated in eleven days. Now that was a case of good military analysis.

The newly created FEMA (Federal Emergency Management Agency) was funding a joint study with the JCS to consider which country could recover faster from a full-scale nuclear exchange, Russia or the United States. The study had become bogged down with inter-service bickering. Because of my experience refereeing those kinds of spats in the TFCA arena, I was assigned to bring order to this study effort. To my surprise, this proved to be fairly easy.

One day the FEMA director sent over word that he was interested in hiring me whenever I retired. In hindsight, I should have given it serious consideration. I didn't.

Six months before my tour on the JCS staff was due to be completed, I called the captain detailer at BUPERS. The same guy was there; apparently they didn't rotate out of BUPERS very quickly either.

"Well," I said after the small talk was over, "I've done my time. Which of those big air bases am I going to get?"

"Sorry," he said. "We have a new policy now. The good bases go to guys coming off sea duty. You've been on shore duty for the past three plus years. You have a choice. You can have one of the small airfields now, or go back to sea and get one of the good ones later."

"Which small air fields can I have now?"

"You can have Cubi Point in the Philippines or Fallon, Nevada."

Neither of those places was suitable for a family with teenagers, especially *our* teenagers. And, besides, I was pissed.

I thought of the detailer who said I could take my family to Bahrain and then sent me solo to Korea; the detailer who said I was needed in an operations research slot in the Pentagon but sent me to a software shop; and now this detailer, who had just backed out of our agreement.

I thought of my disgust at the squabbling over budget dollars that seemed to permeate every waking moment at the JCS.

And I thought of my growing desire to taste the big outdoors: the civilian world. Hell, at forty-three I was still young enough.

"Don't worry about it," I said. "My retirement papers will be on your desk before sundown."

And they were. The ride was over.

But what a grand ride it was. There was no fame and not a hell of a lot of glory. There was tedium, and there was terror. There were shiny uniforms and many sweaty flight suits. But—best of all—there was the camaraderie of those who wore the wings of gold; the ones who came to fly … *and to fly low.*

Old Timer

I hope you enjoyed this story. If so, and if you bought the book from Amazon.com, please go back to the book's Amazon.com page and post a favorable review. It sure helps sales. *B.K. Bryans*

Other books by B.K. Bryans

Those '67 Blues
The Dog Robbers
Flight to Redemption
Brannigan Rides Again
Trouble in Tucson
Arizona Grit

Most of them are available on Amazon.com at:
https://www.amazon.com/author/b.k.bryans

You are also invited to visit the author's personal website at:
http://www.brianbryans.com

The following books were published by:
Patriot Media, Inc.
http://patriotmediainc.com

Those '67 Blues
by
B.K. Bryans

Those '67 Blues is an almost-true story of naval aviators fighting a vicious air war over North Vietnam in the fiery autumn of 1967 ... and of the families waiting for them back home "in the world." The novel covers a two-week period in a day-by-day account of flight operations and the heroic acts of men flying the hostile skies of North Vietnam. Many of the exploits in the book are based on the author's Vietnam War experiences as an A-6 Intruder pilot.

Those '67 Blues is a 6" x 9" glossy paperback novel published by Patriot Media, Inc. The cover art, *Moonlight Intruders*, is courtesy of Craig Kodera, a famed aviation artist whose work is on display in the Smithsonian National Air and Space Museum.

REVIEWS: *The Association of Naval Aviation* reviewed *Those '67 Blues* in the fall 2011 edition of their magazine, *Wings of Gold*, as follows: *Those '67 Blues* by B.K. Bryans. As one reviewer wrote, "This is my kind of book. It has the accurate detail that satisfies the guy who's 'been there and done that' and intrigues the guy who wishes he could have. *Blues* takes you through virtually every aspect of the carrier war in 1967 and does it so precisely you feel as if you are right there getting shot at." This is a story about the aviators who went in harms way big time. "At night," writes Bryans, "Navy all-weather A-6 Intruders went in low and alone." A brief excerpt: "The SAM that hit their A-6 right after weapons release knocked out everything electrical, set the port engine on fire, and caused the plane to shake like a dice cup." Bryans knows his subject. He flew A-6s during the Vietnam war earning a Silver Star and DFC, and commanded VA-35 aboard USS *Nimitz*.

There are numerous four- and five-star reviews for *Those '67 Blues* posted on its Amazon.com web page.

The Dog Robbers

by

B.K. Bryans

After the 1945 Battle of Okinawa, US forces built Marine Corps Air Station (MCAS) Futenma atop the rubble of several small towns. Surviving villagers returning home found that an air base now lay across their land. They could only settle nearby, where they remain to this day, waiting. This real-world conflict serves as background for *The Dog Robbers*.

Lieutenant Deuce Riley, a US Navy pilot, is content to be a flight instructor at Naval Air Station (NAS) Pensacola, FL. Then he's suddenly ordered to Japan to be an aide to Rear Admiral Brewster Brody, who has become enmeshed in the diplomatic argument over MCAS Futenma. Neither officer is real happy about their assignment, but the result is humor, action, and romance.

Flight to Redemption

by

B.K. Bryans

Flight to Redemption is a flying story about an ageing pilot and several classic old airplanes from yesteryear. It is also an adventure story where action is not the sole property of those who are young and strong. Here, two well-seasoned citizens wisecrack their way from crash to crisis and back in a story for the "baby boomer" generation. As this pre-publication reviewer said:

REVIEW: "In *Flight to Redemption*, the author gives us a novel that realistically depicts the drug and alien smuggling problems that challenge our southwestern border country, but he also gives us lingering romance, bantering friendship, and an exciting conclusion. An ageing pilot, reluctantly accompanied by a small-town doc, fly a stolen airplane into Mexico on an ill-conceived rescue mission. This is a page-turner that is difficult to put down."

Robert Jorgensen, Brigadier General, US Army-Retired

Arizona Grit

by

B.K. Bryans

Adventure and nostalgia are all wrapped up in a fast-paced story of stolen women and smuggled guns. Ex-cop Dan Brannigan finds himself trapped in love and danger as he tries to track down beautiful women missing from a TV western being filmed on Old Tucson's dusty movie lot in 1957. If you miss the 50s and their tough-guy heroes, this page-turner is for you.

The author was a teenage cowboy on two southern Arizona ranches before he became the young horse wrangler for a movie company filming television westerns at the Old Tucson movie set. *Arizona Grit* (previously published as *Sand*) is set primarily in the Old Tucson movie lot of 1957, drawing on the author's memories of that time and place.

Brannigan Rides Again

by

B.K. Bryans

Brannigan Rides Again is the sequel to *Arizona Grit*. Once again, ex-lawman Dan Brannigan, a man at home on a horse as well as in a gun fight, saddles up and rides into danger. This time a valuable movie horse has been stolen from the Old Tucson movie town and a cowboy lies dead. Brannigan is hired to track down the thieves and bring back the horse. The ride takes him into Arizona's Mogollon Rim country and then into northern Mexico. Action happens.

Thank you for buying *Flying Low*.

B.K. Bryans